HOW TO

YOUR CHILD

from the NEW AGE

& SPIRITUAL DECEPTION

HOW TO PROTECT
YOUR CHILD
from the NEW AGE
& SPIRITUAL DECEPTION

BERIT KJOS

Originally titled *Your Child and the New Age*

Lighthouse Trails Publishing
Eureka, MT

How to Protect Your Child from the New Age & Spiritual Deception
© 2013 Berit Kjos
Lighthouse Trails 1st Edition
Expanded and updated from original title *Your Child and the New Age*;
published by Victor Books in 1990.

Lighthouse Trails Publishing
P.O. Box 908
Eureka, MT 59917
(see back of book for publisher and author contact information)

Library of Congress Cataloging-in-Publication Data

Kjos, Berit.
  [Your child & the New Age]
  How to protect your child from the New Age & spiritual deception / Berit Kjos. -- First Lighthouse Trails edition.
        pages cm
  "Expanded and Updated from original title Your Child and the New Age; published by Victor Books in 1990."
  "Originally titled Your Child and the New Age."
  Includes bibliographical references and index.
  ISBN 978-0-9846366-3-1 (softbound : alk. paper) 1. New Age movement. 2. United States--Moral conditions. 3. Parenting--Religious aspects--Christianity. I. Title.
  BP605.N48K57 2013
  248.8'45--dc23
                                    2013010857

Note: Lighthouse Trails Publishing books are available at special quantity discounts. Contact information for publisher in back of book.

Printed in the United States of America

With much gratefulness to my Lord for opening my heart to Him and revealing the forces of darkness that are permeating schools, media, entertainment, and even churches—thus training children to love evil and dismiss His truth. May He use this book to equip His families to stand firm in the midst of the spiritual war raging all around us.

> Train up a child in the way he should go: and when he is old, he will not depart from it. (Proverbs 22:6)

Also by Berit Kjos

Books
A Twist of Faith
Brave New Schools
Under the Spell of Mother Earth

Bible Studies
A Wardrobe From the King
David: A Man After God's Own Heart
Heart to Heart
In His Name
Living in His Name

For Children
The Invisible War

CONTENTS

A PARABLE

HIGH ON A ridge overlooking the valley stood the King, framed in the sun's fading light. His form rose like a monument of unyielding strength. Above his head swirled hostile, black clouds. Raging winds snatched at his coat. Yet, he who could quell their assault with a word refused to be distracted. He had fixed his eyes on the valley below. Capturing each tiny detail, he traced the movement of gathering armies. Suddenly, his gaze rested on a shadowy form hidden from ordinary sight. Anger and agony flashed across his noble face.

"I created that imposter," he mused, "but the Prince of Darkness only loved himself. I made him strong and beautiful, but he used my gifts to build his own throne. Did he imagine that his mutinous force could quench my power and hinder my plan? Has he spoken his own lies so often that he has deceived himself as well as my people? His foolish pride kindled this war, but soon even his blinded slaves will see the triumph of my kingdom."

The King's focus moved from the enemy headquarters to the city nearby. Its people slept unconcerned, smug, and oblivious to the scheming, waiting legions.

Tears stung the King's eyes as he spoke to the city he loved. "If only you had listened," he whispered softly. "If only you knew. But you ignored my warnings and went your own way. You followed your own foolish dreams—lies and deceptions that were more pleasant to your ears than my saving truth. My foolish people, open your eyes and see. I came to love and care for you, but you turned away. The thief came to steal, kill, and destroy, and you worship him. If you only knew where you are heading."

Far below, near the edge of the city, where the forest opened to a wide clearing, the grim armies merged into a ghostly, quaking mass. Suddenly, without a sound, a message burst into their consciousness: *The prince has arrived*. As one, they bowed in fearful surrender, breathing their salute, "Hail, Prince of Darkness! Master of the Force! Hail!"

Before them rose the tall, dark figure of the prince. "My friends," he purred, "I hear you have done well!"

A wave of relief swept over the mass.

"Report your progress!" his voice cracked like a whip over the trembling slaves. "Have you captured the city? Are its people ready to follow?"

Silence hung like an ominous sword striking terror into the hearts of the trembling warriors. Brash tyrants away from their master, they cowered like frightened dogs in his presence. Finally, a creature stepped forward. "Sir, the coup is almost complete. The city has yielded to your control."

"How did you win their allegiance?" demanded the prince.

"We followed your plan, Sir. You told us to target the children, to reform their schools, pollute their movies and music, infiltrate their churches—"

"Stop, stop! I want details. Who handled the schools?"

"I did, Sir." A burly figure lumbered to the front line. Under the heavy shrouded cowl, which hid his features, his body was shaking.

"Explain your strategy."

"We followed our ancient plan, Sir. You told us to change labels to fit contemporary tastes—and it worked. First, we whispered doubts about the King's repulsive Book of Truth. Then we planted tantalizing visions of the New World into the minds of educators. We showed them irresistible images of their own greatness, the power of Self, the pleasures of sex, and the peace of global unity under your mighty reign."

"Slow down and describe their response."

"Those open to transformation were thrilled with their new discoveries. They quickly fit your ideas into their curriculum."

"Is that all?"

"No, there's much more! We also told them that the King's

values hinder the freedom, growth, and happiness of Self. To build a better world, they must discard obsolete boundaries and pave new paths to higher consciousness and spiritual oneness. Quick to catch on, the kids are learning to ridicule the King's archaic standards and narrow-minded subjects. Soon they'll hate all who oppose your plan!" He giggled.

"Well done," grimaced the prince, "but control yourself."

Scanning the dark mass, he shouted, "Who's in charge of music?"

A squat, slinking creature crept forward. "I am, Sir."

"Report your progress!"

"We have revived your fool-proof formula: drugs, chants, sensual delights, and throbbing drums. This formula blocks logic, dulls reason, and keeps our connections open. We show them a good time—and make sure they come back for more. With more advanced subjects, we no longer hide your identity. They crave your savage malevolence."

"Well done!" The prince rubbed his hands together in sardonic glee before he shouted, "Next! Who transformed television?"

"We did," answered a shrill voice. A short, stocky figure pushed his way to the front. "One battalion loaded cartoons with wizards amid superheroes winning battles by your cosmic energy. Kids want supernatural power, so we've showed them yours. Camouflaged, of course."

"Splendid!" The prince's cruel voice rose excitedly. "Soon they'll want more, and when they're hooked, they too will be glad to see me. Ha! I will be their god, and they will learn a new form of worship! Go on. Tell me more."

"We have been showing our vision for the New World Order to reporters, producers, and writers," he snickered. "We convinced them that the King's values block progress. Today children choose their own way—or rather, our way. . ."

"My way, you mean!" shrieked the prince.

"Your way, Sir!" quaked the commander.

"You met no resistance?"

"Not much. Your brilliant ideas usually excite them."

"What about the King's subjects?"

"Many don't notice. Since we keep them too busy to study the Book of Truth, they can't tell your plan from the King's. Those who notice are afraid to speak up, and the few fools who do complain face our correction squad. Ridicule and exclusion usually silence them." A cacophony of cheers arose.

For a moment, the prince gazed silently into that dark mass of veiled warriors. Fear and hatred, not love and loyalty, bound these miserable subjects to do his bidding.

"Watch every rebellious subject!" he shouted. "Find loopholes in their armor. Distract and discourage those who pray. And above all, hinder their use of the Book."

Lightning cracked the sky, and the distant thunder grew to a deafening roar. But the King kept his watchful position high above the city, waiting for the precise moment . . .

Suddenly he raised his right arm. "Be still," he cried into the storm. And the storm stilled around the summit.

He raised his left arm, and a battalion of soldiers dressed in white appeared before him.

"It is time! I have awakened my remnant. I have spoken to all who have ears to hear and eyes to see. To everyone not blinded and bound by deception. To those who have not bowed to the Prince of Darkness."

"I have told them to rise, take their swords, and fight for their families and children. You must take your positions at their sides. Sing with them the song of victory, then conquer the forces of evil in the name of the King."

And they overcame him by the blood of the Lamb, and by the word of their testimony; and they loved not their lives unto the death. (Revelation 12:11)

1

CHILDREN AT RISK!

With the sound of their new school bell, the fifth graders at Piedmont Avenue Elementary School here closed their eyes and focused on their breathing, as they tried to imagine "loving kindness" on the playground.[1]—*New York Times*

INDIGO CHILDREN

DURING A FLIGHT delay in Chicago in the late nineties, I spent my time browsing the airport bookstore near my terminal. When a young woman next to me picked up a copy of *Conversations With God*, the first book in the popular series by Neale Donald Walsch, I had to ask, "Are you familiar with that book?"

"A friend told me I should read it," she answered. She then told me she was a Christian.

"But it's not about Christianity," I warned her. "It may sound good and use a lot of Christian words, but its message turns God's truth upside down."

She thanked me and put the book back. My thoughts drifted back to a Christian conference some years earlier where several publishing house editors had concluded that the "New Age movement had peaked." No need for more books on that topic, they said, for the faddish seductions of the "beautiful" side of evil would soon fade away.[2]

They couldn't have been further from the truth. While those early blooms of occult enticements might have peaked in interest among Christians, the seeds of deception sown during the 1960s and 1970s had already taken root in well-cultivated soil across America. Since then, the poisonous fruit disseminated through The Beatles, Napoleon Hill, Shirley MacLaine, Marianne Williamson, Hindu gurus, goddess worshippers, and countless other spiritual advocates of New Age spirituality has sprouted everywhere—in schools, churches, movie theaters, television, books, the news media, and the Internet. Syncretism, mysticism, and a subjective self-focused spirituality have become the norm.

So it was no surprise to learn in January of 2003 that the award-winning movie *Indigo* would be released at select theaters and churches in all fifty states and forty countries. Starring the famed New Ager, Neale Donald Walsch, who scripted his occult *Conversations with God* into the public stream of consciousness, it would surely accelerate America's paradigm shift toward a global "new" spirituality incompatible with the one true God and His Word.

Wondering whether to see the movie or not, I searched the Internet. I discovered that the Indigo child concept was first popularized by the book, *The Indigo Child*, written by husband and wife team Lee Carroll and Jan Tober. "Carroll also portrays himself as a channeler for 'Kryon,'" says one reviewer, "a spiritual entity [demon] who predicted the coming of the Indigo Children."[3]

I found this description of the movie:

> *INDIGO* is a film about loneliness, redemption, and the healing powers and grace of the new generation of Indigo (psychic and gifted) children being born into the world.[4]

The Metagifted Education Resource Organization (MERO) website gave an interesting description of the Indigo personality:

> Being Indigo is not a disorder! It's a Spiritual Evolution that manifests physically and appears to be a Cultural Revolution. This is the new Aquarian energy. . . .

Indigo Children . . . The name itself indicates the Life Color they carry in their auras and is indicative of the Third Eye Chakra, which represents intuition and psychic ability. These are the children who are often rebellious to authority, nonconformist, extremely emotional and sometimes physically sensitive or fragile, highly talented or academically gifted and often metaphysically gifted as well, usually intuitive, very often labeled ADD, either very empathic and compassionate OR very cold and callous, and are wise beyond their years. . . .

Their nonconformity to systems and to discipline . . . will help them accomplish big goals such as changing the educational system. . . . The Indigo Children are the ones who have come to raise the vibration of our planet! These are the primary ones who will bring us the enlightenment to ascend. . . .

About 85% or higher of children born in '92 or later, 90% born in '94 or after and 95% or more born now are Indigo Children![5]

Even two weeks before the opening date, theaters in my state were sold out, but seats were still available in alternative "churches" such as Unity, Unitarian, Congregational, and Christian Science. After much prayer, I bought a ticket from a local Unity "church" and went to the movie.

The Indigo child in the film was the granddaughter of Ray, the character played by Neale Donald Walsch. Arrogant and self-confident, the precocious Grace followed her feelings and conversed with the invisible spirit world that both filled and surrounded her. Mental telepathy, divination, necromancy (communication with the dead), and the "healing touch" came naturally to this Indigo child, for she had intuitively tapped into a "universal force"—a seductive reservoir of occult wisdom, strength, and "prophetic" voices.

According to the movie script and to the promotional message from the producers, all who were touched by Grace's life—including her grandfather—were transformed:

> The dramatic core of the film is the relationship that develops between a man whose life and family have dissolved due to a fateful mistake and his 10-year-old granddaughter with whom he goes on the run to protect her from a would-be kidnapper. Along the way, he discovers the power of his granddaughter's gifts which forever alter the lives of everyone she encounters.[6]

Grace was aloof, willful, sassy, and disrespectful. The list sounds familiar, doesn't it? The profile is typical of television-trained children from today's permissive homes. But in the context of this fictional movie, those contentious attitudes made Grace a valuable change agent within her dysfunctional family. And since the script was written to affirm her condescending ways, I was not surprised by the laughter and cheers from the audience. The fact that contemporary children share many of Grace's characteristics only strengthens its metaphysical message: "Send the energy" to everyone.

Free from the traditional disciplines and boundaries, Indigo Children claim self-determination as their right and follow no authorities but their own inner voice. In light of the supposed interconnectedness between human spirits and the universal force, it all fits together. As the *Indigo* movie and its producers (James Twyman, Neale Donald Walsch, and Stephen Simon) claim, this god is guiding the "evolution of humanity"[7] toward world peace and universal oneness under a socialist/spiritual system.

This is the world today's children have been born into—a world where every child is at risk of being drawn in, influenced, and transformed by the "prince of the power of the air."

CHILDREN AND NEW AGE MINDFULNESS MEDITATION

UNBEKNOWNST to most parents, America's public schools are teaching their children to use mindfulness meditation (Eastern-style meditation or TM). In a *New York Times* article titled "In the Classroom, a New Focus on Quieting the Mind," elementary children in an Oakland, California school are promised peace and loving-kindness if they will learn to meditate. An eleven-year-old explains, "I was losing at baseball, and I was about to throw a bat . . . The mindfulness really helped."[8] While that may sound like a great thing to a lot of teachers, the article acknowledges where this comes from:

> As summer looms, students at dozens of schools across the country are trying hard to be in the present moment. This is what is known as mindfulness training, in which stress-reducing techniques *drawn from Buddhist meditation* are wedged between reading and spelling tests.[9] (Emphasis added.)

A whole new generation of children is being drawn into New Age/New Spirituality, and it is happening right under their parents' noses. While some of us grieve the real-world consequences of this cultural revolution, a rising chorus of voices are now demanding acceptance of today's paradigm shift. Their positive spin inspires visions of an evolved humanity that is bursting out of the old shackles of Christian morality, traditional guidelines, and parental restraints. This new civilization reminds me of Isaiah's ancient warning: "And the people shall be oppressed, every one by another, and

> A whole new generation of children is being drawn into New Age/New Spirituality, and it is happening right under their parents' noses.

every one by his neighbour: the child shall behave himself proudly [insolently] against the ancient [the elder], and the base against the honourable" (Isaiah 3:5).

The promise from the New Age is world peace, but it's not God's kind of peace; thus, it is not a true and lasting peace! As enticing counterfeits develop, they will surely widen divisions among those who call themselves by the name of Christ. While the world calls for unity at any cost (a *whatever it takes* approach), His people can't conform to its ways, visions, hopes, or dreams. "Think not that I am come to send peace on earth: I came not to send peace, but a sword" (Matthew 10:34).

On the other hand, our Lord has promised peace, strength, and eternal hope to all who know, trust, and follow Him:

> Peace I leave with you, my peace I give unto you: not
> as the world giveth, give I unto you. Let not your heart
> be troubled, neither let it be afraid. (John 14:27)

But those who heed counterfeit promises and seek spiritual favors from occult sources become blind to His grace. Deceptions will multiply, and sadly, children are deception's biggest targets. In this precarious situation in which we find ourselves, we should remember the Bible's warnings:

> Beware lest any man spoil you through philosophy
> and vain deceit, after the tradition of men, after
> the rudiments of the world, and not after Christ.
> (Colossians 2:8)

Before we go any further into this book, I want to draw your attention to the Armor of God—God's special refuge for His children—which the Bible tells us to "put on" (Ephesians 6:10-18). Now, perhaps more than ever, our children need its daily protection against the world's deceptive lies and enticing lures.

2

GOD'S ARMOR—
A SHELTER IN THE STORM

Put on the whole armour of God, that ye may be able to
stand against the wiles of the devil. (Ephesians 6:11)

GOD'S ARMOR BRINGS victory because it is far more than
a protective covering. It is the very essence of Jesus Christ
Himself, and with it, we will be able to withstand evil when it
comes our way.

When you put on the armor of God, He becomes your
hiding place and your shelter in the storm—just as He was to
David. Hidden in Him, you can count on His victory, for He
not only covers you as a shield, He also fills you with His life:

> I am the vine, ye are the branches: He that abideth
> in me, and I in him, the same bringeth forth much
> fruit: for without me ye can do nothing. (John 15:5)

Since living in the safety of the armor means abiding in
Jesus, we can expect to share in "the fellowship of His sufferings"
(Philippians 3:10). His struggles as well as His peace. Remember,
God offers us His victory in the midst of trouble—not always
in the absence of pain. So "think it not strange concerning the
fiery trial which is to try you, as though some strange thing
happened unto you: But rejoice, inasmuch as ye are partakers
of Christ's sufferings" (1 Peter 4:12-13).

When you put on His armor, His life surrounds you and keeps you safe in Him. He is your precious friend, and you are His! So "put on Christ" (Galatians 3:27). He is your victory!

> Thou art my hiding place; thou shalt preserve me from trouble; thou shalt compass me about with songs of deliverance. (Psalm 32:7)

How do I "put on" God's Armor?

THIS life in Christ begins with knowing and trusting each part of the armor. The first part is TRUTH—God's revelation of all He is to us, all He has done for us, and all He promises to do for us in the days ahead. This wonderful, everlasting TRUTH is written in the Bible, revealed by the Holy Spirit, and realized through Jesus Christ.

It cuts through all the world's distortions, deceptions, and compromises. When you study, memorize, live, and follow TRUTH, He enables you to see the world from God's high vantage point. For He is the Truth! Putting on the first piece of the armor means feeding on truth through daily Bible reading and making it part of yourself.

To put on the "whole armour"—and enjoy a daily and eternal love-relationship with Jesus Christ, thank Him for what He has shown you in His Word. Know the Scriptures behind your prayer so that your words and faith are grounded in the authority of the Bible. Then pray through each piece. You can use the following prayer as an outline:

• **The Belt of TRUTH:** Thank You, my Lord, for showing me the TRUTH about Yourself, Your plans, and Your ways. Thank You for reminding me that You are the only God, the Creator of Heaven and earth, the King of the universe, my Father who loves me, and my Shepherd who leads me. You are my wisdom, my counselor, my hope, and my strength. You are everything I need each day.

- **The Breastplate of RIGHTEOUSNESS:** Thank You for showing me the truth about myself—that on my own I could never be good enough to live in Your presence. Thank You for taking my sins to the Cross and offering me *Your* perfect, RIGHTEOUS life. Lord, show me any sin I need to confess, so nothing will hinder me from being filled to overflowing with Your Spirit. Thank You for forgiving me and for filling me with Your righteous life.

- **The Sandals of the preparation of the GOSPEL of peace:** Thank You for the Gospel that we can readily share with others, which brings true peace with God, reconciling us to Him through Christ.

- **The Shield of FAITH:** Thank You for helping me have FAITH in You. I choose to count on everything You have shown me about Yourself—and everything You have promised me in Your Word.

- **The Helmet of SALVATION:** Thank You for promising me SALVATION both for today's battles and for all eternity.

- **The Sword of the SPIRIT, the Word of God:** Thank You for the Scriptures You have given me to memorize. Please show me which ones You want me to use to cut through deceptions and gain Your victory in any battle I may face today.

HOW CAN I EXPLAIN THE ARMOR TO MY CHILDREN?

IN a world where public schools, television, movies, and popular music all offer tempting counterfeits of what God promises His people, there is only one safe place for our children: in the loving arms of the Shepherd. So train your child "in the way he should go" (Proverbs 22:6) and help him to wear the "whole armour of God."

1. Memorize Scriptures that show the truth about God and His righteousness, peace, faith, and salvation. Explain that these verses are Scripture swords that counter the main lies of the enemy. Remember, when children know the truth about God, they won't trust popular counterfeits. Knowing God's way to peace and salvation, they won't choose today's numerous counterfeit paths.

21

2. Remind your children that the armor is not like a magic shield they can casually slip on in order to be safe anywhere they want to go.

Years ago, our seven-year-old son asked if he could see a popular movie with some friends.

"No. I'd rather you didn't," I told him.

"Why not?" he asked.

"Because it makes occultism seem both fun and right. Even though your friends know it's fiction, the story and images leave the impression you can win in life by using occult rituals to get supernatural power. Not only does the Bible tell us occultism is evil, it also shows how it destroys people." I started to look up Deuteronomy 18:9-13.

"But I'll put on the armor."

"It won't help. When you go somewhere that you shouldn't, you disobey God and "take off" the breastplate of righteousness. You're not safe if you go somewhere Jesus wouldn't want you to go."

Our son got the message and stayed home. He knew that by himself he was no match for occult forces. But by wearing the special protection God offers us through His armor, he would be able to stand firm against Satan's strategies.

3. To help your children put on the armor, make sure they know and understand the Scriptures I have given in this section so that their prayers will be based on God's Word. Then pray through the pieces of the armor, simplifying each part to fit the ages of your children.

4. You may want to discuss some of the opposing forces that draw children toward all kinds of occult entertainment and tempting thrills. Many of those snares will be discussed and exposed in the chapters ahead. But when we wear God's armor and trust in His Word, He will keep us safe—hidden in Jesus Christ.*

---

*For comparison charts on the armor of God and Satan's counterfeits, visit my website at: http://www.crossroad.to/Victory/Armor.htm.

3

SCHOOLS & THE
WAR ON CHRISTIANITY

Be not deceived; God is not mocked: for whatsoever a
man soweth, that shall he also reap. (Galatians 6:7)

A FIFTH-GRADE TEACHER in a school in Colorado placed a
wide assortment of books in his classroom for students to enjoy
during daily reading times. When a parent complained that two
of the 239 volumes were based on the Bible, the principal told
teacher Ken Roberts to remove them. A judge upheld the school's
order to censor the two books from the classroom. In school, the
children could legally read books on Buddhism, Indian religions,
and Greek mythology—but not on Christianity.[1]

In San Jose, California 300 teachers and school employees
gathered to "improve education" with workshops and lectures
on communication, relaxation, and self-esteem:

> One group sat cross-legged in a darkened classroom,
> learning how to reduce stress with Yoga. While some
> felt self-conscious, others happily released their minds
> to the quieting sounds that flowed from a tape player
> on the desk. In the next room, another group meditated
> behind locked doors.[2]

In another California town, a third-grader pressed his fingers
against his temples, shut his eyes tight, and wrinkled his face
in intense concentration. He was trying to "read" the symbols

touched by the teacher's assistant seated on the other side of a large partition. On the reading instructor's desk lay a book titled *ESP*.[3]

Since the '90s, an explosion of New Age influence has occurred in North American schools—children from as young as pre-school age are being taught about Mother Earth, Yoga, meditation, and just about every kind of pagan religion and Eastern practice.

MASKS OF THE NEW AGE

NEW AGE, or New Spirituality, is actually ancient occultism with a facelift. It is the "beautiful side of evil,"[4] an enticing facade for the kingdom of darkness. Disguised as peace, inner-power, wisdom, and love, this attractive deception pretends to offer everything God promises, yet asks nothing in return—for the moment. Its seductive call to *be like God* dates back to the Garden of Eden (Genesis 3:5). God warned us long ago about deceptions that would lead many to "depart from the faith, giving heed to seducing spirits, and doctrines of devils" (1 Timothy 4:1). The Bible warns:

> [T]he time will come when they will not endure sound doctrine; but after their own lusts shall they heap to themselves teachers, having itching ears; And they shall turn away their ears from the truth, and shall be turned unto fables. (2 Timothy 4:3-4)

Today's most popular myth distorts the character of God and the identity of man. Unwilling to bow to a personal, holy God, multitudes have reshaped their Creator into an image of their own wishful thinking. This imagined god becomes an impersonal power source ready to fulfill the whims of a god-man determined to direct his own destiny.

The New Age shuns Christianity but welcomes all other religions. Each person adjusts what he already believes, adds the desired ingredients, and finds himself immersed in the counterfeit. Almost any combination works:

- Humanism + supernatural power = New Age
- Hinduism + pop psychology = New Age
- Pantheism + confidence in human potential = New Age
- Buddhism + panentheism (God in all) = New Age

Even *crossless Christianity* fits, if we subtract its heart—Jesus Christ and His atonement—and then add some Eastern mysticism.

The New Age is essentially a pseudo (counterfeit) spirituality that is Satan's substitute for Christianity. It offers man a promise of full enlightenment and transformation, not just for himself but also for the entire planet and all of creation—a future filled with peace and love that man can obtain or realize on his own. He doesn't need a Savior who is God because man too is Divine.

In spite of grandiose claims made by New Age/New Spirituality leaders and the effective networking among these groups, we cannot give them sole credit for the phenomenal spread of this deception. Utmostly, that belongs to the mastermind behind the scenes—Satan, who has a brilliant plan and whispers or channels portions of it to any who will listen, anywhere in the world. He intends one day to set up a global government in which he will reign through his puppet, the Antichrist (the long-awaited Aquarian "Messiah").

This counterfeit "Savior" stands in stark contrast to Jesus Christ, the true Messiah of those who have ears to hear, eyes to see, and a heart to respond. The end-time battle will be a duel between the false christ and the true Christ—the New Age "Messiah" and the One True Messiah. For this anti-christ to win, however, he knows he needs to recruit more soldiers. Our children are among those he has targeted and I believe, in fact, are his primary targets today.

For all intents and purposes, Satan can counterfeit almost any good thing God gives us. In his hands, even tools for learning can become weapons loaded with distorted messages aimed at young minds. Look at his three major thrusts toward global society:

◊ Replace biblical Christianity with a self-centered blend of all religions joined in spiritual oneness.

◊ Replace Judeo/Christian values with New Age values— anything that frees a person to follow the desires of self and create his own reality.

◊ Replace nationalism with a one-world government under a spiritually evolved leadership.

WAR ON CHRISTIANITY

HUMANISM has paved the way for the New Age, but most of us didn't notice. Just as termites can chew away at a home's foundation for decades before the damage shows, so humanist educators have sought to undermine the public school system. Suddenly we had to face the fact that many schools teach goals and values that contradict biblical values. And the humanist-oriented educational establishment promotes its beliefs as aggressively as any other religious group. Listen to their war cry:

> The battle for humankind's future must be waged and won in the public school classroom by teachers who correctly perceive their role as the proselytizers of a new faith: a religion of humanity that recognizes and respects the spark of what theologians call divinity in every human being.

> These teachers must embody the same selfless dedication as the most rabid fundamentalist preachers, for they will be ministers of another sort, utilizing a classroom instead of a pulpit to convey humanist values in whatever subject they teach, regardless of the educational level—preschool, day care, or large state university. The classroom must and will become an arena of conflict between the old and the new—the rotting corpse of Christianity, together with all its adjacent evils and misery, and the new faith of humanism, resplendent in its promise of a world in which

the never-realized Christian ideal of 'love thy neighbor" will finally be achieved.[5]

American philosopher and educator John Dewey kindled the fire of educational reform. The first president of the American Humanist Association, Dewey was determined to weed out Christian absolutes and reseed with "truths" that could adjust to changing cultures. *The Humanist Manifesto*, which Dewey signed in 1933, declares the heart of the movement. This is part of its introduction:

> There is great danger of a final, and we believe fatal, identification of the word religion with doctrines and methods which have lost their significance and which are powerless to solve the problem of human living in the Twentieth Century . . . Any religion that can hope to be a synthesizing and dynamic force for today, must be shaped for the needs of this age. To establish such a religion is a major necessity of the present.[6]

Without the 3.2 million-member National Education Association, considered one of the nation's most powerful political machines, Dewey's ideas might have been confined to university campuses. Supported by the NEA, comprised of textbook writers and superintendents as well as professors and public school teachers, Dewey's vision spread like wildfire. Through its militant leadership, the whole educational system became involved—with or without the personal support of local educators, many of whom didn't realize what was happening.

Few textbooks have escaped the watchful eye of NEA censors, who have doggedly followed Dewey's plan to provide a "purified environment for the child." Historical facts that clashed with "progressive education" have been distorted or erased. The NEA has sought total control of curriculum content, control of teachers' colleges, and sex education, free from parental interference. Though a high percentage of American teachers consider themselves moderate or conservative, the NEA supports abortion on demand (without parental consent), preferential treatment of homosexuals, and teaching evolution, while omitting creationism from the classroom.[7]

One book, *Censorship: Evidence of Bias in Our Children's Textbooks*, unveils some alarming facts. Christianity, family values, and certain political and economic positions have been systematically banished from children's textbooks. For example, in 670 stories from third-and sixth-grade readers:

◊ No story features Christian or Jewish religious motivation, although one story does make American Indian religion the central theme in the life of a white girl.

◊ Almost no story features marriage or motherhood as important or positive. . . . But there are many aggressively feminist stories that openly deride manhood.

◊ In an original story by Isaac Bashevis Singer, the main character prayed "to God" and later remarked "Thank God." In the story as presented in the sixth-grade reader, the words "to God" were taken out and the expression "Thank God" was changed to "Thank goodness."[8]

While some elementary history textbooks still tell about Thanksgiving, they do not explain to whom the Pilgrims gave thanks. Pilgrims were defined as "people who make long trips." The Pueblo Natives "can pray to Mother Earth—but Pilgrims can't be described as praying to God."[9] Overt attacks on Christianity through distortion, depreciation, and ridicule have caused even more damage than omissions. Many of the books students are required to read refer to boring church services, self-righteous ministers, and lustful evangelists. One psychology text equated the historical Jesus with mythological gods:

A great many myths deal with the idea of rebirth. Jesus, Dionysus, Odin, and many other traditional figures are represented as having died, after which they were reborn, or arose from the dead.[10]

When children are subjected to such suggestions and pressures year after year, many yield to the hostile forces that oppose their beliefs.

The chart on the following page lists several of the humanistic standards that are being passed down to a new generation of young people and compares these with traditional Christian values.

A MODEL SCHOOL FOR FUTURE LEADERS

BILL CLINTON'S Governor's School—one of many "Governor's Schools" across America—demonstrates tragic results. For six weeks each summer, the school isolated selected Arkansas high school students from the outside world and immersed them in liberal ideology, sensual literature, group dialogue, and mystical thrills—both real and imagined.[11]

"Students, do me a favor," urged author Ellen Gilchrist, a guest speaker at the school. "Totally ignore your parents. Listen to them, but then forget them. Because you need to start using your own stuff, your real stuff that you have."[12]

Her aim was to free students from "obsolete" family values, not promote a healthy personal independence. They must reject the old ways and become "open-minded"—ready to accept the unthinkable practices that would bombard their minds.

By the time they left the Governor's School, their utopian dreams seemed more real than the actual world. Like the results of Soviet brainwashing, they had been weaned from truth, facts, and reality. With seared consciences, new ideals, and volatile emotions, they would now face the old world they had left behind only six weeks earlier.

The Marxist change agents behind this transformation are too numerous to list, but behavioral psychologist Kurt Lewin gives us a simple formula. Linked to psychological research institutes in London (Tavistock) and Germany (Frankfurt Institute), Lewin moved to America when Hitler began his

SECULAR HUMANISTS BELIEFS VS. CHRISTIANS BELIEFS

Secular Humanists	Christians
There is no God.	We trust in a living, personal God.
The world is self-existing.	God created the world.
Everything exists for the fulfill-ment of human life.	"For of him, and through him, and to him, are all things: to whom be glory for ever." (Romans 11:36)
The goal. . . is a free and universal society where people cooperate for common good.	Our goal is to "know" Christ and the "power of his resurrection." (Philippians 3:10)
Man is responsible for the realization. . . of his dreams.	"In God is my salvation and my glory: the rock of my strength, and my refuge, is in God." (Psalm 62:7)
Values are relative and chang-ing, determined by human need.	Biblical values are absolute and unchanging. (Matthew 24:35)
Man has within himself the power to create a new world.	"The things which are impos-sible with men are possible with God." (Luke 18:27)

This and other helpful charts can be found at: www.crossroad.to.

reign. His influence spread through Massachusetts Institute of Technology and other universities, then paved the way for "sensitivity training" and the formation of National Training Laboratories that would prepare transformational tactics and textbooks for public schools.

Lewin outlined his program with a 3-step formula:

1. UNFREEZING minds: Questioning the old ways through facilitated dialogue, peer pressure, and group "experience"—real or imagined.

2. MOVING students to the new level: Using cognitive dissonance (mental, moral, and emotional confusion), peer pressure, and manipulated consensus to shift loyalties from the old ways to the new.

3. FREEZING group minds on the new level: The new views become the norm. They feel good! The old views become offensive as well as wrong![13]

For the students, the transition back to reality—to home, family, and normal life—was painful. For some it was lethal. "When I came back home, I sort of wrote a suicide note to myself," confessed LeAndrew Crawford. "Not actually wanting to kill myself, but wanting to kill the reality of what society had been teaching me for so long. . . . I was totally down, because my family just didn't feel like my family. . . . I didn't want to be back."[14]

A student by the name of Brandon Hawk did kill himself within a year, however. Hearing about his death, other concerned parents contacted Brandon's parents.

They see the same thing in their kids that we saw in Brandon," the father explained. . . . "They just sort of walk off and leave the family."[15]

But Brandon wasn't the only one who chose death rather than life. After the third suicide, the Joint Interim Education

Committee of the Arkansas legislature held hearings that exposed some of the problems. Perhaps the most revealing testimony came from Brandon's mother, who read from her son's log. In his first entry, he wrote, "Moms are the best people around, and my mom is the best mom on earth." But three weeks later, he wrote, "My mom is so closed minded I feel like we will have a standoff soon over issues." And his final entry stated, "After I came back from the [July 4th] break, my friends and I could tell that we had suddenly been transformed into free thinkers."[16]

Another mother testified that, "My son came back from Governor's School and his favorite line was 'There are no absolutes; there are no absolutes.'"[17] It didn't take long to change the students' minds and hearts, did it? Yet few parents were aware that this subversive agenda was going on.

Back in 1982, Professor Benjamin Bloom, an internationally known behaviorist, defined "good teaching" as "challenging the students' fixed beliefs and getting them to discuss issues."[18] He stated:

> [T]he evidence collected so far suggests that a single hour of classroom activity under certain conditions may bring about a major reorganization in cognitive as well as affective [attitudes, values and beliefs] behaviors.[19]

The most revealing evidence that this scheme really "works" comes from those who participated in the Clinton's Governor's School. The following six points sum up some of the strategies of the school as derived from the video, *The Guiding Hand*.[20]:

1) Isolate Students From Traditional Family Values

> For the six weeks . . . they are not allowed to go home except for July the Fourth. They are discouraged from calling home. . . . They can receive mail but they are encouraged to have as little contact with the outside world as possible. (Shelvie Cole, Brandon's mother)

> I felt I needed not to talk about it. I don't know why. Maybe because we were supposed to stay here and the fact that we couldn't leave. . . . No one . . . who had gone before would talk to me about it. (Kelli Wood, former student)

The "effectiveness" of such mandatory separation may help explain why (1) educational change agents want to put three-year-olds in pre-school programs and (2) why "Obama says American kids spend too little time in school."[21]

2) REINFORCE NEW LIBERAL, ANTI-CHRISTIAN VALUES

> We watched movies like *Harvey Milk*. We learned about gay life—those things that your parents say, "This is wrong. . . . You shouldn't see this type of thing because, hey, that's just not right." (LeAndrew Crawford, former student)

> [The instructors] tear down their authority figure system and . . . help establish another one. . . . They convince the students that "You are the elite . . . you're not going to be understood when you go home—not by your parents, your friends, your pastor or anybody." (Mark Lowery, former director for Governor's School publicity)

3) EMPHASIZE FEELING-CENTERED TEACHING (AFFECTIVE, NOT COGNITIVE)

> Rather than learning what 2 and 2 equals, they would be asked what they *feel* about 2+2. Right now we have a move going on in our Arkansas schools called restructuring, where they are trying to get away from more objective, substantive learning into this subjective area of feelings. (Mark Lowery)

You would think that there would be some academic challenges . . . getting ready for college . . . The main textbook that I remember from there is a book called *Zen and the Art of Motorcycle Maintenance,* and the book is totally Hindu religion defined. (Steve Roberts, former student)

4) Shape a Personal, All-Inclusive Spirituality

A lot of places. . . even Christian camps, you get that stress about 'What am I doing wrong?' . . . There it was like, hey, I can talk to God! Me and God are one, the world is one . . . Jump up and down, you know, just twirl around.

It was kind of like that Baha'i idea. How you have Islam, Baha'i, Muslim, Christianity . . . They're all different kinds of trees, but underneath, its root system grows together [and] is the same god. (Steven Allen, student)

5) Instill the Target Beliefs—A "New" Social & Political Agenda

The next quote from *The Guiding Hand* fits Bill Clinton's experience. He was selected as a potential future leader—a Rhodes scholar—worthy of the required indoctrination:

I think the whole intent of the Governor's School in taking 350—400 students per summer, is to pick out the four, five or six students that could be political leaders and then to mold their minds in this more liberal and humanistic thinking. (Mark Lowery, former director)

They're bringing a political agenda in the guise of academic excellence. . . . It was something that was well orchestrated, well organized, it was mind-bending and manipulative. (Steve Roberts)

Prominent themes promoted by this school include radical homosexuality, socialism, pacifism, and a consistent hostility toward Western civilization and culture, especially [America's] biblical foundations. (Jeoffrey Botkin)

6) BUILD ALLEGIANCE TO THE NEW COMMUNITY

You could dress just about any way you want. We had almost naked people. It was real liberal . . . an awful lot of cursing. (Mike Oonk, former student)

The students . . . say, "This is the perfect place. I never want to go home." I caught myself saying that several times. (Mike Oonk)[22]

Indoctrinating students with diverse beliefs, socialist values, utopian dreams, and idealized love leads to deception, disillusionment, corruption, and chaos. Today's change agents need chaos and crisis to justify their oppressive action. Not only does it unravel the old social order, it gives an illusion of newfound freedom—from family values as well as moral restraints.[23] Bill Clinton did not hide his enthusiasm for the project when he stated, "It would be impossible for me to describe to you just how exciting and unusual this educational adventure is."[24]

It wasn't exciting for re-programmed students who returned home. But that problem may soon be resolved. Through "service-learning" and other long-term re-learning projects, today's students can stay rooted in the new environment—even if they sleep at home.

This is where we are headed, dear friends! During one year, three students at a top-rated high school in California committed suicide—one of the many consequences of today's emotional confusion. One evening, as desperate parents met with school officials to seek solutions, a fourth student attempted suicide at the nearest railroad crossing. He was pulled off the track seconds before the train thundered down the track.[25]

Embracing Eastern Mysticism

> One of the biggest advantages we have as New Agers is, once the occult, metaphysical and New Age terminology is removed, we have concepts and techniques that are very acceptable to the general public. So we can change the names . . . demonstrate the power [and] open the door to millions who normally would not be receptive.[26]—New Age leader **Dick Sutphen**

THOUGH religious in fervor and commitment, humanism failed to meet man's spiritual needs. As the front door of the school closed to God, the back door swung wide open to New Age teaching. Disguised as stress reduction, relaxation, or transpersonal education—or just tucked unnamed into a traditional curriculum—it added spiritual power to the existing man-centered program.

Few educators have resisted the "positive" new approaches to learning and "wholeness." The counterfeit god (the Source, Force, Cosmic Consciousness, Universal Mind, Self, etc.) has satisfied anti-Christian humanists and New Agers, well-meaning teachers, and adventurous children. And it has completed the lie. Humanist selfism added to New Age spirituality formed a plausible picture of reality—one that fit human nature and sanctioned the trappings of old-time paganism.

Paganism? You mean trance-inducing drumming, sensuality, orgies, and witchcraft? Right. However, the New Age preferred to hide its dark, sinister side until it had popularized its light, appealing side. Introduced in disarmingly noble and affirming terms, the counterfeit has fooled all but those who have studied the genuine. Take a look at some of the charts I have on my website* that show the enticing similarities to biblical truth and its striking contradictions.

An increasing number of American classrooms have become workshops where children can learn and practice New Spirituality

---

* You can find these charts at: http://www.crossroad.to/charts/1-Index.html.

precepts. While some well-meaning teachers turn to meditation and guided imagery just because they think "it works," others base their actions on personal faith in New Age doctrines. Those who believe in oneness with the cosmic source of peace, wisdom, and creativity see an obvious way to help their students: Connect them to the Source!

Some teachers who forbid prayer to Jesus Christ in their classrooms see nothing wrong with Hindu-based meditational exercises that connect young minds with other gods.

Deborah Rozman is co-founder of HeartMath, a program that trains health professionals to handle stress through meditation. Rozman is also founder of one of the first private children's schools in "holistic education" in Northern California, and she has spent time training teachers. She has a master's degree in child psychology and a doctorate in the psychology of consciousness. In her book, *Meditating with Children*, she thanks "the Universal Mother of Compassion found in all of nature . . . and Paramahansa Yogananda."[27] She dedicates the book to "all children, everywhere, that they may evolve towards their spiritual destiny."[28]

Rozman's meditations delight teachers, quiet children, and invoke a dangerous spiritual force. Consider this drill: The children sit cross-legged in a circle on the floor and discuss the nature of spiritual energy. They straighten their backs so the "energy from the Source within can flow up . . . our spine into our brain."[29] The teacher then is supposed to lead the children in a visualization exercise. One begins:

> Sitting very still with eyes closed. . . imagine that you are floating out of your spiritual eye (the point between the eyebrows) and into the leaf of the plant.. . feel the oneness of the source of all life everywhere.[30]

Or she may use this visualization:

> Meditate and go into the Source within, and in that
> One Source feel that you are One with everyone else's
> Light, Intelligence, Love, and Power. . . . Chant 'Om'
> softly to fill the whole circle and the whole room with
> your experience of the Source within.[31]

The final step invites the children to extend their arms and be channels "for healing energy from the Source through you to another." The teacher tells the children to "feel energy traveling from the Center within down the arm and out . . . into the object or person." She explains that this is a way they "can help each other feel better."[32]

With each session, the children risk taking another step toward spiritual bondage. Few teachers realize that any contact with the occult can open the door to demonic strongholds and oppression. Invoking spiritual forces and channeling their power usually results in blindness to God and a wide range of oppressive personality changes.

Stephanie Herzog first heard Ms. Rozman speak about meditation at a school district in-service meeting. Impressed, she began using meditation in her own classroom the next day. To avoid criticism from parents, she called it "centering" and "concentrating our energies."[33]

After years of unhindered classroom meditation, Ms. Herzog wrote her own book promoting these spiritual exercises. Its title, *Joy in the Classroom*, illustrates the appeal of New Age deception. She claims that the student can find joy, peace, wisdom, and strength by enjoyable, seductive exercises that raise her consciousness and connect her with her true god-Self.

Such programs may be called confluent or wholistic education, transpersonal psychology, and accelerated learning. They are usually presented as stress management, suicide prevention, or self-esteem programs.

In addition to the possibility of occult bondage, children face a subtle challenge to their faith. If they learn that their imaginations can produce the reality they desire, why follow Jesus Christ? If pleasant meditations can connect them with the cosmic god, why choose the Cross? Their spiritual needs are being met, or so it seems.

Parents need to know what schools are teaching our children. Dr. Shirley Correll, herself an educator, shares our concern about the newer forms of education. She describes a program called Quieting Reflex and Success Imagery:

> Trusting children are psychologically manipulated into involvement with spirit guides, Eastern religion, hypnosis, altered states of consciousness, and occult activities forbidden to Christians.

> In one case, a little girl refused to pray in the name of Jesus after her imaginary wise person, or spirit guide, directed her not to. Children are often subtly conditioned not to discuss these programs with their parents, and some children are reluctant to admit the programs' existence.[34]

Many textbooks, while silent on the subject of Christianity, don't hesitate to teach Buddhism and Hinduism. A textbook on world cultures even told students to pretend for several days that they were Hindus.[35] A health guidance text devoted several pages to the process and benefits of Eastern meditation. Picturing a teenage girl in Yoga position, it defined meditation as "a technique used to alter the states of consciousness and trigger relaxation response."[36]

A speech teacher in a high school in California told his students to give impromptu talks on the topic, "What I want to be in my next life."[37] Did he assume that reincarnation is now generally accepted among the youth?

This embrace of spiritual propaganda reaches beyond the seemingly *bright side* of the New Age. Defiantly challenging the patience of God and the cruel power of Satan, many schools now welcome the dark occult. In an article by Mary Ann Collins titled "Is This America?," Collins stated:

> Public school students . . . are taught to put themselves
> into a trance and get counseling from imaginary friends,
> including Pumsy the Dragon. This teaches children to
> use "spirit guides" . . . The Pumsy curriculum was used
> in forty percent of American public schools some years
> ago.[38] . . . Some school children have been taught to
> make "worry dolls" to ward off evil spirits, and to make
> representations of Hindu gods.[39]

Native Spirituality is now being introduced into many schools. Nanci des Gerlaise is a Canadian Cree First Nations woman. In her book, *Muddy Waters: an Insider's View of North American Native Spirituality*, she tells how dream catchers are being used in public school settings and describes the nature of dream catchers:

> [U]sing a dream catcher in its intended purpose is
> nothing more than a form of practicing occultism.
> How can an inanimate object "catch" evil spirits,
> much less bad dreams? . . . Using dream catchers is an
> open invitation for more spiritual works of darkness.[40]

An increasing number of schools are telling students to research the occult, to role-play occult fantasy games, and to seek esoteric knowledge through horoscopes, I Ching, and Ouija Boards. Needless to say, the children are playing with an incredible fire that neither they nor their teachers can control.

In this chapter, I have tried to paint a picture of what is happening to our children in the public schools and how the New Age, which unfortunately many parents don't even know or refuse to believe exists, is having a dangerous and significant influence on young people's lives. There is victory to be had—it begins with knowing and loving God and His truth. From the living Word, our children can learn genuine wisdom, discern evil, conquer giants, walk in peace, and experience God's freedom—but we have to be there to teach them, guide them, and pray for them.

4

WHAT CAN PARENTS DO ABOUT THE WAR ON CHRISTIANITY?

For we wrestle not against flesh and blood, but against principalities, against powers, against the rulers of the darkness of this world, against spiritual wickedness in high places. (Ephesians 6:12)

NOW THAT WE see the conflict, let's take a look at the invisible war behind the visible facts. Remember that the battle is infinitely greater than any potential conflict between your child and his school. Teachers and principals, many of whom share your values, are not the enemy. Neither are the humanist "new" spirituality missionaries in the NEA. The real enemy is the one who opposed God's plan from the beginning—Satan, who uses his blinded victims to carry out his hidden agenda.

Though the spiritual war grows fiercer all around us with each passing day, this is not a time to fear, despair, get angry, or lose hope. History has proven that times of ease and acceptance produce complacency, while repression and persecution produce strong, solid Christian believers who wholeheartedly trust in Him and are not afraid to contend for the faith and protect their children.

God is our strength in this struggle against a counterfeit force, and He will accomplish His purposes through us. As we trust Him to give us courage and strength, He will remove any fear we have of contending for the faith and doing what we must to protect our children, even if it sometimes means we are standing alone.

Nehemiah faced a battle similar to ours. When Satan sent human agents to mock, ridicule, incapacitate, and destroy God's people, Nehemiah prayed. God answered with a foolproof plan that can also work for us today:

Nehemiah	Christian Parents
1. They "made [their] prayer unto our God, and set a watch against them day and night." (Nehemiah 4:9)	"Put on the whole armour of God . . . Praying always . . . and watching . . . with all perseverance." (Ephesians 6:11, 18)
2. They stationed families to stand guard together. (4:13)	As a family, teach and discuss truth; help each other resist deception.
3. They carried their weapons continually. (4:13, 16-18)	Know God's Word—your spiritual weapon.
4. At the sound of the trumpet, they joined together. (4:20)	Christian families—stand, pray, and fight deception together.

STEP ONE: BE ALERT & ALWAYS KEEP ON PRAYING

Pray! For as Jesus said, "[W]ithout me ye can do nothing." (John 15:5). The battle begins *and ends* with prayer. Pray for open and trusting communication with your child. Pray for discernment to detect teaching that contradicts God's truth. Pray for wisdom to know when to speak up and what to say.

• **Pray for your child.** Pray that he learns to discern error on his own and that he will be bold enough to speak truth with courage and to stand alone when all his friends follow after other gods. Pray that pleasing God will be more important than pleasing teachers and peers.

• **Pray together as a family.** Put on the "whole armour of God" daily. Remember that "having your loins girt about with truth" means more than merely declaring it done. It means reading (or hearing) and following the Word, and knowing it well enough to discern error. Read and discuss Ephesians 6:13-17. Memorize the parts of the armor.

• **Pray that you might meet other Christians who also understand the problem.** Pray for faithful Christian friends for your child. Pray for other parents who will stand with you. Since you see the need to get involved in your child's schooling, pray for direction.

• **Pray for the school, teachers, principals, counselors, the curriculum committee, and the school board.** Pray that they learn God's truth, discern deception, choose the best curriculum, and make wise decisions.

• **Trust God, not yourself.** "Trust in the Lord with all thine heart; and lean not unto thine own understanding. In all thy ways acknowledge him, and he shall direct thy paths" (Proverbs 3:5-6).

Step Two: Know What Your Child Is Learning in School

• **Talk with your child.** Listen for clues that help you spot good as well as questionable teaching. Be objective and model appreciation of schools and teachers.

Perhaps you have a child who gladly gives detailed accounts of all events from the time he left for school that morning. My boys preferred to answer all my questions with a brief "Good!" or "Okay." But I discovered that a tasty snack after school could produce at least five minutes of sharing. When my son was fourteen, a sandwich at a local deli boosted our conversations immensely.

I also found that communication mysteriously wilted when my sons suspected that my motive was cross-examination rather than having fun together or if I kept so busy at home that I couldn't stop and listen.

If you and your child have been too busy to really listen to each other, it is not too late to begin now. Don't start by asking a lot of questions about school, especially if you have a teenager. She probably won't be ready to share openly until she knows she can count on your empathetic response, non-judgmental attitude, and genuine interest in her. If she has found that her sharing produces anxiety, agitation, anger, and an impulsive trip to her teacher resulting in confrontation on any level, she will probably make a point to keep hidden from you most, if not all, questionable information. No child wants to be an accomplice to an emotional or embarrassing confrontation.

• **Volunteer to assist the teacher in the classroom.** You will gain firsthand knowledge as well as easy access to the teacher's listening ear.

• **Scan elementary textbooks, take-home papers, and fliers.** Check to see if significant facts are deleted or distorted. Consider their effects on your child. Ask yourself the following questions about the above material:

> » Does it censor out important facts about the influences of Christianity in the development of our country? Does it imply that Christianity is unimportant, old-fashioned, or a hindrance to progress? Does it ask your child to discuss his faith in front of the class—thus leaving him open to embarrassment and ridicule? With new proposals for bringing religion back in schools, look carefully at the kinds of religions which are being promoted and ways in which these religions will be taught. It could mean wide open doors to more counterfeits.

> » Does it present an imbalanced view of Christians? Are pastors, evangelists, missionaries, and other Christians denigrated, maligned, and ridiculed—or never described favorably?

» Does it emphasize, promote, or give detailed descriptions of other religions, while ignoring Christianity?

» Does it require your child's participation in spiritual exercises? Does it give instructions in Yoga, meditation, channeling, or guided imagery?

» Does it include a blatant pro-homosexual slant?

» Does it ask your child not to share information with his parents?

Discuss your findings with your child. Express your appreciation for the good things you see. Explain any area of concern. Teach discernment by pointing out contradictions to God's truth.

Step Three: Know & Exercise Your Privileges as a Parent

If you suspect a problem, you may need to talk with the teacher and, if necessary, ask to see the teacher's manual and classroom projects. But first—

• **Discuss your plan with your child if his age and understanding level permits.** Explain that God made you, not the school, responsible for his training and education. Therefore, you have the right to know what he learns and the responsibility to guard his spiritual development. In obedience to God, you must act when God shows you areas of spiritual danger or distortion.

• **Pray together as a family for God's wisdom and direction**—for His love and message to be communicated through you. Pray for openness and responsiveness in the people you find yourself in a position of having to address.

Keep in mind that many teachers try to do the best they can and would not consciously try to subvert your children. They merely apply the latest techniques presented to them at teachers' seminars, conventions, or in-service sessions. These new ideas are like the tail of an elephant—they rarely reveal the character of the whole.

Convinced their intentions are good, most teachers and principals will naturally become defensive if you confront them with anger or harshness. Pray, therefore, that God will enable you to express genuine appreciation for their well-meaning efforts.

- **Let the teacher know you care.** Realize that a major reason why the school has assumed the responsibility for educating your child is its belief that most parents have abdicated theirs. Have you shown interest by helping with classroom activities, joining in school activities, or perhaps driving for a field trip?

- **Make an appointment with the teacher or school official you need to see.**

- **Let your outward appearance reflect God's peace and order.** Even how you dress could affect their attitude toward you, as well as your own sense of confidence.

- **Bring written notes of the facts that concern you.** Be prepared to suggest possible solutions to the problem.

- **Bring a tape recorder and ask permission to use it.** Recording the conference helps me review conversations, follow suggestions, and share information with my husband.

Be spiritually and emotionally ready to face resistance, defensiveness, and denial, but don't expect them. Cyndie Huntington, author of *Combat Handbook for Parents with Children in Public Schools,* tells about one encounter with school officials:

> When you reach this step, it is not unusual to be told, "Mrs. Jones, your child doesn't seem to have the problem, you do. Now what can we do to make YOU feel better?" or "We're the experts, let us raise your children."
>
> [One parent] was told by the principal to consider counseling for herself. Upon the recommendation . . . she

went to a secular counselor for two months of therapy.

She stated that she . . . counseled the counselor more than the counselor counseled her. It was then suggested by the school that she take the STEP (Steps to Effective Parenting) course. The school said that this would help her "interact" better with people and her children. So she signed up.

At the second session, the instructor made the following statement: "No longer does the biblical principle of the wife being submissive to her husband and the children being submissive to both parents [apply] in society today. We are all equal."

. . . The mother asked the instructor what she should do if her ten-year-old did not want to clean her room. She was told that the room was the private property of the child and she should close the door if it bothered her; she had no right to enter without permission!

She resigned herself to the fact that *she* did not have the problem, *her* child did not have the problem, the school system had the problem. She took her child out and put her in a private school.[1]

• **Be familiar with the laws written to help you carry out your responsibilities.** For example, if school officials refuse to show you special classroom projects, you can remind them of your legal rights as a parent.

> » The Protection of Pupil Rights (Hatch) Amendment states that "all instructional material, including teacher's manuals, films, tapes, or other supplementary instructional material which will be used in connection with any research or experimentation program or project shall

be available for inspection by the parents or guardians of the children engaged in such programs or projects."[2]

» The "Equal Protection" Clause of the Fourteenth Amendment affirms that humanist or New Age educators have no more right to promote their religious views than do Christians. The constitutional interpretation that forbids prayer in school can work in our favor.

» Your state and school district may have other helpful laws. Check to see which ones would apply to your situation. Write to your U.S. senator and request federal and state level "Freedom of Information Acts."

According to the U.S. Department of Education's "Parents' Guide to the Family Educational Rights and Privacy Act," parents have the right to:

◊ Access their child's education records, such as report cards, transcripts, disciplinary records, and class schedules.

◊ Review their child's education records.

◊ Protect their child's privacy.[3]

STEP FOUR: ENLIST THE SUPPORT OF OTHER CHRISTIAN FAMILIES

• **Find other parents who share your concern.** Your influence increases when parents stand together.

• **Pray with other Christian parents.** Always have prayer backing when you need to confront. And remember this verse:

Be careful [anxious] for nothing; but in every thing by prayer and supplication with thanksgiving let your requests be made known unto God. (Philippians 4:6)

- **Get together with other parents** to discuss issues, compare notes, seek God's guidance, and plan strategy. Go to the board meetings regularly and speak out! One strong and wise but gracious voice can wield tremendous influence.

- **Show your child you understand the loneliness he may feel in an anti-Christian classroom,** and remind him he is not alone. Today, God is training many children to follow His truth, no matter what it may cost. Pray together that God will provide a Christian friend who shares his commitment and can stand with him for what he believes. (This presupposes that he really knows and understands what he believes. So keep teaching God's truth.)

- **If you have a less-than-desirable communication pattern with your child,** pray that God will provide another adult confidant—someone for whom your child has or could have a great deal of respect for and who also shares your views.

- **Inform and warn all who will listen.** "[N]ow I send thee, to open their eyes, and to turn them from darkness to light" (Acts 26:17-18).

EQUIPPING YOUR ELEMENTARY CHILD TO DEAL WITH DECEPTION

- **Know that you are the most important teacher in your child's life.** So take time to share her struggles, read together, and help with homework.

- **Make sure your child has entered into a personal relationship with Jesus Christ**; otherwise she will not be able to understand biblical truth and discern the counterfeit.

- **Continue to read and talk about God's Word.**

- **Explain the differences between God's truth and the counterfeit New Age spirituality.** Study the charts that can be found on my website.

- **Make a game of discovering examples of New Age spirituality.** Explain each conflict from God's point of view. As your child learns to see beliefs contrary to the truth, she will grow in discernment.

- **Alert your child to some of the New Age buzzwords and phrases** such as: centering, visualizing, meditation, contemplative prayer, inner space, "imagine yourself flying," "feel yourself becoming," etc.

- **Warn your child that meditation, guided imagery, Yoga, visualization,** and other spiritual or psychic techniques are not neutral exercises. They can bring her into contact with dangerous, supernatural forces—which God has told us to avoid. Discuss Deuteronomy 18:10-12 together:

  » There shall not be found among you any one that maketh his son or his daughter to pass through the fire, or that useth divination, or an observer of times, or an enchanter, or a witch, Or a charmer, or a consulter with familiar spirits, or a wizard, or a necromancer. For all that do these things are an abomination unto the LORD.

- **Explain the significance of God's armor.** Practice putting it on together. Assure your child that this armor will keep her spiritually safe. Remind her that if coerced into being physically present during meditations, séances, or guided imagery, she need not be afraid or participate mentally. Instead, she should thank God for keeping her safe in the armor.

EQUIPPING YOUR TEENAGE CHILD TO DEAL WITH DECEPTION

Equip your children to discern evil and resist compromise. "Be not deceived" (1 Corinthians 15:33).

- **Be available.** Your teenage child needs your participation in his life. He needs to see you as more dependable, caring, and understanding than his peers and teachers. Take time to enjoy as well as discipline, to play as well as pray.

• **Listen!** Give undivided attention! Be patient. Pray for understanding. Don't react with shock, dismay, or fear when your teenager shares what's happening in his world. Respond with gentle wisdom and compassionate love.

• **Show appreciation.** All too often, I catch myself correcting and reminding more frequently than affirming and thanking. Ask God to show you good things to affirm daily.

• **Provide information on New Age influences in the school.** Suggest interesting books and articles he can read. Then plan times to discuss their relevance either one-on-one or as a family.

• **If you question whether your teenager has a personal relationship with Christ, pray daily for openness to truth.** Contact with Christians and an opportune moment with you or another Christian might lead him or her to Christ.

• **Encourage your child to read the Bible each day.** He needs to wear God's armor as much as you do—and that requires regular feeding upon and exposure to truth.

• **Share a meal.** In *Seducers Among Our Children*, retired Investigative Sergeant Patrick Crough suggests sharing a meal at a restaurant or pizza parlor with your teen as a way to "learn about what goes on in our children's daily lives . . . not to gather intelligence for disciplinary action but to assist you in keeping them safe."[4]

- **Get in the habit of praying together.** When you share your needs (with discretion) and ask for prayer, your teenager will find it easier to share his. When you show appreciation for God's answers and His wise, loving participation in your life (according to your teenager's capacity to listen), you are encouraging your teenager to know, trust, and follow God.

Be a friend as well as a parent. Show respect, trust (where earned), and genuine appreciation. By your attitude and words—make sure they match—you can give your child a vision of what God wants to do in his life. Then walk with your child—not pulling from ahead or pushing from behind—but at his side, gently encouraging, sharing, and supporting.

> Children are a precious gift, an awesome responsibility, and your greatest investment.

Children are a precious gift, an awesome responsibility, and your greatest investment. Training them to follow God challenges your faith, demands your time, drains your energy, forces you to your knees, shows you God's sufficiency, and delights your heart. Hang in there—and "count it all joy" (James 1:2).

5

SCHOOLS & THE PROMOTION OF CORRUPTING VALUES

Wisdom resteth in the heart of him that hath understanding: but that which is in the midst of fools is made known. Righteousness exalteth a nation: but sin is a reproach to any people. (Proverbs 14:33-34)

SHOULD SCHOOLS TEACH values? They inevitably do. So the essential question is: Whose values?

Years ago, history books presented honorable heroes who modeled faith, courage, honesty, and integrity. Elementary readers introduced children to memorable characters who demonstrated genuine love, not a fleeting loving feeling, but the deep, laying-down-your-life kind of love that is so often ridiculed today.

A daring curriculum took their place—texts that have been carefully combed for any trace of biblical bent. Literature free from "biased" words like wife, husband, or marriage. Books that emphasize reality and relevance by modeling adultery, homosexuality, dishonesty, and drug abuse.

Called "values clarification," this "progressive" program challenges our children to defend or deny all the cherished goals and guidelines of earlier days. It insists that the only true values are those a child chooses himself in response to his immediate needs, desires, and circumstances. It tells him, "Do your own thing!" The result is a growing social chaos among people who, like Israel during the time of the Judges, do what is "right in [their] own eyes" (Judges 17:6 and Judges 21:25).

A mother from Kenosha, Wisconsin felt the painful effects of what her children were learning in school:

> By the time my first two children had reached third grade, I realized something was wrong. The child I took to school in the morning was not the child I picked up after school in the afternoon. If this change had been a positive change, reflecting academic progress, I would have been delighted. However, the change I noticed was in their value system. They seemed to be desensitized to the morals I had been trying to instill in them as their mother, and I thought that I had failed. . . .
>
> I failed because I had assumed the schools my children were attending were like the schools I had attended.
>
> I found instead that the thrust of schools had turned from education to indoctrination. I found the values I instilled in my children were not reinforced or respected by the schools, but were systematically challenged in the classroom.[1]

Spreading like cancer, this values transformation extends from the very core of our educational system to all its parts. In the name of progress, it promotes a self-centered kind of freedom from commitment and self-control.

Junior and senior high school students in Michigan were told to relax and "fantasize" in order to design a device for birth control "they would enjoy using." They were to discuss the criteria used for planning and the advantages of one design over another. Finally, they compared their design with existing contraceptives.[2]

What do students learn from this kind of exercise? The answer lies in the common goals of the humanist NEA, the New Age movement, and Planned Parenthood—three social forces that are surging forward together, dead-set on accomplishing their purpose. All three of these groups see a need to break free of "traditional" and "religious" authority that places God above human "needs" and hampers the desires of young people for sexual expression and activity according to whatever proclivity and lifestyle they desire—so long as we can keep unwanted pregnancy in check. As Planned Parenthood founder Margaret Sanger put it, sex is the "radiant force" enabling mankind to "attain the great spiritual illumination which will transform the world, which will light up the only path to an earthly paradise."[3]

> Luring children into this sensuous, self-centered lifestyle is Satan's most effective way of turning them away from God.

Such hedonistic philosophy cannot bring fulfillment. Instead, it stirs insatiable cravings. Luring children into this sensuous, self-centered lifestyle is Satan's most effective way of turning them away from God. If they embrace sin, they cannot see God's glory (2 Corinthians 4:4).

BACK TO "NATURE"

HUMANISM inflamed the intellectual community because it mirrored what they already believed. Likewise, Darwin's theory of evolution became an instant hit because he put a plausible "scientific" framework around a myth that had already found acceptance—thus validating it. This explains why "creative" scientists could produce a full-bodied drawing of their mythological missing link from fractions of bones and get away with it. Though admittedly false, the familiar monkey-to-man line-up may remain in textbooks—as if true—until evolutionists find better "proof" for their popular beliefs. The probabilities of chance-evolution have been likened to that of a tornado sweeping through a scrap yard and accidentally forming a Boeing jet.

Far more than an attempt to explain origins, evolution has become a social philosophy—the way to view all of life. Evolutionists see man simply as a higher form of animal. Since we train animals to serve society, why not use psychological techniques like behavior modification in the classroom? Why not free children to exercise their natural instincts, satisfy their evolving animal nature, and thereby fulfill their human potential?

Humanist goals have not changed since Darwin's days. In fact, the educators who signed the Humanist Manifesto II in 1973 stressed a "natural" and evolutionary way of life:

> In the area of sexuality, we believe that intolerant attitudes, often cultivated by orthodox religions and puritanical cultures, unduly repress sexual conduct. The right to birth control, abortion, and divorce should be recognized . . . Moral education for children and adults is an important way of developing awareness and sexual maturity.[4]

Even before the signing of the revised manifesto, two innovative humanists, William Glasser and Sidney Simon, showed the way to implement it. Published in 1969, Dr. Glasser's book, *Schools Without Failure*, presented a "daring new program"[5]: The class, led by the teacher, would become a counseling group. Somehow, by airing uncomfortable circumstances and feelings each day, this encounter group was supposed to teach social responsibility and solve behavioral problems. Consider the effect of this suggestion by Dr. Glasser:

> Children will often become very personal, talking about subjects that ordinarily are considered private. . . . The teacher should keep in mind that in class meetings, free discussion seems to be beneficial and that adult anxieties are often excessive. Nevertheless,

a child who discusses drunken brawls at home might quietly be asked to talk about something that has more relationship to school.

Changing the subject in this way is sometimes unwise, however because it is just those drunken brawls at home that have the most relationship to his school progress.[6]

Professor Sidney Simon went a step further. His book, *Values Clarification—A Handbook of Practical Strategies for Teachers and Students*, is packed with classroom exercises which filtered into text-books and public schools. A popular strategy called values voting is "a simple and very rapid means by which every student in the class can make a public affirmation on a variety of values issues."[7]

The teacher simply asks a question. The students respond affirmatively by raising their hands. They give a negative reply by pointing their thumbs down. If undecided, they fold their arms. To pass, they do nothing. After the teacher has asked about ten questions, the class discusses the answers. Each child is forced to take a public stand—even if he passes. Imagine the effect of this kind of peer pressure on a child who feels insecure.

The teacher asks, "How many of you:

» think there are times when cheating is justified?"

» regularly attend religious services and enjoy it?"

» think that women should stay home and be primarily wives and mothers?"

» would like to have a secret lover?"[8]

Simon recommends this list for all ages. For secondary students, he adds questions such as: "How many of you think sex education instruction in the schools should include techniques for lovemaking, contraception?" and "How many of you think you will continue to practice religion, just like your parents?[9]

CLARIFYING VALUES CLARIFICATION

PARENTS and teachers across the nation have agonized over the emotional damage caused by the psychological manipulations of *values clarification*. In response to their outcry, the Department of Education held hearings in seven locations across the country to implement the Protection of Pupil Rights (Hatch) Amendment.

Hundreds of parents testified at the hearings held in Seattle, Pittsburgh, Kansas City, Phoenix, Orlando, Concord (New Hampshire), and Washington, D.C. An amazing book by Phyllis Schlafly titled *Child Abuse in the Classroom* reported violations from the official transcripts of the proceedings. They fell into these categories:

• **Bias against Christian values.** A mother from Oregon, whose son became "very confused as to the rightness or wrongness of stealing," shared this testimony:

» Young children are expected to fill in sentences such as, "the trouble with being honest is _____." They are asked, what would be the hardest thing for you to do: "steal, cheat, or lie?"

» This question was discussed in the third grade: "How many of you ever wanted to beat up your parents?"[10]

• **Bias toward humanist/New Age values.** A first-grade lesson in "sex equality" shows the cruel pressure to conform.

» The students each had two naked dolls, one male, the other female. They were asked to dress the dolls in work clothing to show that both genders could work at any job. . . . there were no dresses. All clothing was male-oriented. Then the teacher had the students sit in a circle while she pulled out objects from a sack, like a pancake turner or a tape measure. She asked, "Who uses this, mom or dad?"

» If the students did not answer the way she had wanted, she would say, "Well, who *else* uses this?" Finally one little boy raised his hand and said, "I don't care. Men ought to be doctors and ladies nurses."

» The teacher then asked how many of the students agreed with him. By the tone of her voice, they knew no one should raise a hand, so no one did. The little boy was so humiliated by the peer pressure and class manipulation . . . that he started to cry.[11]

Striving with religious zeal to convert children to "moral relativism" or "situational ethics," humanist educators argue that anything other than "value-free" teaching is religion. To them, only values that fit man's desires are valid. For if man is his own god, he has divine authority to choose his own rights and wrongs. Frequent changes in terminology block the kind of "clarification" that exposes the mental manipulation. Programs might be called "values education," "self-awareness," "decision-making," "self-acceptance," or "interpersonal relationship skills."

Values clarification is neutral, argues Simon, since every value is as valid as any other. To him, the only wrong position is one that believes in absolute values—and therefore opposes his belief that all values are relative.[12]

• **Bias against traditional authorities such as parents and the church.** An eighth-grade sex education curriculum, titled, "Are You Ready for Sex?" used in Manistee, Michigan, asked questions such as: "Do you know why your parents and/or religion have taught that intercourse should wait until marriage? Do you accept these ideas? If so, would you be creating a lot of inner turmoil to go against your own beliefs?"[13]

Parents from New Jersey "could not find . . . in any of the hypothetical situations, a single portrayal of parents in a positive manner. Parents were shown to be overreaching, nagging, unfair, and overcritical of their children's friends." No wonder many children are confused about values, question their faith, and resist their parents.[14]

- **Denial of the right to privacy.** Values projects often require students to keep journals about their own and their parents' private activities. They are warned to tell no one.

Another popular technique described in *Child Abuse in the Classroom* makes home problems the focus of classroom discussion:

> Earlier this year, my fifth grader came home from school telling me about a new classroom activity called Magic Circle. . . . He told me the children sit in a circle and tell each other positive and negative things about each other. The teacher is not a trained psychologist, and this type of group therapy can be harmful to a child if done improperly.
>
> I also resent the probing questions asked by the teacher in this setting:
>
> "How many of you have unemployed parents?"
> "How many of you have divorced parents?"
> "If any of you are abused sexually, I want you to tell me, because by law I have to report it."

One mother summarized her feelings, "I consider this curriculum an invasion of family privacy, a subtle effort to erode all authority and undermine the traditional values that have made this nation great.[15]

- **Practice of dangerous and destructive psychological techniques.** The following attempts at Values Clarification, in a program called Preventive Guidance and Counseling, occurred in Lincoln County, Oregon. The parents learned about the program after they determined to find out why their children came home agitated on certain days. Some of the instances were:[16]

60

» An eleven-year-old girl was placed in front of her counseling class to tell her feelings when she found her father dead. Upon disclosing this information, she was later hassled by classmates with teasing questions.

» A second child was forced, under threat of discipline, to stand in front of the class and tell how it felt to have parents going through a divorce.

» A third child answering a questionnaire said, "Daddy spanks me, and sometimes pulls down my pants to spank me." Dad was then taken to the police station.[17]

• **Concealment of strategies from parents.** Many of the ways schools gain private information about the home life of its students are so subtle they escape notice. Often personal projects are hidden in curriculum that appears unrelated, such as physical education, English, or history. A teacher in the Lansing, Michigan school district observed:

» Students are all treated as in need or as having problems. Children are being pre-tested, then subjected to an affective [relating to feelings] values program as treatment for the disturbed child; then the child is post-tested to see what measurement of change has been produced by the affective values program.

» No parent has ever been notified or allowed to view the materials, nor have they ever consented to psychological diagnosis or treatment by an unlicensed psychologist or a psychiatrist. The children have even been promised that their parents won't be allowed to see their answers, "so be honest."[18]

Are you wondering what happens to the data gathered by tests and experiments? The above information on values and behavior is fed into computers and kept in student files in an extensive data bank. Does this sound like "Big Brother" watching?

Peer pressure is used for conforming children to group standards—or to the values of the more popular students. Concerning "sexual identity," Sidney Simon says, "The schools must not be allowed to continue fostering the immorality of morality. An entirely different set of values must be nourished."[19] One of Simon's strategies, the *values continuum*, asks students to choose a position between two value-loaded alternatives:

How do you feel about premarital sex?

| Virginal Virginia wears white gloves on every date. | Mattress Millie wears a mattress strapped to her back. |

Sometimes students tend toward compulsive moderation in taking positions publicly. They place themselves right in the middle, thereby hoping to avoid conflict or the need to think critically. One thing the teacher can do if this occurs frequently is to simply eliminate the middle of the continuum.[20]—*Values Clarification—A Handbook of Practical Strategies for Teachers and Students*

• **Bias against self-sacrifice and toward self-gratification.** Former Secretary of Education, William J. Bennett, and Edwin Delattre exposed the following strategy, which was recommended for mealtime family discussion:

» Your husband or wife is a very attractive person. Your best friend is very attracted to him or her. How would you want them to behave?

• Maintain a clandestine relationship so you wouldn't know about it.

- Be honest and accept the reality of the relationship.
- Proceed with a divorce.

Commenting on this exercise, Bennett and Delattre wrote:

> Typically the spouse and the best friend are presented
> as having desires they will eventually satisfy anyway;
> the student is offered only choices that presuppose their
> relationship. All possibilities for self-restraint, fidelity,
> regard for others, or respect for mutual relationships
> and commitments are ignored.[21]

Apparently, educational psychology aims to "free" students to satisfy selfish cravings without ever feeling guilty. So they replace God's idea of service with the lie that man exists primarily to serve himself. In the end, what kinds of relationships will this attitude produce? What happens to a child's sense of self-worth when he and his peers learn to worship only themselves?

The student is led to believe that he or she has freedom to choose among meaningful alternatives, which on one level is partly true. But at the critical meta-ethical level, no choice or even mention of serious alternatives are presented. In fact, whenever other positions are mentioned, they are almost without exception presented in a highly biased language.[22]

Sex Education: Promotion or Prevention?

Adolescents need to know the physiology of sex and the dangers of promiscuous encounters. Their minds do not need to be steeped in envisioned delights and techniques of sexual intercourse.

Unfortunately, Planned Parenthood's philosophy pervades today's sex education: that children must be set free to indulge in sexual adventures without fear of pregnancy. Working together for social change, the NEA, Planned Parenthood, and SIECUS (The Sex Information and Education Council of the United States) have prepared a titillating display of movies, textbooks, props, and promotional material. Most encourage rather than discourage sexual activity.

Sexuality and Man is a collection of articles written and compiled by SIECUS board members. One of its authors, Lester Kirkendall, Ph.D., unveils the SIECUS philosophy:

> The purpose of sex education is not primarily to control and suppress sex expression, but to indicate the immense possibilities for human fulfillment that human sexuality offers. The individual must be given sufficient understanding to incorporate sex most fruitfully and most responsibly into his present and future life.[23]

During the 1990s, a much-used "value-free" text, *Changing Bodies, Changing Lives,* stated: "People aren't born knowing how to be in sexual relationships, so you have to learn a lot with each partner."[24] Attempting to broaden this learning, it explains anal and oral sex and suggests that students may

Like values clarification, sex education seems to be most "effective" in changing lifestyles when discussed openly.

discover homosexual tendencies. "For some, that self-awareness and understanding is a natural and positive thing."[25] It tells how gay men make eye contact with strangers and hints that lesbians can meet through "shared political work in the women's movement."[26] To students confronted by parents who don't want them to "be sexual at all until some distant time," it suggests that they may have to "tune out their [parents'] voice entirely."[27]

Like values clarification, sex education seems to be most "effective" in changing lifestyles when discussed openly. Therefore, the curriculum usually includes questions that stimulate the imagination, which in turn, helps in overcoming modesty. Consider the discussion that could follow this question from the popular health guidance text, *Masculinity and Femininity*, "What are the advantages and disadvantages of using withdrawal to prevent conception?"[28]

While this text does mention abstinence as a possible means of birth control, it adds this comment: "Although agreeing that it works, many people do not consider abstinence to be a satisfactory choice."[29]

Obviously not. Studies show that today's teens generally believe they are entitled to enjoy sex. Anything goes, as long as they don't hurt or force anyone. Of course, "force" becomes a highly subjective term when many (who have learned to affirm their greatness and follow their feelings) believe that a resisting partner secretly wants to be forced.

Assuming that children will indeed be sexually active, Planned Parenthood, together with the Center for Population Options, has planted school-based health clinics on campuses across America. These clinics provide birth control information, contraceptives, and abortion referrals for children as young as twelve. While a school cannot dispense an aspirin without a parent's consent, abortion clinics can provide abortion on demand without parental knowledge.

Ponder this chilling observation: In *The Aquarian Conspiracy*, Marilyn Ferguson quotes sociologist John Cuber, who observed that the youth of 1969 had rejected the old sexual code:

> It is a comfortable cliché among the middle-aged that the restive young, when faced with responsibilities, will settle into traditional viewpoints. That is not so for this generation. . . . As long as the sinner acknowledges his guilt, there is a chance that he may reform and repent. *But*

the key to this generation is precisely its freedom from guilt.'[30] (emphasis changed, caps in original)

If people discredit truth and quench the conscience, how will they live? God points us to the answer:

> This know also, that in the last days perilous times shall come. For men shall be lovers of their own selves, covetous, boasters, proud, blasphemers, disobedient to parents, unthankful, unholy, Without natural affection, trucebreakers, false accusers, incontinent, fierce, despisers of those that are good, Traitors, heady, highminded, lovers of pleasures more than lovers of God . . . Yea, and all that will live godly in Christ Jesus shall suffer persecution. (2 Timothy 3:1-4, 12)

> But evil men and seducers shall wax worse and worse, deceiving, and being deceived. But continue thou in the things which thou hast learned and hast been assured of, knowing of whom thou hast learned them. (2 Timothy 3:13-14)

What I have shared here in this chapter is heavy and certainly could be cause for despair. And apart from God, we have *every* reason to be discouraged. But God is greater than the social forces corrupting our world, and we know that our Redeemer lives. Someday, maybe not on this Earth, we will live in a Holy land with our King. He has promised this to those who name the name of Jesus Christ. In the meantime, let us remember that in the light of His sufficiency, we can face unafraid the future of our children, and we pray daily for His wisdom and His guidance in the way in which we should go.

6

HOW TO GUARD YOUR CHILD AGAINST CORRUPTING VALUES

And these words . . . shall be in thine heart: And thou shalt teach them diligently unto thy children, and shalt talk of them when thou sittest in thine house, and when thou walkest by the way, and when thou liest down, and when thou risest up. (Deuteronomy 6:6-7)

WHETHER WE LIKE it or not, we know that our strongest messages flow through our lifestyles. Yet, even if we could live God's values perfectly, the model is incomplete without explanation. Our children need to know that our values come from God's Word and not just from a personal preference. They need to hear and discuss God's ways until they can confidently explain them to others.

Children need to know *why* as well as *what*. Hard-hitting questions will surely come from those who challenge their faith. Knowing the basis for their convictions, they will not waver when others declare that God's ways have become obsolete and outdated.

STEP ONE: ENCOURAGE YOUR CHILDREN TO LOVE GOD

• **Show your children how much you love God.** Let them hear you pray, sing, thank Him, talk about Him, and make choices that honor Him.

- **Show your own enthusiasm and commitment** to knowing and hearing God speak to you through His Word.

- **Read and discuss other books** that tell about God, and share what God shows you. Tell how He helps you.

- **Pray with your children each day for wisdom and strength.** Ask God to live His life in and through you. Show that you rely on Him.

- **Thank Him together for answers to prayers.** Be specific.

- **Help them to see that you put your trust in the Lord,** leaning not on your own understanding (Proverbs 3:5) but wholly relying on Him for all your needs, including the ability to walk a godly life.

- **Practice living God's truth together** as you play games, eat meals, participate in sports, ride in the car, and share your resources with others. Remember that all activities are opportunities to live for God and affirm your appreciation for what He values.

STEP TWO: SHARE GOD'S VALUES WITH YOUR CHILDREN

- **Ask God to show you how to communicate in natural age-appropriate ways.** The simplest way is to discuss your own personal experiences from God's perspective during your ordinary encounters—when you *sit, walk* (or drive), *lie down*, and *get up*.

You may want to use the following topics for meal or bedtime discussion or for special family evenings. Choose items appropriate to your children, adjusting the words to their age-level.

- **Explore the meaning of values:**

  » What does it mean to value something?

> » What do you value? Least? Most?

> » What determines your values?

> » What costs are you willing to pay for what you value? Rejection, teasing, not seeing certain movies?

- **Discuss what God says about things He loves:**

> » Honoring and obeying parents: Exodus 20:12, Ephesians 6:1

> » Respecting authority: Romans 13:1

> » Following God—our highest authority: Acts 5:29; John 10:4

> » Love: 1 Corinthians 13:1-7

> » Forgiving and caring for others: Luke 6:27-36

- Discuss what God says about things He hates.

> » Lying: Proverbs 12:22

> » Stealing: Matthew 19:18

> » Cheating: 1 Corinthians 6:8-9

> » Greed: Luke 12:15

> » Rudeness and swearing: Ephesians 5:3-5

> » Proverbs 6:16 has a list of what God hates.

- **Talk about what would happen if everyone followed this guideline:** Do whatever feels right.

> I have never asked my children's opinion about the truth of this value claim [that torture is wrong] and do not intend to do so, just as I never asked them their opinion about the law of gravity. . . . Rather, I teach them the truth of this value and expect them both to believe it and to base their action on it.[1]—**Richard A. Baer, Jr.**

Step Three: Train Your Children To Be "Ambassadors" For God

- **Tell your own experience of standing up for what you believe.** Let your children feel your inner battle to choose God's way. Assure them that you understand their struggles—and that God's favor is worth far more than peer approval. No matter how we feel, we who belong to Him are His ambassadors (2 Corinthians 5:20).

- **Take time to read together stories about courageous Christians.** Nobody outgrows the richness of family reading.

- **Practice sharing your convictions with each other (1 Peter 3:15-17).**

Step Four: Know What Values the School Teaches

America's obvious moral deterioration has fueled a growing demand for values education. Offered in an atmosphere that rejects biblical roots, values teaching will continue to grow out of the sandy foundation of moral relativism.

- **Talk with your children about classroom activities.**

- **Scan texts, take-home projects, and fliers.** Discuss movies and special classroom activities. Ask: Do they:

  » Put down Christian values? Imply that honesty, loyalty, obedience, and sexual purity are outdated or negotiable?

  » Present a negative view of parents? Suggest that parents are old-fashioned, too strict, or intrusive? Recommend that students ignore parents' advice and dismiss their guidelines?

  » Require students to reveal or discuss private family matters? Ask embarrassing personal questions?

  » Tell your children to keep secret an assignment or project?

  » Use peer pressure to conform children to popular standards and class consensus?

  » Promote self-gratification rather than actions that produce patience, perseverance, and maturity?

- **If any answer is yes, speak with the teacher or school officials.** Follow the guidelines in chapter three of this book.

- **Examine the sex and/or AIDS education program.** If it promotes sexual activity, join with other parents and suggest alternatives.

STEP FIVE: WORK TOGETHER WITH YOUR CHURCH

- **Know what it offers your children.** Find out what children's programs and youth groups are teaching. Ask:

  » Do they teach the basic tenets of Christianity (e.g., the deity of Christ, the substitutionary atonement, the virgin birth)?

  » Do they have a plan for teaching biblical values? The Ten Commandments is a simple and basic outline of God's values. The Sermon on the Mount (Matthew 5—7) shows the utter impossibility of keeping God's Laws by our own strength and therefore reminds us to acknowledge our need and trust in His sufficiency.

- **Encourage each other.** Parents need to agree on standards so children realize that other families follow the same guidelines.

- **Build a resource center.** Share books, information, experiences, and concerns with other parents.

  » Make sure that someone who has spiritual discernment is overseeing the resource center. Today, there are many books published by Christian and secular publishers that are promoting New Spirituality concepts.

PROJECTS FOR ADOLESCENTS

- **Talk together about the basic goals of sex education.** In most places, these goals are not to prevent sexual activity but to release children from parental authority to a "new" sensual lifestyle. This fits the New Age demands for a return to nature and for pleasure. It also closes doors to Christianity—most sexually active teens will shut out voices that question their chosen lifestyle.

- **Define and discuss words like:**

  » Love. What kinds? Based on what? (See 1 Corinthians 13:1-7; John 15:12-14; 1 John 4:7-12.)

  » Commitment. What is it? What are the costs?

  » Respect. Who are some of the people you respect? Why?

  » Intimacy. What is it? How can teens be intimate without having sex? How can sex hinder intimacy?

  » Chastity or virginity. What do they mean? Why are they good?

  » Dating. Advantages of group dating? Disadvantages of group dating? How can you show love without sex?

» Abortion. Study these Scriptures for insight: Jeremiah 1:4-5; Psalm 127:3; 139:13-16; Luke 1:41-45.

- **Know what God says about your body** in 1 Corinthians 3:16-17; 6:15-20.

- **Know what He says about sex outside marriage** in Ephesians 5:3; 1 Thessalonians 4:3-5; and Genesis 39:7-9.

God made sex the most beautiful expression of intimacy and love possible between a man and a woman who are committed to each other. But outside of marriage, it cripples both the body and the mind—and with excruciating emotional pain and lasting wounds.

STEPS TO VICTORY

- **See yourself as special and unique,** belonging to God—created, planned, set apart, and guarded by Him.

- **Be wise.** Study God's guidelines (Ephesians 5:15-18).

- **Know your own weaknesses.** Trust in God's strength. Choose to say NO to disobedience before you take the first step. Avoid compromising situations (1 Timothy 4:7-8).

- **Remind yourself:**

  » His grace is sufficient in my weakness (2 Corinthians 12:9-10).

  » "Christ liveth in me" (Galatians 2:20).

  » "I can do all things through Christ." (Philippians 4:13).

Trust in the Lord with all thine heart; and lean not unto thine own understanding. In all thy ways acknowledge him, and he shall direct thy paths. Be not wise in thine own eyes: fear the Lord, and depart from evil. (Proverbs 3: 5-7)

7

SCHOOLS &
NEW AGE GLOBALISM

He alone, who owns the youth, gains the Future![1]—
Adolph Hitler

The traditional Christian family has been a continual obstacle to the globalist vision of solidarity. . . . the United Nations
and its mental health gurus have fought hard to eradicate
those old "poisonous certainties" that stood in their way. .
. . The results can be disastrous. Students trained to scorn
God's guidelines and conform to the crowd are . . . soon
driven by evolving new notions that undermine all truth and
certainty. [2]—**Carl Teichrib** (research journalist)

A COUNTERFEIT HOPE surges through our society today: We
can do it! We can re-create the earth and complete the evolutionary process. When we eliminate national and spiritual barriers,
we will be one. By becoming a part of the "cosmic" stream of
consciousness around the world, we can become a superrace, the
true global family of God.

The seeds of this utopian dream were sown by John Dewey.
Nurtured by the warm friendship between humanist NEA and
UNESCO, one-worldism sank its roots deep into every level of
public education. The late Dr. Robert Muller, former Under-
Secretary of the United Nation's Economic and Social Council,
unmasked the movement's spiritual nature in his book on global
education, *New Genesis: Shaping a Global Spirituality*:

On a universal scale, humankind is seeking no less than its reunion with the "divine," its transcendence into ever higher forms of life. Hindus call our earth Brahma, or God, for they rightly see no difference between our earth and the divine. This ancient simple truth is slowly dawning again upon humanity . . . as we are about to enter our cosmic age and to become what we were always meant to be: the planet of God.[3]

To "evolving" New Agers, the end goal of global oneness justifies any questionable ways or means. It is not surprising then to find classrooms teaching steps and carrying out curricula that work toward fulfilling this lofty vision. The formula that substitutes counterfeit values for God's wisdom can also change the world: crush the old; then out of the ashes will rise a new earth—a world free from guilt, fear, oppression, and poverty. The time is ripe to buy the lie.

This transformation has vastly accelerated as millions around the globe await the New Age/New Spirituality world of harmony, love, and oneness—a world of evolved god-men all following the wisdom of Self. Discernment Research Group at the Herescope blog explains the crucial role that education (the transformation of it) plays in bringing this new world to the forefront:

> Education is a key vehicle to implement Robert Muller's "vision" for a New Age. . . . [Muller's] education curriculum served as a spiritual and political model, based on the metaphysical beliefs of Theosophy, for education reform in the United States and around the world. Muller's spiritual framework was particularly appealing to globalists and futurists, many of whom were the architects of the transformation of education.[4]

THE NEW AMERICAN HISTORY

THE New Age/New Spirituality balloon has two major flaws. It ignores the selfish, sinful nature of man and rejects the perfect and righteous plan of God. Yes, the Bible tells us that a one-world government *will* rise to power waving the banner of peace. But it will unleash unimaginable cruelty and oppression. Like ancient Babylon, it will demonstrate both the captivating power of Satan and the base depravity of man separated from God.

History has shown time and again that when people adhere to the "end justifies the means," it usually results in the means foretelling the end. We can catch a glimpse of a future New Age world by looking at the ways in which its people pursue their goals. And if they deceive during the pursuit, they will surely deceive in the end.

We know that totalitarian governments distort historical facts in order to control their people—but America would never stoop to that level now, would it? In their book, *What Are They Teaching Our Children?*, Mel and Norma Gabler present some chilling facts:

Who deserves more attention in an American history text: George Washington or Marilyn Monroe? One fifth-grade text devoted seven pages to Miss Monroe, while mentioning George Washington only eight times.[5]

• Name the nation you think is being discussed in this passage from another fifth-grade text: "No nation on earth is guilty of practices more shocking and bloody than is _____ at this very hour. Go where you may and search where you will. Roam through all the kingdoms of the Old World. Travel through South America. Search out every wrong. When you have found the last, compare your facts with the everyday practices of this nation. Then you will agree with me that, for revolting barbarity and shameless hypocrisy—has no rival." Give up? The country so honored is the United States.[6]

• Name six major culture areas of the world. If you included the United States and Western Europe, you're wrong—at least according to a world history text which selects: the Soviet Union,

Latin America, China, India, Africa, and the Middle East.[7]

• Fill in the blank. "[In China] _____turns the people toward a future of unlimited promise, an escalator to the stars." The missing word is Marxism.[8]

While other nations whitewash their own pasts, our country grants global-minded educators the freedom to reduce our nation's image to that of a greedy, aggressive tyrant. They warned us, but we didn't believe it could happen. In their Manifesto II, humanists told us that they "deplore the division of humankind on nationalistic grounds" and aim to "transcend the limits of national sovereignty."[9] They are determined to build "a world community"—with the help of our children. A textbook for teachers says:

> Allegiance to a nation is the biggest stumbling block to the creation of international government. National boundaries and the concept of sovereignty must be abolished. The quickest way to do this is to condition the young to another and a broader alliance. Opinion favorable to international government will be developed in the social studies in the elementary school.[10]

PEACE EDUCATION

THE depreciation of the entire Western world and the proclamation of the globalist view of peace are programming children to accept four New Age goals:

• A New World Order, which implies a one-world government.

• A new world religion. The New Age medley (syncretism) of humanism, Hinduism, and every other religion—except genuine Christianity—fits the bill perfectly.

• A new economic system to redistribute the world's wealth.

- A spiritually evolved global citizenry ruled by the most advanced and most aware.

To steer students into the one-world camp, globalists use a strategy called "Management by Crisis." Their prod is fear, and the programming may begin as early as kindergarten. This "peace curriculum" first immerses the children in genuine concerns blown to crisis proportion—such as the horrors of nuclear war and ecological disaster—then uses predetermined reactions for political purposes.

To avoid confrontation with "right-wing Christian groups," a memorandum from the Seattle Public Schools dated April 19th, 1985 recommended using terms other than "Global Education." A "temporary, safe term is multicultural/international curriculum development."[11]

With the excuse that children's fear had to be brought out in the open, globalist educators found ways to produce the needed fear. Children watched films showing mutilated victims from the Hiroshima and Nagasaki bombings.[12] They were told to discuss the long-term effects on "those who are not immediately killed by the explosion."[13] They pondered the ongoing pain of radiation sickness. They studied pictures drawn by Hiroshima survivors. They played games to stir thoughts about their own death. They imagined the devastation from far larger nuclear explosions in their own state, county, and neighborhood. And they became afraid.

They heard strange accounts about America's aggressive, uncooperative policies. They learned to sympathize with Russia's struggles with unfriendly neighbors. They played games to prove American wealth and greed in the face of a starving world community.

They became angry and felt ashamed. At that point, a trained teacher could direct their fear, anger, and national guilt into desirable action—make scrapbooks on peace, tell adults about disarmament, share at community forums, write letters to their senators—and to the President.[14]

If global education taught facts rather than feeling, discernment rather than sympathy, and reality rather than propaganda, we would applaud it. But it doesn't. It teaches children to scorn Western democracy (calling it capitalism), favor Marxism (calling it social justice), and despise national leadership. It leads children to sincerely, but arrogantly, believe their naive solutions are better than those based upon the wise consideration of historical data, the oppression of dictatorships, and the horrendous injustices of Communism and Marxism.

Deploring this political subversion in our schools, William Bennett, then United States Secretary of Education, remarked:

> Nor is it proper to use American classrooms for "creating a grassroots network of educator activists" as Educators for Social Responsibility . . . described its goal.

> Wishes will not replace the fact that American citizens share almost nothing of their political life with the subjects of a totalitarian government. . . . All men are created equal, but all political and social systems are not.[15]

THE HUNDREDTH MONKEY

To inspire children with a sense of power to change their world, many peace programs use the following fable as a guiding principle. The fact that it evolved from real events makes the fiction all the seemingly more credible.

The story began with a group of Japanese scientists who studied macaque monkeys on the island of Koshima in 1952. When they left some sweet potatoes—a new treat—on the beach, a young female monkey improved the taste by washing off the sand in nearby water. First, the younger monkeys imitated her actions, soon the others followed.

Here, factual reporting gives way to New Age myth-making. In the fictional story used by several peace programs, Imo, a young female, taught the trick to her mother. Then her smart little play-mates who copied her taught the trick to their mothers. The next point is significant: "Only the adults who imitated their children learned this social improvement. Other adults kept eating the dirty sweet potatoes."[16] At this point, the myth mushrooms into the realm of magic.

> In the autumn of 1958, a certain number of Koshima monkeys were washing sweet potatoes—the exact number isn't known. Let us suppose that when the sun rose one morning there were ninety-nine monkeys on Koshima Island who had learned to wash their sweet potatoes. Let us further suppose that later that morning, the hundredth monkey learned to wash potatoes. THEN IT HAPPENED!

> By that evening almost everyone in the tribe was washing sweet potatoes before eating them. The added energy of this hundredth monkey somehow created an ideological breakthrough!

> But notice. The most surprising thing observed by these scientists was that the habit of washing sweet potatoes spontaneously jumped over the sea—colonies of monkeys on other islands and the mainland troop of monkeys at Takasakiyama began washing their sweet potatoes!

> Thus, when a certain critical number achieves an awareness, this new awareness may be communicated from mind to mind. Although the exact number may vary, the Hundredth Monkey Phenomenon means that when only a limited number of people know of a new way, it may remain the consciousness property of these people. But there is a point at which if only one more person tunes in to a new awareness, a field is strengthened so that this awareness reaches almost

everyone! . . . Your awareness is needed in saving the world from nuclear war. You may be the "Hundredth Monkey."[17]

Like Darwin's theory of physical evolution, the hundredth monkey allegory has been highly touted as the "scientific" basis for the New Age/New Spirituality vision, both inside and outside the field of education. No wonder! It presents the ultimate in spiritual evolution. And in the subjective atmosphere of the New Spirituality, you don't question a revelation. You just believe!

The tale of the hundredth monkey became a popular urban legend—powerful enough to shape New Age thought. People believed it—and acted on it. For example, Randolph Price, co-founder of The Quartus Foundation for Spiritual Research, called for a special day of global meditation. He stated:

> We see that the world consciousness is quickly moving toward critical mass. . . . Doing whatever is necessary to change our individual consciousness, we will begin to break up some of the dark pockets of negative energy in the race mind. Through our collective efforts on December 31, 1986, we can literally turn on the Light of the World, dissolve the darkness, and begin the New Age of spirituality on Planet Earth.[18]

A NEW WORLD RELIGION

To inspire a consciousness explosion, many New Age leaders are determined to win a critical mass of minds. Children will be the prime target of the "missionary" efforts, and schools their greatest battlefield.

William Bennett exposes this ominous blend of public school curriculum, New Age spirituality, and cosmic dreams:

> Another legacy from the Age of Aquarius that has been enshrined in too many of our social studies curricula

is a disturbing anti-rational bias. Curriculum guides for . . . global education are shot through with calls for "raised consciousness," for students and teachers to view themselves "as passengers on a small cosmic spaceship," for classroom activities involving "intuiting," "imaging," or "visioning" a "preferred future."

Two proponents of such curricula have offered a candid caution: "These exercises may seem dangerous to your logical thought patterns. For best results, suspend your judging skills and prepare to accept ideas that seem silly and/or impractical." Well, if we're going to give up critical judgment, we'd better give up the game of education altogether.[19]

While "raised consciousness" and "visioning" sound too mystical for admission into many schools, a new form of religious education does not. Teaching about the major world religions such as Buddhism, Hinduism, Islam, and Christianity, the curricula emphasize the universal "truths" and historical values of each. That sounds fair and innocuous, until we remember that New Age globalism calls for a one-world religion—a persuasive union of all supposed paths to eternal life. Since biblical Christianity doesn't fit the formula, some of these courses have—in the hands of "progressive" teachers—become a platform for criticizing Christian exclusiveness and promoting Eastern meditation. Speaking to many of the world's religious and political leaders, the former Archbishop of Canterbury, Robert Runcie, articulated this New Age formula for spiritual oneness in a global community. Notice the apologetic and compromising version of "Christianity":

Behind [this resurgence of religions] lies a widespread pessimism about the future of humankind, and unsatisfied longing for alternative paths to salvation. All the centuries that the Spirit of God had been

> working in Christians, He must also have been working
> in Hindus, Buddhists, Muslims, and all the others. . . .
> This will mean that some claims about the exclusiveness
> of the Church will have to be renounced.[20]

In April of 1988, representatives of Christianity, Buddhism, Hinduism, Islam, and Judaism met with political leaders from over forty nations to "solve" the world's problems. This Global Conference of Spiritual and Parliamentary Leaders on Human Survival was sponsored by the Temple of Understanding, a global interfaith organization, which was founded with the support of such dignitaries as the Dalai Lama, Indian Prime Minister Nehru, Eleanor Roosevelt, Popes John XXIII and Paul VI. The Temple is an inveritable "hotbed of international dialogue and outright promotion of Eastern mysticism," working in a "consultive status" with the United Nations and offering interfaith programs for youth. Guest speakers have included such New Age advocates as Donald Keys, David Spangler, and Benjamin Creme (who has heralded the coming of Lord Maitreya, "The Christ," for many years).[21]

> For there shall arise false Christs, and false prophets,
> and shall shew great signs and wonders; insomuch that,
> if it were possible, they shall deceive the very elect.
> (Matthew 24:24)

Just to show you what really lies behind the New Age plan for a coming "Christ," listen to Benjamin Creme describe this "Messiah":

> In the esoteric tradition, the Christ is not the name of an
> individual but of an Office in the Hierarchy. The present
> holder of that Office, the Lord Maitreya, has held it for
> 2,600 years, and manifested in Palestine through His Dis-
> ciple, Jesus, by the occult method of overshadowing, the

most frequent form used for the manifestation of Avatars. He has never left the world, but for 2,000 years has waited and planned for this immediate future time, training His Disciples, and preparing Himself for the awesome task which awaits Him. He has made it known that this time, He Himself will come.[22]

The Bible tells us that one day, a man will come on the scene who will proclaim himself to be God and will demand that all of humanity worship him. Children throughout the world are being conditioned to accept him even now.

Let no man deceive you by any means: for that day shall not come, except there come a falling away first, and that man of sin be revealed, the son of perdition; Who opposeth and exalteth himself above all that is called God, or that is worshipped; so that he as God sitteth in the temple of God, shewing himself that he is God. (2 Thessalonians 2:3-4)

MYTH-MAKING & GLOBAL TRANSFORMATION

AN assignment from the "Kids" page of the United Religions Initiative (URI) website illustrates the mind-changing tactics that speed this global transformation. The page is subtitled, "Individual Spiritual Growth: Create Your Own Religion." Working with UNESCO and its partners around the world, the URI envisions a united world "freed" from the bounds of biblical absolutes. Its march toward solidarity must exclude our almighty God—the actual Creator and Sustainer of our planet. It accepts only those who can walk the broadly traveled popular road together toward inclusive spirituality and collective thinking.

By the time this assignment is given, most young minds— Christian or not—have already been introduced to all kinds of alluring gods, goddesses, nature spirits, and chi forces. Here's their opportunity to practice visualizing their favorite spiritual blend:

experience death and at that moment you will see yourself rise to the ceiling of this room . . . [and be] content in your new state.[29]

Gregg L. Cunningham was an official in the Education Department's regional office in Denver until he wrote a candid report exposing the globalist program of the Center for Teaching International Relations. Ponder his observation:

> For unsurpassed morbidity . . . students can consider a lament that our culture does not "encourage visits" from "the spirits of the dead" (described as an "open and joyous" experience in contrast with American "uncomfortable" attitudes toward the dead).[30] They are then taught to "create their own altar honoring the dead" (in a manner reminiscent of ancestor worship).[31]

Who promotes these courses that encourage depression and suicide? Ecologists who want to reduce the world's population to save resources? Proponents of eugenics who, like Hitler and Margaret Sanger, envision a super-race rid of its "weaker" or more "dissident" members? Militant social reformers who want to desensitize youth to organized euthanasia and other forms of social killing? New Age missionaries who want to present death as a way to escape the present for a better tomorrow through reincarnation? Or New Age visionaries preparing our youth for the prophesied purge of all who commit the sin of separateness—who hinder the plan by not joining the march toward the new global society?

Most likely, all of the above. God says, "all they that hate me love death" (Proverbs 8:36). The counterfeit army that hates God's people embraces death education and other treacherous philosophies.

THE "SIN OF SEPARATENESS"

BECAUSE unity is essential for creating the critical mass, many New Age leaders join in condemning the hindering influence of the church. Their objection? Its "negative energy" blocks the envisioned, long-anticipated evolutionary breakthrough. As you have seen, this belief has filtered into the classroom.

Thus, anyone who follows God becomes guilty of the only sins in the New Age: unbelief and separateness. Christians who refuse to share the global vision and join the evolutionary march will reap persecution as Scripture indicates (e.g., 2 Timothy 3:12). For Satan, the counterfeit angel of light, hates all who shine the true light of Christ into the world. The New Age book *Spiritual Politics* lays out the plan for the "Age of Aquarius" where all are united and all believe they are God. Unity among all humanity will be essential and non-negotiable, they believe, for this global unification and *divinity realized* to take place:

> According to Ageless Wisdom, there really is only one sin—separateness. In the early years of World War II, Alice Bailey noted that we will achieve peace in the world only after we first create unity. . . . The persistence of war is more likely to spring from rampant nationalism, ethnocentrism, and intolerant religious fundamentalism--all extreme and separative attitudes.[32]

God is not surprised at this diabolical deception. Long ago, He warned us that the Antichrist would one day rule the world and persecute Christians:

> And it was given unto him to make war with the saints, and to overcome them: and power was given him over all kindreds, and tongues, and nations. And all that dwell upon the earth shall worship him, whose names are not written in the book of life of the Lamb slain from the foundation of the world. (Revelation 13:7-8)

Meanwhile, God calls us to remain separate. As His holy people, we cannot join the forces of the Antichrist:

> Be ye not unequally yoked together with unbelievers: for what fellowship hath righteousness with unrighteousness? and what communion hath light with darkness? And what concord hath Christ with Belial? . . . And what agreement hath the temple of God with idols? for ye are the temple of the living God; as God hath said, I will dwell in them, and walk in them; and I will be their God, and they shall be my people. Wherefore come out from among them, and be ye separate. (2 Corinthians 6:14-17)

Since our children belong to God, He takes care of them. If they have to share in some of the persecution, He will be with them to protect, shield, and render unto them spiritual compensations that far exceed their physical suffering. Let Him encourage your family with these words:

> Be strong and of a good courage, fear not, nor be afraid of them: for the Lord thy God, he it is that doth go with thee; he will not fail thee, nor forsake thee. . . . fear not, neither be dismayed. (Deuteronomy 31:6, 8)

While world leaders seek "helpful" religions that serve their purposes, our gracious, almighty, and omnipotent Lord watches over those who have wholly put their trust in Him. Refusing to compromise, they walk the narrow road—but never alone. Their Shepherd walks with them no matter how rocky the road or lonely the miles.

Like His faithful pilgrims through the ages, they know Whom to thank whether their days are filled with sunshine or rain, and freedom or restraints. Trusting His love and His faithfulness, they praise Him for His strength through life's storms and for peace amidst problems. For He has promised never to leave them. So "in all these things we are more than conquerors through him that loved us" (Romans 8:37).

> And we know that all things work together for good
> to them that love God, to them who are the called
> according to his purpose. (Romans 8:28)

Our children are not immune to the world's messages. They hear the same tempting voices, the same "positive affirmations" that others hear and follow. Concerned about their spiritual safety, our Shepherd reminds them:

> And be not conformed to this world: but be ye
> transformed by the renewing of your mind, that ye may
> prove what is that good, and acceptable, and perfect,
> will of God. For I say, through the grace given unto
> me, to every man that is among you, not to think of
> himself more highly than he ought to think; but to
> think soberly, according as God hath dealt to every
> man the measure of faith. (Romans 12:2-3)

Unless we help our children build a mental framework and filter based on biblical truth, the world's philosophies will squeeze them into its mold. Therefore, it is essential that they see God as the only ultimate source of wisdom, power, and triumph.

The Lord is my rock, and my fortress, and my deliverer; my God, my strength, in whom I will trust; my buckler, and the horn of my salvation, and my high tower. I will call upon the Lord, who is worthy to be praised: so shall I be saved from mine enemies. (Psalm 18:2-3)

8

WHAT CAN PARENTS DO ABOUT NEW AGE GLOBALISM?

Now all these things happened unto them for ensamples: and they are written for our admonition, upon whom the ends of the world are come. (1 Corinthians 10:11)

THE OLD TESTAMENT has some of God's most practical truths. He told His precious people that success would come from knowing, loving, trusting, and following Him. On the other hand, if they were to spurn His counsel, they would lose His protection and become slaves of foreigners.

His people forgot. Growing strong and comfortable in the rich land God had given them, they became complacent and ignored His warnings. The result? They lost everything—possessions, lives, God's favor, the Promised Land, God's protection, and the comfort of God's presence. Longing to save us from similar consequences, God reminds us through Paul, that those events are "examples, to the intent we should not lust after evil things" (1 Corinthians 10:6).

When Israel followed God's guidelines, the people enjoyed His protection, peace, and prosperity. This same principle applies in the spiritual Kingdom where we, God's people, live with our King. On either home front, the key to success lies in His ancient instructions to Israel when he told them to love God with all their hearts, souls, and might, and to diligently teach their children the way to walk (Deuteronomy 6:5-7). In Deuteronomy 8:10-14, it says:

> When thou hast eaten and art full, then thou shalt bless the LORD thy God for the good land which he hath given thee. Beware that thou forget not the LORD thy God, in not keeping his commandments, and his judgments, and his statutes, which I command thee this day: Lest when thou hast eaten and art full, and hast built goodly houses, and dwelt therein . . . . and all that thou hast is multiplied; Then thine heart be lifted up, and thou forget the LORD thy God.

While these verses are not talking about America or our present world today, much can be learned from them, and the principles can be applied. Today America (including many proclaiming Christians, unfortunately) has gone down a very dangerous path. In her pursuit of other gods, she has forfeited freedom and morality. Is it too late? Some think so. And maybe that is true. But as believers, let us turn wholeheartedly to God, and let us do all we can to protect our families from this explosion of spiritual apostasy. Whether it is too late for America, as a nation, we cannot know for certain, but regardless of the outcome at a national level, let us work earnestly while it is still day to train and protect our children.

STEP ONE: KNOWING & LOVING GOD

- **Continue a family Bible reading program appropriate to your child's age.** Look at God's character together, see Him as He really is—not as the world depicts and distorts Him.

- **Help your child see that his identity should be in Christ.** Every one of us is a citizen of some country (e.g. Americans, Canadians, Africans, Australians, Britains, etc.), but more importantly, if we are believers in Jesus Christ, if He truly is our Savior and Lord, then we are citizens of God's kingdom. He is our only hope for genuine and lasting peace, no matter what happens around us (Philippians 3:20; 1 John 3:1-3; Ephesians 1:1-10).

- **Help your child to appreciate God's hand in providing a country** in which democracy and freedom have been established. Teach him about:

  » The historical foundation for democracy. Point out that many people fled to both Canada and the United States because they had experienced religious persecution. Seeking God's guidance, they carefully established a system of governmental checks and balances in order to preserve their precious new freedom—that which would become the foundation for the development of these two free countries.

  » The influence of faithful Christian believers who trusted God, followed His ways, and helped build His truths into the fabric of democracy.

- **Train your child to understand:**

  » The worth of our freedom to worship and follow God. Tell about faithful historical figures who laid down their lives so others could have freedom, which some of today's citizens seek to wholly discredit, deny, or take for granted.

  » The worth of the privilege to influence public policies on all levels of government. America's willingness to hear all kinds of ideas—even revolutionary ones—proves its tolerance and freedom. However, apart from God, this freedom can destroy our nation.

STEP TWO: KNOW GOD'S INSTRUCTIONS & WARNINGS

- **As a family, read Deuteronomy 6—8.** Study a portion each day. Write and discuss what He tells you to do and what He promises to do for you. Agree to help each other to follow His guidelines and receive His promises.

- **Show your child that while charity and respect should**

be shown to all human beings, the New Age/New Spirituality quest for a global community is based on the evolutionary presumption that man—not God—controls and can save the world.

• **Summarize the differences** between Western world democracy and the aggressive, authoritarian, and anti-Christian policies of Communist governments, radical Islamic governments, and military dictatorships.

• **Show how commitment to truth has its roots in and stems from biblical values.** While loving the world's people, we cannot trust rulers who oppose God and reject His values.

One of the most misunderstood and misquoted Scriptures in the Bible is Luke 6:37: "Judge not, and ye shall not be judged." God is not telling us to close our eyes to evil and tolerate beliefs and behavior that deny Him. Rather He reminds us to have "righteous judgment" (John 7:24).

Hinduism teaches New Agers to tune out unpleasant realities. But no amount of creative visualization or individual, group, or collective meditation will even begin to create a perfect world. The fact is that mankind, apart from God, still suffers from a deadly urge to conquer and control.

STEP THREE: GUARD AGAINST INFLUENCES OPPOSING GOD

SCAN all textbooks, fliers, extracurricular information, and school newsletters. Keep in mind that globalism may be disguised under other titles. Ask:

• **Do they indicate that New Age directives and global propaganda** have infiltrated into traditional areas of study such as English and science?

• **Do they suggest that meditative exercises may be used in the classroom** to encourage children to visualize a New Age world community or world peace? Remember that such consciousness-raising exercises are usually hidden behind innocuous names or scripted into regular classroom subjects.

• **Do they sensationalize or exaggerate the problems and dangers** of global pollution, overpopulation, and global warming? Do they use this information to direct children toward planned, biased political action?

• **Do they emphasize suicide?** Do they condone suicide as a viable solution to pollution or overpopulation?

• **Do they promote any form of eugenics or euthanasia** to solve the problems of overpopulation? Does your child participate in survival games that force him to choose who should live and die in hypothetical situations?

STEP FOUR: ACT ON WHAT GOD HAS SHOWN YOU

• **Pray alone and as a family** for wisdom and for the capacity to love the deceived while abhorring the deception.

• **Learn about U.S. education agreements** with Russia, China, and other countries to work together in developing a global curriculum. Robert Muller said in March 1985, "A world core curriculum might seem utopian today. By the end of the year 2000 it will be a down-to-earth, daily reality in all the schools in the world."[1]

• **Share your concerns with officials.** Your voice can make a difference. Write your Senators at the Senate Office Building, Washington, D.C. 20510. Write your Congressman at the U.S. House of Representatives, Washington, DC 20515.

• **Consider an alternative to public school.** After praying and seeking God's guidance, you may choose to remove your child from the public school system. Millions of children have either been enrolled in private schools or are homeschooled. There are currently over two million homeschooled children in the U.S.[2] A 2012 *Education News* article titled, "Number of Homeschoolers Growing Nationwide" states:

> Researchers are expecting a surge in the number of students educated at home by their parents over the next ten years as more families spurn public schools. . . . Any concerns expressed about the quality of education offered to the kids by their parents can surely be put to rest by the consistently high placement of homeschooled kids on standardized assessment exams.[3]

If you choose to homeschool, there are excellent online resources to help you along the way.[4] Currently, homeschooling is allowed in all fifty states of America and in all the Canadian provinces, but be sure to check your state's or province's specific regulations.

• **Finally, discuss and memorize this promise below.** Count on it! Live it!

Therefore, my beloved brethren, be ye stedfast, unmoveable, always abounding in the work of the Lord, forasmuch as ye know that your labour is not in vain in the Lord. (1 Corinthians 15:58)

9

THE MIND-CHANGING VISUAL MESSAGES IN MOVIES

We live in a culture where television, movies, the printed page, and now the Internet wield a great influence . . . the New Age movement has experienced stupendous growth because of these vehicles of communication. . . . Even the smallest influence can be a step in the process of fulfilling this obvious paradigm shift.[1]—**Ray Yungen**

IN 1977, A youth pastor took our thirteen-year-old son Todd to see *Grease*. You probably remember it—a movie musical written for the 1970s that showcased the '50s. The next evening my husband and I went to see it. I was shocked to think that a trusted church leader had brought junior high boys to a movie that modeled promiscuity and applauded a heroine who turned from morality to permissiveness.

"Don't worry," said the youth leader a few days later. "I taught them how to evaluate the movie. It can't hurt them."

Can't it? What about the exposure to pictures—the holographs or indelible imprints that are stored in the brain? What about the memories of a process that makes morality seem narrow-minded, cold, and judgmental, and makes evil seem kind and good? What about the manipulation that occurs when youngsters identify with the hero and participate emotionally with the good and bad choices of the characters?

Sensual pictures, mystical visions, and tempting suggestions don't immunize their viewers against wrongs. Rather, they desensitize the conscience and stir a craving for more. Stored in the brain, the enticing stimuli continue to influence the mind whether one recognizes it or not.

Discussing the movie afterward doesn't erase those stored images. Glimpses of immoral activities, identification with characters who oppose God, and memories of the apparent triumph of evil—all of these become building blocks in a child's value system.

When I saw *Grease*, I too felt the pull of the world's value system. First, I silently cheered the sweet, innocent girl who stood firm in what she believed. But the growing tension between the hero's unsatisfied sexual desires and the heroine's moral stand kindled a desire for a resolution. In the end, the heroine donned black, sexy, skintight wrappings—the symbol of her choice to discard the values that "deprived" the one she loved.

> Children are continuously exposed to an incredible onslaught of counterfeit messages.

While disgusted with her foolish decision and destructive modeling, I found myself sharing the audience's relief for what seemed to be the only comfortable solution to the problem.

Did my values change? No. But for a moment, I was tempted to view God's wise standards as archaic and the world's ways as more appropriate to our times.

Do you see the danger? Can you identify with the struggle? Then ponder the dangerous conflict our children face. Most of their values have not been tested and affirmed or proven and practiced as have yours and mine. They don't yet have the knowledge needed to discern error. Yet they are continuously exposed to an incredible onslaught of counterfeit messages.

THE MINDS BEHIND THE MOVIES

THE *Star Wars* epics put America in touch with "the force." Their thrilling cosmic intergalactic battles mesmerized millions, inspiring dreams of connecting with the same power system. Few bothered to examine the source of that "force." The appealing images and visions of contemporary movies bombard our children, making them doubt God and seek "better" ways to powerful living. Many young people create an imaginary world that seems more real and exciting than true reality. Quick to believe that nothing is impossible, viewers grasp for illusive dreams of adventure, power, mystical experiences, and promiscuity without consequences.

In *The Empire Strikes Back*, Yoda employed the "good side" of the force to raise Luke Skywalker's spaceship out of the swamp, showing his spellbound audience that man can accomplish anything he wants through faith in the "God of forces" (from Daniel 11:38, meaning false god).

Visions and values taught in movies are not accountable to truth and reality. They are accepted, not on the basis of reason but because they excite the emotions, challenge the imagination, and manipulate minds.

In this chapter, I can't even begin to cover all the movies that could readily qualify in this regard. There are just too many. But I will talk about a few of them, ones that are very indicative of the nature of movies for youth today.

THE SPIRIT BEHIND THE LION KING

BETRAYED, rejected, running from responsibility, growing strong through adversity . . . Disney's box-office hit, *The Lion King*, was full of seemingly biblical parallels, colorful characters, and personal struggles that help us identify with a lovable lion that thinks like a man. But watch out! Behind the spectacular scenery and noble sentiments hides the timeless earth-centered view of reality that has always lured God's people from truth to counterfeit truths.

In other words, *The Lion King*—like the movie *Aladdin*—demonstrates an alarming shift in values. While the old fairy-tale cartoons like *Snow White* linked sorcery to the evil characters, *The Lion King* uses tribal magic for "good." While most children in the seventies knew enough truth to place divination in the forbidden realm of the occult, today's children—who often feel more comfortable with occult games than biblical truth—see nothing wrong with pagan practices.

The Lion King opened with a spectacular celebration in honor of Simba, the newborn prince. The animals of the land flock to Pride Rock, where the mystical baboon Rafiki cracks open an egg-like gourd, dips his finger into the dark liquid, and anoints the little lion with a mark on his forehead.

While Pride Lands worships its royal heir, Simba's devious uncle, Scar, wishes Simba dead. As soon as the infant king grows to cubhood, he becomes a target for Scar's cruel schemes. The first plot fails, but the next assault kills King Mufasa. Scar blames Simba for his father's death, sends the heartbroken cub into the wilderness, and tells three savage hyenas to finish the execution.

Simba escapes through a web of thorns and collapses under the hot African sun. A warthog and a meerkat find the little prince, revive his exhausted body, and teach him a new philosophy: No worries! Hakuna matata!

Back in Pride Lands, Scar and his hyenas reign. The land lies dry and barren. One day, Rafiki looks into his magic gourd and sees Simba's living image. He sets out to find the reluctant heir to the throne, then demonstrates a worldwide pagan tradition: Reliance on help from ever-present ancestral spirits.

"I know your father," says Rafiki.

"My father is dead," answers Simba.

"Nope! He's alive. I'll show him to you." The shamanic baboon leads Simba to a pool of clear water. "Look down there."

First Simba sees his own reflection, then the face of his father.

"You see, he lives in you!" says Rafiki.

Simba hears a familiar voice call his name. He looks up. His father's ghostlike image appears among the stars.

"Look inside yourself," says the apparition. "You must take your place in the circle of life. Remember who you are." The vision fades.

Simba believes. He sees that the dead are not separated from the living, nor earth from the realm of spirits. Everything is connected. Empowered by a new sense of identity, he races back to Pride Lands to challenge his uncle, win the throne, and restore the land. Soon, Pride Lands celebrates the birth of the next lion prince, the son of Simba and his cubhood friend Nala. Again, Rafiki lifts a royal infant for all to worship. Everything comes full circle, and the circle of life continues. Consider the following five concerns:

1. King Mufasa tells his son, "Look at the stars. The great kings of the past look down on us from those stars. They will always be there to guide you . . . and so will I." This fatherly advice blends the world's timeless trust in astrological guides, spiritism, ancestral worship and multiple gods. The Bible tells us to shun all such expressions of paganism. (Deuteronomy 4:19; 18:9-13)

2. "Simba, everything you see exists together in a delicate balance," explains Mufasa. "As king, you will need to understand that balance and respect all creatures because we are all connected in the great circle of life."

In light of the earlier reference to the "circle of life," we know this statement moves beyond a biological food chain and natural cycles. Mystical connectedness, the spiritualized circle of life, and respect or tolerance for everything—no matter how evil by God's standards—fit right into contemporary multicultural and environmental teachings. Educators, entertainers, and media-leaders promote these pagan concepts as moral ideals needed to save the earth and usher in global oneness. In sharp contrast, God's Word tells us that nature worship and oneness with pagan cultures bring destruction both to land and people (Deuteronomy. 11, 28; Romans 1:18-32).

3. To "look inside" for wisdom and guidance usually implies that anyone—Christian or not—can tap into an inner source of uncorrupted wisdom, because all are one with some sort of pantheistic deity or cosmic intelligence. Liberated from outside authorities, children can freely follow the destructive ways of ancient Israel, where "every man [did] whatsoever is right in his own eyes" (Deuteronomy 12:8).

4. Today's attraction to the vile, wicked, and cruel can be gauged by audience responses to evil or ill-mannered characters. In *The Lion King*, the devilish Scar, the bloodthirsty hyenas and the flatulent warthog drew the loudest laughter. Like the sordid success of Beavis and Butthead, this phenomenon reminds us that in our culture bad is good, and good is boring.

5. *The Lion King* matches the new earth-centered paradigm or worldview that is transforming children's view of reality. While God told us to communicate truth to our children when we sit . . . walk . . . lie down and . . . get up (Deuteronomy 6:7), today's culture trains children to see reality through a global, earth-centered filter. This "new" mental framework distorts truth, stretches the meaning of familiar words, and promotes spiritual "insights" that are incompatible with Christianity. Packaged as entertainment, this message usually bypasses rational resistance, desensitizes opened minds, and fuels general acceptance of pagan spirituality.

Families that have already seen *The Lion King* may still use its pagan context to show the contrasts between God's truths and earth-centered religions. Look together for the many parallels, and point out the vital differences. Remember, the most deceptive spiritual counterfeits look most similar to God's truth. Discuss Scriptures that counter the deceptions. Then thank God for His genuine truth and His life at work within those who follow Him.

ATLANTIS RISES AGAIN: NEW AGE SPIRITUALITY FOR NEW MILLENNIUM CHILDREN

LONG ago, the Greek philosopher Plato introduced humanity to a mysterious civilization, which supposedly flourished 9000 years before his own time. He called it Atlantis and inspired his followers with grandiose descriptions of its power and politics, its amazing flying machines and its majestic temple to Poseidon, the Greek god of the sea. But Zeus, the reigning god on Mt. Olympus, wasn't pleased. And so, we are told in the *Dialogues of Plato* how the island continent with its magnificent city was swallowed up by the Atlantic Ocean in a massive cataclysmic event.

This violent finale breathed lasting life into the myth. Exciting stories don't die quickly, and the magic of Atlantis[2] seems to rise out of obscurity whenever a culture is ripe for pseudo-historical visions of popular occultism. It happened in the 1930s, when Edgar Cayce, the "sleeping prophet," linked Atlantis to Mayan land and, while in a trance, described its technological marvels and the re-incarnations of its inhabitants.

It happened five decades earlier, when Madame Helena Blavatsky was writing *The Secret Doctrine* for the Theosophical Society. It told about "revelatory spirits from the Orient" who brought insights from Atlantis and described its people as one of humanity's seven "root" races.[3] Blending western occultism with Hinduism, she founded Theosophy with its occult hierarchy of ascended masters and laid the foundation for the New Age movement.

The list of leaders that followed in Blavatsky's theosophical footsteps include Rudolf Steiner, who founded the Waldorf Schools; UN leader Robert Muller, whose World Core Curriculum provided a framework for global education; and Dr. Shirley McCune, keynote speaker at the 1989 Governor's Conference on Education. In the book Dr. McCune co-authored, *The Light Shall Set You Free*, the mesmerizing myth of Atlantis soared into new realms of mysticism. Basing her understanding of spiritual realities on a blend of Buddhism and channeled messages from various spirit guides, she wrote:

> All humans have the natural ability to perceive
> dimensions higher than the Third . . . In Atlantis,
> humans in embodiment accepted this mode of
> operation and perception as normal behavior. The
> Atlanteans operated on this superior level of existence,
> connected to their Higher Selves. With the fall of
> Atlantis, humanity experienced a struggle for survival
> and became aware of the lower self, dominated by
> the will of the ego. Now after thousands of years of
> evolution, most people have forgotten . . . how to
> connect with higher dimensions.[4]

Today, some of the most demonic facets of this occult belief system is marketed to our children through Disney's 2001
animation, *Atlantis: the Lost Empire*. Featuring a brilliant but
unappreciated Harry Potter look-alike named Milo Thatch, it
quickly draws young audiences into a captivating quest to find
the mythical city and turn fantasy into reality.

Milo's knack for ancient languages unlocks the secret that
puts Atlantis on his map. And when stodgy old civic leaders
mock his dreams, the determined young seeker gains support
from a Yoga-loving old friend of his deceased grandfather. With
such diverse companions as a karate-kicking feminist and a crude
creature called Mole, he begins his quest.

At the end of a noisy, fast-action journey, the adventurers find
a civilization bathed in New Age imagery, colors, and idealism.
Ancient symbols, especially variations of the ever-present spiral and
triangle, are carved into ceremonial stones and painted on masks that
resemble the ritual attire used in historical Native Spirituality. "I've
seen them back in North Dakota," observes a member of Milo's crew.

A life-giving power source energizes all life, lights, and flying vehicles in Atlantis. Each person is connected to this force
through a personal crystal amulet worn as a pendant. Princess
Kida uses her amulet to heal Milo's bleeding wound after she
scratched him—apparently to see if he was truly a flesh-and-

blood person like herself. Later she uses the same magic amulet, like a car key, to start a vehicle.

This spiritual life source was not the only deity in Atlantis. Blending ancient polytheism (many gods) with Westernized Buddhism and New Age cosmic consciousness, the Disney movie gives its own reason for the city's disappearance: The "gods became jealous." In this story, the otherwise immoral Greek gods showed a politically correct intolerance for the Atlantean capitalism, which had replaced the virtuous oneness of earlier times.

This timely moral message is stressed by the Dalai Lama in his foreword to *Spiritual Politics*. The book's co-author, Corinne McLaughlin, taught mediation (group consensus) strategies at the Department of Education, at the EPA, at the Pentagon, and to former President Clinton's Council on Sustainable Development.[5] In her book, she summarizes one of many occult messages given to Theosophist Alice Bailey by her *spirit guide*, the ascended master Djwhal Khul. Notice how her vision of a collective society matches UN ideology:

> According to Ageless Wisdom, during the time of Atlantis there was a tremendous battle on the astral [emotional] level between the Forces of Light, who wanted to lift human evolution of materialism and separateness, and the involuntary Forces of Darkness, who wanted to enslave human will and more deeply immerse humanity in matter. This resulted in the sinking of that ancient continent.[6]

It seems fitting, then, that Milo's final battle should be against the heartless materialism of two mutinous team members who had stolen both the life-giving power source and Princess Kida. Actually, the two have become one. Having merged her own being with the life force, the princess appears translucent as crystal—perhaps as pure energy or spirit, like the ascended masters of Blavatsky's Theosophy.

Naturally, the "good" hero wins over the capitalistic villain. In the end, the glowing, trance-like princess floats down from the skies in a beam of light and melts into Milo's arms where she regains consciousness and her human, flesh-and-blood form. The two gaze in awe at the glorious city now rising from the fiery waves.

The temple that emerges seems to be a blend of Hindu and Mayan temples. Yet the film's featured symbol—a stylized eye in a triangle—resembles the peak of the Masonic pyramid on our dollar bills. It, in turn, combines the Egyptian symbol of the all-seeing eye with the ubiquitous triangle featured in Eastern as well as Western magic. All these occult images and subtle suggestions lead the audience through a virtual experience in 21st century multiculturalism that should please any globalist educator.

Children and parents go home with a fresh appreciation for "the beautiful side of evil." They might even stop and buy Disney's new Atlantis toys and Milo action figures on the way home. Few will be able to shut the doors of their minds to the movie's enticing legends, symbols, delusions, and worldview. Disney's mighty marketing arm will keep the lights burning for a long time.

CRUSHING CHRISTIANITY

YOU may remember when major motion picture movie studios produced biblical spectaculars such as *Ben Hur* and *The Ten Commandments*. Back then, movies honored Christian values and morality, and God's ministers were portrayed as kind, wise, and faithful. Not anymore. Today, ministers are portrayed either as foolish or corrupt or as liberal and unbiblical. Christians appear wimpy, immature, and out of touch with the real world. While most Americans call themselves Christians, they laugh along with the world at the biased portrayal of the church.

The anti-Christian bias, so visible through movies and television, shows an incredible double standard. Other religions are apparently safe and acceptable, but Christianity alone is judged dangerous and must be eliminated or altered in such a way that fits the "new" Christianity, which lines up far more with the New Age/New Spirituality outlook than with the Bible. Yet when Christians voice concern about immorality and violence, the angry media cries, "Censors!"

The furor surrounding *The Last Temptation of Christ* left no doubt in any discerning Christian's mind about Hollywood's hostility toward Christianity. In choosing a story by Nilcos Kazantzakis, it popularized the Greek novelist's philosophy—a contemporary blend of Buddhism, Lenin, Christ, Spinoza, Darwin, and Nietzsche—and gave birth to a mythological Jesus, who like other man-made gods, suits this present time. Like the gods of ancient Greece and Rome, this Jesus portrays the weaknesses of human nature rather than the triumph of spiritual obedience.

To Kazantzakis, God was the sum total of consciousness in the universe, expanding throughout the course of human evolution. Even back in 1927, he envisioned a union of higher, evolved individuals with paranormal power, who were joined in a superhuman effort to create for themselves a new world.[7]

A student editorial for the a local high school newspaper said:

> The controversial film, *The Last Temptation of Christ*, has been condemned and boycotted by many religious people. Their religious ignorance has made them scorn a movie they probably have not seen. If more of these misguided people watched this movie, they might actually approve of it. The film is powerful, gripping, beautiful, and very much on a human level.[8]

It's far easier to identify with a confused, fallible, questioning Jesus than to accept the biblical Jesus' challenge to trust God for victory over sin. Discipline, self-denial, and the Cross have no place in a society where "humanness" has become a virtue, where Self reigns as God, and where people are evolving into the "world's highest creators."

Angry that Christians would resist Hollywood's artistic license-taking with God's Word, Jack Valenti, the late long-time president of the Motion Picture Association of America (MPAA), declared, "[The] only issue is whether. . . self-appointed groups can prevent a film from being exhibited to the public or a book from being published."[9] In response, columnist Patrick Buchanan asked and answered a question worthy of our consideration:

> Would Mr. Valenti defend a film titled *The Secret Life of Martin Luther King, Jr.* that depicted the assassinated civil rights leader as a relentless womanizer—a point of view with more foundation in truth, and surely, less of a profanation than showing Jesus of Nazareth as a lusting wimp?

> Of course not. We live in a day and age where "tolerance" is shouted from the roof tops when it comes to just about anything or anyone . . . except Christians. In that case, any kind of ridicule and mockery is permitted without a bat of the eye from most.[10]

Bad Is Good

By banishing or twisting Christian truth and values from the screen, Satan has cleared the way for counterfeit messages. Without God's standard, anything goes. The world watches as Hollywood presents good as bad, morality as boring, and evil as delightful. The three main thrusts we saw in education—counterfeit religion, counterfeit values, and a counterfeit world system—illuminate movie screens across our nation. These three thrusts are examined below:

• First, a new religious system is replacing Christianity—primarily a mixture of humanism, hedonism, Hinduism, and occultism. Whether the beautiful or the ugly side of evil, it testifies to the respectability that cloaks the New Age movement.

In the mythological setting of *Willow*, which is threaded with biblical allusions, occult wonders, and macho prowess, George Lucas tells a new set of youngsters a familiar message: The force is with you. Now garbed in ancient sorcery rather than space-age light sabers, the cosmic force shines through ugly trolls, pretty pixies, good as well as evil witches, and a courageous dwarf called Willow. Notice the messianic emphasis:

> A baby girl is born whom the *prophets* declare will be the savior of the land, and evil Queen Bavmorda vows to destroy the child. She's discovered like Moses, in the bulrushes on the banks of a river by Willow Ufgood, a tiny Newlyn and aspiring sorcerer.[11]

This spiritual medley accomplishes two of Satan's purposes. By identification with occult symbols and cultural myths, it weakens the Christian message. And the same association veils the counterfeit in an aura of traditional credibility.

• Second, you can't miss the degrading values. Violence, immorality, profanity, and lawlessness (lying, cheating, disrespect toward authority) are standard fare—even in children's movies. For example, *Who Framed Roger Rabbit?* (still popular today in DVD format), which could have been a delightful family movie, was tainted with sexist humor, sadistic violence, and vulgar comments.

• Third, the globalist's vision of a transformed world takes on many forms. Man wields psychic forces, races through time, crushes the boundaries of death, and connects with evolved extraterrestrials. Impossibilities become realities; for nothing is impossible to the imagination. Many of today's shows transcendent powers put real life to shame.

Notice how the mythological story, *Dark Crystal*, illustrates Hindu-based global oneness. The movie begins with a look at two dying species: the kind Mystics and evil Skeksis. Long ago, "in the age of oneness," when the radiant Crystal transmitted harmony to everyone, the two were joined. But damage to the Crystal divided good and evil into two opposing forces. The damage can only be reversed if . . . the crystal's missing chip is replaced. No time to lose, for the three suns have almost reached alignment.

As in the computer game bearing the same title and characters, *Jen*, the crystal's chosen healer, overcomes all obstacles with the help of astrology, mystical chanting, telepathy, clairvoyance, and other psychic tricks. Finally, just before the three suns are aligned, he drops the chip into place. The crystal lights up, energy flows, good and evil merge into one, and harmony returns to the land. The parting message from the perfected beings: "[W]e all are part of each other. Now we leave you the Crystal of Truth. Make your world in its light."

This pantheistic message grows more disturbing when we remember that Jim Henson, who wrote, directed, and produced this movie, was also the mind behind the Muppets—the popular stars of Sesame Street as well as a number of movies.

The purpose behind these entertainment creations is a deification of man and a diminishing of God. Hollywood long ago, like the educational establishment and media elites, caught Satan's vision: Absolve people who turn against God, and justify an alluring lifestyle of sensual pleasure, spiritual misadventure, and readiness for a new and overtly permissive kind of world.

THE MIND-CHANGING MYTHS OF AVATAR

> When I woke up this morning after watching Avatar for the first time yesterday, the world seemed . . . gray. It was like my whole life, everything I've done and worked for, lost its meaning. . . . I live in a dying world.[12]

IMAGINE a new world! Visualize its beauty! Flow with your feelings! Become one with all! But what about reality?

With their cat-like eyes, pointed ears, snarling hisses, and balancing tails, the James Cameron's tall Na'vi humanoids fit right into a spiritual network that supposedly links everything together on Pandora, a lush distant moon. Environmentally attuned, they ride through the skies on powerful birds, climb the stony walls of magnificent hanging mountains, and worship their goddess. Naturally, they despise the corporate monstrosity that has invaded their habitat in search of priceless resources.

Those earthly intruders intend to excavate Pandora's most sacred spot. To avoid war, they brought a scientific team trained to befriend the indigenous Na'vi people and persuade them to move.

That team includes latecomer Jake Sully, a paraplegic Marine replacing his slain twin brother. After some training, his mind and consciousness would periodically be transferred to his Na'vi-like avatar—a body originally made to match his brother's DNA.

The Hindu word avatar refers to an incarnation or manifestation of a Hindu god. The most common avatars are incarnations of the god Vishnu, and they include the mischievous flute-playing Krishna and the bow-and-arrow carrying Rama. Both are usually pictured with bluish skin—just like the native Na'vis.

Testing his new avatar legs, tail and body, Jake heads for the forest, admires the flowers, and faces a rhino-sized beast. This strange world is nothing like the gray, polluted earth he left behind![13]

Moments later, a snarling panther-like thanator chases him deeper into the woods where he meets the beautiful Neytiri who aims her bow and arrow at him. Fortunately, she receives a message from her mysterious goddess through a cloud of white flower-like creatures that settle on Jake—a clear sign that the goddess [Eywa] wants Neytiri to befriend this ignorant stranger. But first she scolds him for causing the death of other terrifying pursuers.

Hmmm. Do you wonder why Neytiri carries a bow and arrow when all life is one?[14]

Jake does his best to follow the sure-footed Neytiri (climbing, leaping, etc.) back to Hometree, her clan's sacred domain. She introduces him to Mo'at, her psychic mother who happens to be the tribal tsahik (shaman to the pagan goddess "Eywa"). She tells her daughter to train this "dreamwalker" in their native ways. Some of the clan warriors look skeptical.

Jake is a good pupil, and his lessons on pantheistic unity soon shift his loyalty from his worldly mission to the tribe and Eywa. So when his commander prepares to destroy Hometree and much of the sacred forests, Jake springs into action. Through psychic linkage, he tames and rides the fiercest bird of all—the mighty Toruk, who became his "spirit animal" through a prior ritual Spirit Quest.[15] Speeding above the forests, he gathers Pandora's tribes for war.

He prays to Eywa for help, and she answers his plea. She summons birds and beasts of every kind. With such an army, how could they lose?

Her final "miracle" is to transfer Jake's life from his injured earthly body to his Na'vi avatar. The earthly human dies, then awakens to new life in a pantheistic "paradise." By putting his faith in the pagan goddess, Jake had earned the honor of a counterfeit resurrection. Now, he's one of them!

It all sounds good to earthlings who love the myth of mystical oneness! No wonder thousands of viewers became depressed (even suicidal) after their virtual experience of Pandora's wonders. To them, dropping their 3-D glasses into the recycling bin at the exit meant a dreaded return to a dull reality! Ponder the potential effect of this seductive journey on those who love fantasy more than reality:

> Ever since I went to see *Avatar* I have been depressed. Watching the wonderful world of Pandora and all the Na'vi made me want to be one of them. I can't stop thinking about all the things that happened in the film . . . I even contemplate suicide thinking that if I do it I will be rebirthed in a world similar to Pandora.[16]

The reality behind this mind-bending, feeling-based mythology is the existence of an occult spiritual system. Avatar's promotion of pantheism and panentheism point to the "spiritual unity" at the heart of Hinduism, Native American shamanism, and the worship of Mother Earth. They all clash with God's truth.

> Woe unto them that call evil good, and good evil; that put darkness for light, and light for darkness. (Isaiah 5:20)

Filling minds with occult visions and evolutionary ideals will surely immunize the masses against the Truth of God. His reality is incompatible with *Avatar's* mystical illusions! Yet people have, through the ages, chosen to compromise God's truths with their imagination. Remember the moral condition of the masses back in Noah's days: "[E]very imagination of the thoughts of his heart was only evil continually" (Genesis 6:5).

Filling minds with occult visions and evolutionary ideals will surely immunize the masses against the Truth of God.

Similar conditions now prevail and will continue to become more pervasive right up to the point of Christ's second coming (see Luke 17:20). Today's occult movies and computer games, preying on the imaginations of impressionable children, could open a "Pandora's Box" of paganism and spiritual bondage. So let's heed His warnings.

HARRY POTTER

The premiere of *Harry Potter* the movie will lead to a whole new generation of youngsters discovering witchcraft and wizardry. . . . Increasing numbers of children are spending hours alone browsing the Internet in search of Satanic websites and we are concerned that nobody is monitoring this growing fascination.[17]—**Peter Smith,** former general secretary of the Association of Teachers and Lecturers, UK

It's taken away a lot of the fear. People are more accepting of things like witchcraft and magic after Harry Potter came out.[18]—A psychic bookstore manager

THE Harry Potter books and movies hit the scene in the late nineties and have had a major impact in the lives of millions of youth. Even many Christian families have allowed their children to stand in the lines so they could be some of the first to obtain the latest Harry Potter book. On my website, I have written several articles about the Harry Potter series since the year 2000. Through this continued research, I have seen a consistent pattern in J. K. Rowling's Harry Potter of the occult and witchcraft.

The following are twelve reasons why parents should not allow their children to view or read the Harry Potter movies and books. I further discuss Harry Potter in a later chapter as well.

1. God shows us that witchcraft, sorcery, spells, divination, and magic are evil. He hates those practices because they blind us to His loving ways, then turn our hearts to a deceptive quest for self-empowerment and deadly thrills. Harry Potter's world may be fictional, but the timeless pagan practices it promotes are real and deadly. Remember the stern warning from Scripture mentioned earlier in this book regarding witchcraft (Deuteronomy 18).

2. The movie's foundation in fantasy, not reality, doesn't diminish its power to change beliefs and values. Imaginary (or virtual) experiences and well-written fantasies can affect the mind and memories as much, if not more, than actual experiences.[19] Designed to stir feelings and produce strong emotional responses, a carefully constructed myth with likeable characters can be far more memorable than the less exciting daily reality—especially when reinforced through books, toys, and games as well as movies.

Small wonder Harry's fans have been counting the days until their next fantastic journey into Hogwarts classes on sorcery, divination, potions, and spells.

> But they hearkened not, nor inclined their ear, but walked in the counsels and in the imagination of their evil heart, and went backward, and not forward. (Jeremiah 7:24)

3. Each occult image and suggestion prompts the audience to *feel* more at home in this setting. Children identify with their favorite characters and learn to see wizards and witches from a popular peer perspective rather than from God's perspective. Those who sense that the occult world is evil face a choice: Resist peer pressure or rationalize their imagined participation in Harry's supernatural adventures.

The second choice may quiet the nagging doubts, but rationalizing evil and justifying sin will sear the conscience and shift the child's perception of values from God's perspective to a more "comfortable" cultural adaptation. Even Christian children can easily learn to conform truth to multicultural ideals and turn God's values upside down.

4. God tells us to "[a]bhor that which is evil" and "cleave to that which is good" (Romans 12:9). But when Christian children and teens love the Harry Potter plots, delight in the movies, and read the books again and again, they are desensitizing their hearts and minds to its evil. Turning God's truth upside down, they are learning to "love" what is evil. The next natural step is to reject God's wise boundaries and "abhor" what He calls good. "Thou lovest evil more than good" (Psalm 52:3).

5. Immersed in Hogwarts beliefs and values, children learn to ignore or reinterpret God's truth. They lose their natural aversion for the devious spirits represented by the creatures and symbols in this eerie world. Caught up in the exciting stories, they absorb the suggested values and store the fascinating images in their minds—making the forbidden world of the occult seem more normal than the Kingdom of God.

6. This inner change is usually subconscious, for the occult lessons and impressions tend to bypass rational scrutiny. After all, who will stop, think, and weigh the evidence or the consequences, for that matter, when caught up in such a fast-moving visual adventure? Fun fantasies and strategic entertainment have a special way of altering values, compromising beliefs, and changing behavior in adults as well as in children. All in the name of entertainment, they will leave impressions lasting for years to come.

> Turn away mine eyes from beholding vanity; and quicken thou me in thy way. (Psalm 119:37)

7. The main product marketed through Harry Potter is a new belief system. This pagan ideology comes complete with trading cards, computer and other wizardly games, clothes, and decorations stamped with HP symbols, action figures and cuddly dolls, audio books and DVDs that could keep the child's mind focused on the occult all day and into the night. But in God's eyes, such paraphernalia entices and lures while becoming an open doorway to deeper involvement with the occult. In contrast, listen to God's description of someone He calls "blessed":

> Blessed is the man that walketh not in the counsel of the ungodly, nor standeth in the way of sinners, nor sitteth in the seat of the scornful [mockers]. But his delight is in the law of the Lord; and in his law doth he meditate day and night. And he shall be like a tree planted by the rivers of water, that bringeth forth his fruit in his season; his leaf also shall not wither; and whatsoever he doeth shall prosper. (Psalm 1:1-3)

8. The implied source of power behind Harry's magical feats tends to distort a child's understanding of God. In the movies, as in the books, words traditionally used to refer to occult practices become so familiar that children begin to apply the same terms to God and His promised strength. Many learn to see God as a power source that can be manipulated with the right kind of prayers and rituals—and view His miracles as just another form of magic. They base their understanding of God on their own feelings and desires and not on His revelation of Himself.

> For as the heavens are higher than the earth, so are my ways higher than your ways, and my thoughts than your thoughts. (Isaiah 55:9)

9. Blind to the true nature of God, children will blend (synthesize) biblical truth with pagan beliefs and magical practices. In the end, you distort and destroy any remnant of true Christian faith. For our God cannot be conformed to the image of pagan gods.

> For my people have committed two evils; they have forsaken me the fountain of living waters, and hewed them out cisterns, broken cisterns, that can hold no water. (Jeremiah 2:13)

10. God tells us to "train up a child in the way he should go" (Proverbs 22:6). It starts with teaching them God's truths and training them all day long to see reality from His point of view and not the world's perspective. To succeed, we need to shield them from contrary values until they know His Word and have memorized enough Scripture to be able to recognize and resist deception. Once they have learned to love what God loves and see the world from His perspective, they will demonstrate their wisdom by choosing to say "no" to Harry Potter.

> We will not hide them [God's laws] from their children,
> shewing to the generation to come the praises of the
> Lord, and his strength, and his wonderful works
> that he hath done. For he established a testimony in
> Jacob . . . which he commanded our fathers, that they
> should make them known to their children: That the
> generation to come might know them . . . who should
> arise and declare them to their children: That they
> might set their hope in God, and not forget the works
> of God, but keep his commandments. (Psalm 78:4-7)

11. While some argue that Harry and his friends model friendship and integrity, they actually model how to lie and steal and get away with it. Their example only adds to the cultural relativism embraced by most children today who are honest when it doesn't cost anything, but who lie and cheat when it serves their purpose.

> And even as they did not like to retain God in their
> knowledge, God gave them over to a reprobate
> [depraved] mind, to do those things which are not
> convenient; Being filled with all unrighteousness,
> fornication, wickedness, covetousness, maliciousness;
> full of envy, murder, debate, deceit, malignity;
> whisperers, Backbiters, haters of God, despiteful,
> proud, boasters, inventors of evil things, disobedient
> to parents, Without understanding, covenantbreakers,
> without natural affection, implacable, unmerciful:
> Who knowing the judgment of God, that they which
> commit such things are worthy of death, not only do
> the same, but have pleasure in them that do them.
> (Romans 1:28-32)

12. God has a better way. When His children choose to follow His ways, He gives them a heart to love Him, spiritual eyes that can understand and delight in His Word, a sense of His presence, and a confidence in His constant care—no matter what happens to them. Harry Potter's deceptive thrills are beyond worthless when compared to the wonderful riches our Shepherd promises those who will ignore evil and walk with Him.

"SNOW WHITE & THE HUNTSMAN"—CORRUPTING MINDS & MOCKING OUR GOD

UNLIKE Disney's 1937 cartoon fantasy, today's bewitching *Snow White* movie features real-life characters that popularize the occult through shocking thrills and unforgettable suggestions.

The setting for this movie is medieval Europe with its pagan beliefs and Renaissance magic. It also resembles the dark practices of ancient Canaan, Egypt, Assyria, Babylon, Greece, and early Rome. They all worshipped their regional "gods" and idols that "sold" their favors through heartless sorcerers.

> Throughout the ages, biblical faith has been the greatest obstacle to the occult. But today, as God's Word and values fade from the Western world's consciousness, the darkness is spreading fast.

Throughout the ages, biblical faith has been the greatest obstacle to the occult. But today, as God's Word and values fade from the Western world's consciousness, the darkness is spreading fast. Mystical games and movies feed the growing appetite for magical thrills.

This movie is targeted at the age sixteen and over crowd, but I saw parents bringing young children. After all, *Snow White* is just a fairy tale, isn't it?

As the movie ended, I walked out behind a family of five. The children looked a bit stunned. With the father's permission,

I asked his two older boys, ages eight and twelve, what they thought of the movie. They both shrugged and said, "It was okay." Were they aware of the raging battle between good and evil?

"God is going to change," wrote Naomi Goldenberg in *Changing of the Gods: Feminism and the End of Traditional Religions.* "We women . . . will change the world so much that He won't fit anymore."[20]

She is wrong about God. But she's right about our changing culture.

In the movie, the powers of the occult are featured through two strong, dominant leaders—a current and a future queen. Together, they demonstrate the light and the dark side of evil. Neither would hesitate to fight and kill. Viewers simply flow with the action and passively absorb new values.

Snow White's homeland is attacked by "black warriors" conjured by the evil Ravenna. The king's army fights back, and the mystical invaders shatter like glass. As planned, the king's soldiers find a beautiful woman (Ravenna) inside a carriage. The widowed king, Snow White's father, immediately falls in love with her.

Soon after their marriage, Ravenna mysteriously poisons her royal husband, then puts a dagger through his heart. Determined to be the sole ruler of the land, she has stationed her actual army (not the magical imitation army that was shattered) outside the castle. She opens the gates and her soldiers burst into the castle.

By order from Queen Ravenna, a huge mirror is brought into her throne room. She asks a familiar question: "Mirror mirror on the wall, who's the fairest of them all?" The mirror melts down, then rises and assumes the shape of a faceless gold-covered statue that answers: "You are fairest. . . ."

Imprisoned in the castle tower, Snow White mechanically recites the Lord's Prayer to two dolls that apparently represent her dead parents, the former king and queen. Her rapid recitation sounds more like a ritual than a heart-felt genuine prayer.

The land suffers and poverty reigns across the land. A father and son were caught stealing from the Queen's transport and are brought into the throne room for judgment. When the son stabs Ravenna in her belly, the queen—like a vampire—sucks the life from his heart.

Ravenna stares at her new wrinkles in the mirror. Her power has weakened, but she knows the solution. She asks for a young girl, then sucks out her youthful beauty.

Once again, the queen questions her magic mirror: "Who is fairest?" The faceless golden figure answers, "[Y]ou are fairest, but another has come of age who threatens to take your place." Snow White! The mirror suggests a solution to the Queen's dilemma: "[I]f you consume her heart, your power will be immeasurable, and you will never grow old again."

Ravenna sends her brother to fetch Snow White, but she escapes through a sewer pipe that leads to a hole in the castle wall above the surf. She jumps into the water and swims to shore where a beautiful white horse happens to be waiting for her.

Pursued by Ravenna's soldiers, Snow White hides in the Dark Forest where everything is corrupt, rotten, menacing, and surrounded by deadly gases.

The drunken Huntsman, a grieving widower, agrees to lead the search for Snow White. The Queen had promised to "resurrect [his] wife," but he soon realizes that this promise was simply a convenient lie. He finds Snow White and teaches her how to stab an enemy through the heart.

They meet seven unfriendly old dwarfs who eventually show them some hospitality. Together they enter a fairy forest—an oasis with beautiful flowers and magical animals. Snow White's magical essence brings strength and beauty to the plants and animals.

Meanwhile, the Queen still wants Snow White's heart! Like a shamanic shape-shifter, she assumes the appearance of a young man and tricks Snow White into biting an apple. Coughing and choking, Snow White collapses.

When Ravenna lifts her arm to stab her unconscious foe, the Huntsman appears with his axe. Ravenna dissolves and reappears at her castle.

Snow White seems to be dead. Her lifeless body is brought

to a chapel and placed on a bed. The Huntsman kisses her, then leaves. Snow White revives.

As her friends plan their attack on Ravenna's castle, the revived Snow White appears. She shows the dwarfs how to enter the castle through the sewer pipe and open the gates for the army. While the battle rages, Snow White heads for Ravenna's throne room. The queen wields her magical powers, but Snow White remembers the Huntsman's lessons. She blocks Ravenna's dagger and stabs her through the heart.

Snow White becomes the queen—the sovereign ruler of her kingdom.

On September 11th, 2012, the DVD version of the movie was released. No doubt, countless children will watch it again and again until its thrills and values are rooted in their imagination. Will it desensitize viewers to the spreading evil? I am sure it will have a lasting and negatively profound effect as so many other movies like it.

Loving Evil

An advertisement for the movie *The Unholy* said it well: "Evil has never been so irresistible . . . or so deadly."

We might add, "or so prevalent." That dark, ugly face of the occult that hides behind the beautiful, enticing masks of the New Age—now shows its ugly countenance everywhere. Children are learning to love its scary, grotesque faces.

Notice how horror movies have changed with the times. In *Halloween 4: The Return of Michael Myers*, Michael evolves beyond a mere homicidal maniac. Reflecting today's fascination with human potential and supernatural power, he now appears with supernatural strength, while his fellow actors exhibit cartoon-like qualities such as falling off roofs without injury.

Did you see *Gremlins* some years ago? Promoted as a children's movie, it turned into a nightmare. Yet kids loved it. Typical of the New Age, the movie softened hearts with the bright, happy side of evil: a lovable and intelligent little Mugway called

Gismo. But happiness turned to horror when Gismo's evil off-spring became an army of ugly, lizard-like, demonic gremlins who destroyed everything in their path.

A scene where the vicious gremlins pushed against a door—their horny claws and red, cruel eyes peeping out from the crack until Billy, the hero, pushed the door shut—brought back memories from my own life.

In my third year as a Christian, I knew little about "pulling down" demonic strongholds (2 Corinthians 10:3-5) and freeing the oppressed. But I had pondered the triumphs of Jesus and His disciples over demonic forces. I longed to know the secret of victory both in my own life and in the more intense struggles that seemed to crush others.

One day a church leader asked me to counsel a young, depressed mother. Trusting that God's wisdom would be sufficient in my weakness, I accepted. A few days later, Sue and I spent seven hours together seeking and applying God's answers for her guilt, anger, and confusion. When she finally went home, Sue was radiant.

But I heard terror in her voice when she called late that night. Her spiritual battle exceeded anything I had imagined. God quickened my mind, prompting me to ask her, "Sue, have you been involved in the occult?"

Her answer raised goose bumps on my arms. "Yes," she sobbed, "I worshiped Satan for three years. . . . The name they gave me is the name I gave my daughter. . . ."

I heard myself telling Sue to return the next week. We needed to pray together for release from the demonic bondage and op-pression. I didn't know how, but trusted God would show me. I knew He had promised conquering power for battling evil in His name.

The next day, God miraculously trained me for warfare through the timely phone call of a stranger. And three days later, on the day He scheduled, He set Sue free. But the battle wasn't completely over. Through Luke 11:24, God reminded me to be on guard, lest the "unclean" evil spirits return.

Sue promptly began to memorize, meditate, and keep her mind filled with Scriptures, for she might be tested very soon.

Indeed, she was. Eight days after God freed her, she experienced an onslaught of incredible terror. That night Sue and I battled against the demonic forces that tried to regain their "right" to a territory no longer theirs. The images she described to me were identical to the demonic gremlins pushing against the door in the movie.

"Horrible, ugly demons are pressing on my mind," she cried. "I'm trying to shut the door, but I can't. Their hideous eyes are staring at me. . . . I can't get away from those eyes. . . . Help me!"

After a twenty-hour battle, Sue shut the door for good—by faith—and the demons departed. During the following year, as Sue fed on a daily diet of biblical truth, God completed her healing. She joined a neighborhood Bible study and later became one of the leaders. God is faithful! He can set free anyone who turns to Him in faith and obedience!

We need to ask ourselves and our children: "Do we want to be entertained by the ghastly, demonic creatures so prevalent in movies, on television, in toys, and comic books? Can God's children delight in the symbols of darkness and still enjoy God's presence and protection? I believe not. Listen to His warning:

> Ye that love the Lord, hate evil: he preserveth the souls
> of his saints; he delivereth them out of the hand of the
> wicked. (Psalm 97:10)

And remember, God has something far better in store for those who say no to evil in order to follow Him.

10

HOW TO GUARD AGAINST MIND-CHANGING MESSAGES

Love not the world, neither the things that are in the world. If any man love the world, the love of the Father is not in him. For all that is in the world, the lust of the flesh, and the lust of the eyes, and the pride of life, is not of the Father, but is of the world. And the world passeth away, and the lust thereof: but he that doeth the will of God abideth for ever. (1 John 2:15-17)

"**MOM, WHY CAN'T** I see Beetlejuice?

"We talked about that yesterday."

"I forgot what you said."

Sandy felt exasperated. She didn't like to tell Tim that some of the movies "all" his friends enjoyed were out of bounds for him. Yet, she just couldn't ignore certain standards. They had debated this issue all the way home from school yesterday, and she felt too weary to take up the challenge again today.

"Mom, where does the Bible say that I can't see Beetlejuice?" Tim wasn't ready to accept no for an answer.

Sandy glanced at her son as she pulled away from the curb. His wide, blue eyes expressed sincere questioning, not rebellious disagreement. She knew he wanted to follow God's way but thought it sometimes seemed just too narrow. He hated to be different from everybody else.

"Help me, Lord," she prayed silently, then took a deep breath and began.

"Tim, the Bible doesn't mention Beetlejuice any more than it mentions rock music or crack. But God does make it very clear to us what He likes and what He hates. If you choose to do things He hates, it becomes harder and harder to walk with God. You lose your sense of what is right, and you begin to rationalize what is wrong. Then you begin to think like those who don't know God—based on what you want, rather than what God wants."

"But how do you know God hates Beetlejuice?"

"We saw the advertisements, remember? I have talked with some people who have seen it. So have you." She glanced at him again, and saw the telltale look of reluctant assent. "Remember the Bible verses we looked up yesterday that show us what God thinks about spiritism, spells, and those kinds of things?"

"But everybody else gets to see stuff like that. . ."

"You're different. You belong to God. Therefore, you can't do what everybody else does."

"Nothing happens to the kids who see those movies."

"Yes, it does. It just doesn't show right away. People can't watch all that corruption and not begin to change their attitude toward life and people. After a while, they can't tell the difference between right and wrong."

"I know the difference. Can't you trust me, Mom?" Tim sounded so confident that Sandy almost laughed.

"You asked me that last week, when you were choosing a video to take home. Remember the ones you wanted to see? In some areas of your life, you haven't yet shown that you have the wisdom to make wise choices. But I trust you to ride your bike safely into town and back." It was Tim's turn to be silent.

"Tim, when we get home, I'll show you some passages in the Bible that will help you understand God's thoughts and teach you to be wise."

"God's thinking is very different from the way most people think, isn't it?" he asked thoughtfully.

"Nowadays it is," answered Sandy. She shivered as the awareness of the widening chasm between God's ways and the world hit her like an icy cold wind. "Precious Lord," she prayed silently, "help Tim choose Your ways, even when it means rejection and embarrassment. Teach him Your wisdom, so that He will want to choose Your way."

Sandy sensed both the danger of a movie's persuasive power and the need to teach her son discernment. She also experienced the frustration we feel when faced with a child we long to please as well as protect and spiritually train. How do we fulfill our responsibility in training a child in God's ways? Are our concerns grounded in reality? For answers, let's look again at the conflict.

The movie industry has amazing power. As a film forces viewers to make continual choices, it dulls their awareness of choosing, weakens their mental resistance to its pull, and becomes a persuasive tool for social change.

How do we help our children choose movies appropriate to their ages and faith? How do we prepare them to face the unexpected distortion they surely will encounter—even in a "good" movie? How can we encourage them to follow God's way, when it means saying "no" in so many instances?

STEP ONE: FINDING THE RIGHT MOVIE

How do we find "safe" movies for our children? Are there any? Checking each possible choice personally would be a time-consuming undertaking—time many parents simply do not have. And the present rating system has failed to keep up with the changing film content. Introduced in 1968, it merely follows the shifting standards, which slip further and further away from God's unchanging guidelines.

This relaxed rating system doesn't warn us that behind an innocent-sounding title and a PG rating hides four-letter words, a slew of sexual innuendos and references, and subtle promotions of evolution, homosexuality, abortion, and a basic disregard for godly standards. Today's rating system doesn't reveal that sending our teenager to a PG-13 movie exposes him to sex scenes that once signaled an R rating. And there's no warning whatsoever of the assault on Christianity, the promotion of counterfeit religions, or the ghoulish, grotesque images so popular today.

While movie reviews can help us avoid bad choices, they cannot replace your own discernment and judgment. Even many so-called "family friendly" films are tarnished with New Age/New Spirituality messages that belittle the God of the Bible and exalt man as divine. This makes it all the more vital to equip your child with understanding of spiritual deception in the light of God's Word.

STEP TWO: BE PREPARED

- **Pray together for continued wisdom and direction.**

- **Agree ahead of time to leave if the movie turns out to be worse than expected.**

- **Research the subject.** Discuss biblical events or principles that relate to the movie's vision (e.g., does it deal with a futuristic New Age utopia, or does it present the biblical view of the future).

- **Be ready ahead of time to view counterfeit messages from a Christian perspective.** Before seeing *Field of Dreams* with a friend, our then fourteen-year-old read newspaper and other reviews. He went fortified with the following questions, which we discussed afterwards when we met the boys for ice cream.

> » Why does the movie make people "feel good"?

> » Where does it sound like Christianity but contradict the Bible?

> » What did it say or imply about God, His values, or heaven?

> » Did you see anything supernatural? What was its source—God or Satan?

- **Put on the whole armor of God.** If we go to enjoy a movie without the armor—without choosing to count on truth as our filter, the life of Jesus as our righteousness, and faith in our Shepherd as our shield—we may begin to absorb some of the movie's counterfeit values. We will be allowing the world to squeeze us into its mold.

If we go somewhere God does not want us to go, we may not be protected from the consequences. We can't put on the "breastplate of [God's] righteousness" (Ephesians 6:14)—which assumes our assent to His will—then go our own way rather than His. It is essential to understand what God does and does not promise to do. If I presume that God's protection extends beyond His promise, I will become disappointed and frustrated. His armor may not always protect me against the storms of the world (Matthew 5:45). But it will protect me against the assaults of Satan, whose arrows use the circumstances of the world and our bad choices to crush and destroy far more than could any storm.

In other words, God may not take me out of my circumstances, but He will bring victory in the midst of the trial. He will protect me against discouragement, despair, hopelessness, and worthlessness—all the destructive emotions and fears that rise up from deep within me to disturb my peace, deny my resources in Christ, and quench my joy in Him.

I learned that lesson the hard way. During my first three years as a Christian, I worked with the chaplain's service in a local VA hospital. Both patients and chaplains encouraged me to attend a "new, transforming" group therapy session, which had "freed them up" to relate to others with more love and transparency. Curious and open to adventure, I went.

The session didn't impress me. I heard nothing new, only the same profanity I had been exposed to on other days. But something had changed in me. Suddenly God seemed distant and my mind seemed out of tune with His.

Later I realized why. My Lord had not sent me. I went to the session to satisfy my own curiosity, to please others, and to gain knowledge that opposed His truth. Because I failed to protect my mind, the profanity I heard found entrance and gained a foothold. For the next three months, four-letter words would burst into my thoughts. Daily I begged that God would cleanse and renew my mind. When the onslaught ended, I had learned my lesson. When I go where my Shepherd sends me, no evil can drive a wedge between Him and me. But if I choose my own way, no matter how much I affirm the armor, I suffer the consequences.

STEP THREE: OTHERS GO, BUT YOU CANNOT

As parents, sometimes you just have to say no. It's hard! Your children's friends are all excited about a popular movie, but you can't allow your son or daughter to go along. You hurt with them and wish you could shield them from the pain—but you cannot without compromising your faith. Suffering for Christ's sake is an unavoidable part of a disciple's life. You just hope to see the pain produce wisdom and maturity rather than bitterness and rebellion. How can you encourage them?

A one-on-one talk and a fun activity may help. But only God's comforting Word and promises can change their attitudes, build wisdom, and produce the kind of maturity parents long to see in their children.

The following Scriptures will deepen her understanding of what it means to be a Christian. You may want to choose a Scripture each morning, then discuss it at a predetermined time later in the day.

As you read the Scripture passages, ask yourself these questions: What does it say? What is God saying to me? How can I apply it to my life?

- **Look at what God wants to accomplish:**

  James 1:2-4 * Romans 5:3-5 * 1 Peter 5:6-10

- **Listen to what God tells you to avoid.**

  Romans 12:9 * Ephesians 4:17-20 * Deuteronomy 18:10-13

- **Know that God has wonderful plans for those who trust in Him.**

  Matthew 5:11-12, 13-16 * Romans 8:16-18 *
  2 Corinthians 4:16-18

The object of our focus changes our lives. When we focus on immorality and violence, these mental pictures mold our thinking and behavior. But when we focus on God and His truth, He fills us and makes us more like Himself. The transformation the world offers can't compare to what God promises His children:

> But we all, with open face beholding as in a glass the glory of the Lord, are changed into the same image from glory to glory, even as by the Spirit of the Lord. (2 Corinthians 3:18)

To resist its lures, follow Job's example. He had committed himself to look away from distractions that might cause his mind and emotions to sin against God:

> I made a covenant with mine eyes; why then should I think upon a maid? For what portion of God is there from above? . . . Is not destruction to the wicked? and a strange punishment to the workers of iniquity? Doth not he see my ways, and count all my steps? (Job 31:1-4)

What we see affects our thoughts and values. To help us guard our spiritual purity and safety, Jesus reminds us that forbidden imagery and scenarios are out-of-bounds to our eyes as well as our hearts: "[W]hosoever looketh on a woman to lust after her hath committed adultery with her already in his heart" (Matthew 5:28).

Like pornography and sensual images of violent thrills, occult visions inspire occult cravings. Delighting in forbidden fantasies will dull our understanding of reality no matter how well versed our minds have become in knowing the difference between the two. Focusing our thoughts on a particular subject contributes to shaping the mental filter through which we understand reality and make our daily choices. Jesus said, "Where your treasure is, there will your heart be also" (Matthew 6:21). The only safe guide to peace and purity in a pagan world is His Word. It tells us:

[W]hatsoever things are true, whatsoever things are honest, whatsoever things are just, whatsoever things are pure, whatsoever things are lovely, whatsoever things are of good report; if there be any virtue, and if there be any praise, think on these things. Those things, which ye have . . . seen in me, do: and the God of peace shall be with you. (Philippians 4:8-9)

11

SHAMELESS CORRUPTION THROUGH TELEVISION & DIGITAL MEDIA

If readers would hear the term New Age in television, they would most likely relate it to popular shows such as "Medium," about a psychic housewife, or "Crossing Over," a show about psychic Jonathan Edward, or most likely Montel Williams' talk show, which regularly features best selling author and psychic Sylvia Browne. But the real situation is far more profound in scope and impact.[1]

TEACHING THAT TRANSFORMS

NO ONE CAN dispute television's power to teach and model good values and useful skills to generations of children. Experience has proven its effectiveness. For example, in one *Happy Days* episode, Fonzie gets a library card. Soon afterward, libraries across the country reported a noticeable rise in the number of children requesting cards.

Unfortunately, television also wields the same potential for modeling profanity, promiscuity, permissiveness, and counterfeit power. We have seen both the good and the bad, but in the tug of war between two forces, the latter is winning by a landslide.

"It used to be that children didn't understand much of the adult world until they were old enough to read about it in books," observes Dr. William Dietz, former chairman of the American Academy of Pediatrics Subcommittee on Children and

Television. "With the advent of television, children are exposed to more sophisticated messages at earlier ages."[2]

What then does television teach our children? The spectrum is broad and varied. But let's look at key categories and consider how the media message molds young minds.

[Only] the TV machine . . . holds such a devastating potential for brainwashing, mass programming, and the destruction of individualism—with, of course, reinforcement from the other mass media. This threat is every bit as disastrous for the future of mankind . . . as is pollution, overpopulation, or atomic and biological warfare.[3]

• **Laugh at religion.** Whether they like it or not, media leaders can't ignore Christian memorials like Easter or Christmas, but they can exclude Christ. By laughing at poor examples of or ineffective representatives from the church, they display a lifeless, inept, and materialistic substitute—which is not Christianity at all.

If it feels good, do it. Prime-time sitcoms, soaps, reality shows, mini-series, and mysteries model a seamy and sordid medley of yesterday's sexual and spiritual taboos, for this is the "liberated generation"—hopelessly addicted to entertainment.

Profanity, crudeness, sarcasm, and cynicism are then thrown in to spice things up. Have you noticed how quickly children have assimilated these negative qualities into their conversations and humor? Kindness doesn't fit unless it serves self-interest, but impudence is cool. Respect for parents is downright embarrassing, but following your own rules earns peer respect—or at least elicits approving laughter.

- **Experiment with magic.** The bright, beautiful gods and dark, cruel gods both draw power from a single source. So when Papa Smurf conquers evil with magical charms or when Teddy Ruxpin's friends trust in the divining power of crystals, or if the CareBears transform their world with loving vibes, they are all teaching counterfeit spirituality.

Thousands of children watched the young Houdini perform magic, not by illusions, but rather through a force from which he learned the trade secrets from a wise, old Indian shaman.

Others saw Hooperman seeking help from a frustrated channeler to solve a murder. The last scene showed the police chief, who at first resented involvement with the supernatural, sneaking in a visit with the triumphant psychic.

A Smurf episode shows Mother Earth guiding the forces of nature with her magic wand. When her wand breaks, an earthquake frees a wizard determined to steal the Smurfs eternal-life stone. In the end, good (or white) magic conquers evil, the wand is restored, and the earth is healed.[4] Though the Smurfs television shows are from the 1980s, a 2011 Smurf movie was a box-office success, grossing over 500 million dollars, and *Smurfs 2* is a 2013 release.

Magic, packaged for every age, prepares youngsters to accept occult forces without questioning their source. Appealing to their desire for secret knowledge and power to control their world, the supernatural has infiltrated almost every kind of program—including ads.

- **Pursue a new world order.** With television, mass programming has become a chilling reality. Media spokesmen wield power to censor facts, select information, ridicule vital principles, build illusive expectations, and redirect America's thinking. Today's information glut has produced an audience ill-equipped to argue with the "experts."

Some years ago, the late Dr. Francis Schaeffer spoke at a National Religious Broadcasters' convention. One participant summarized some of his key points:

> My clear impression, received from Dr. [Francis] Schaeffer's revelations, is that our nation is being systematically conditioned [by the media, public schools, and legislature] to accept a totalitarian, humanistic, elite ruling class. The rationale used for the concept of a one-world, all-powerful ruling class is that it is the only way to save the world from collapsing economically and socially.
>
> This is the reasoning of the self-appointed social "elite" who feel they are the only ones who have the intelligence and power to prevent mankind from destroying itself. And, if in the process of saving the world they have to destroy the Constitution of the United States and the personal freedom and dignity of the American people, then so be it! The threat to the Constitution is no fairy tale. It is very real.[5]

- **Don't hide from the horror and the paranormal.** It isn't just on Halloween anymore that children can tune in to horror shows or shows about the paranormal. They seem to be available all year long. And the effects they have on children can be lifelong. One study reveals direct evidence that in children five and younger, "scary movies can produce acute cases of anxiety. The symptoms of this anxiety include sleeping disorders, aggressiveness and self-endangerment."[6]

"Just turn it off!" argue network spokesmen, refusing to take any responsibility for what viewers happen to see. One woman shared her response to this kind of overly simplistic advice in *U.S. News and World Report*:

My heart is palpitating. Sweat pops from my forehead. The chair clings to my body. Back-to-back sequences of supernatural carnage unfold before me. Unsuspecting young victims are wrenched with soul-shivering cries into a world of malignant forms, satanic demons, and evil incarnate.

Each day's end brings terrifying commercials for yet another terrifying horror film. . . . Against my will I have become familiar with Jason of Friday the 13th and Freddy of Nightmare on Elm Street. Against my will, I've seen the faces of little children placed in the wake of sickness dredged from the depths of adult deviancy.

I do not now, nor will I ever, deny others their right to fright. I am only asking that it not be forced upon me and my small children, who've learned to "duck for cover" while we wait for the black horror to pass. I agree to give you the spooky, the scary, the startling. In return, give me back my family viewing hours and let me nestle softly among those I love, free from fright.[7]

ALIENS, UFOS, & A (FALSE) NEW AGE CHRIST

THE invasion of monsters began decades ago, and it quickly transformed the world of entertainment. With little resistance, an army of cute-ugly creatures swept into toy stores, television, and movies. They now adorn children's clothes, bedding, wallpaper, lunchboxes, and books. And many have pushed their way into children's hearts on the backs of seductive and misleading fables that mold their thoughts and manipulate their imagination.

Some of these monsters are crude and cool like Stitch, Shrek, and the serpentine aliens of *Men in Black*. Others appear wise and honorable like Yoda in *Star Wars*. But the creatures that win the prize for thrills and chills are the dark and deadly looking ones like Darth Maul, Tolkien's Orcs, and the ominous aliens in *Signs*.

They all serve a set of strategic social and spiritual goals: They entertain. They shift a person's attention from the real world to a more titillating realm created by those who write the myths and steer the imagination. They tempt Christian fans to re-imagine or reinvent both God and themselves in the new context—thus bending the old realities to fit the re-envisioned ones. They desensitize their fans to mystical images and symbols of evil. And they stir a craving for more intense excitement of the same kind.

Eventually the real world of nature, families, work, and biblical truth becomes too boring to be enjoyed. Who cares about truth and facts when folklore and fantasies seem far more titillating and exciting?

Today's techno-progressive mystical-oriented world has little tolerance for biblical watchfulness. Instead, it embraces its mythical heroes with a driving passion that often eclipses both family and reality. The more shocking, crude, insidious looking, and ugly, the more cool and captivating the product. Hollywood and toy makers know that well.

Perhaps you remember the Madballs from the late eighties. The grotesque bouncing heads bore matching names like Wolf Breath, Swine Sucker, and Screamin' Meenie. With shrewd foresight, their inventor, Ralph Shaffer, suggested that his successful minispheres would "take the world of cute-ugly into a new direction."[8]

He was right. The horrific-ugly as well as the cute-ugly began turning a corner and pulling Western culture along with it. Grotesque, demonic-looking creatures with fiery eyes infiltrated toy stores and sold like hotcakes. Many were mutants—part animal and part human, or an admixture of animal and monster. And most could wield the kind of supernatural power featured in their respective legends and stories.

They won incredible popularity. Children quickly overcame their natural aversion to scary images and learned to treasure these ugly, hybrid, mutant supernaturals. Few noticed their resemblance to the demonic creatures described in the Bible.

One of those early creatures of darkness, Black Star, would ride on a green horse with huge bat-like wings and a long dragon tail. Its eyes were glowing red and a long tongue dangled from its mouth. Another popular invader, Dark Dragon, had black wings and a huge tail with red scales along the sides. Hiding a skull in its chest, it had a lion's mouth, teeth, and claws. Its eyes were glowing red, and out of the center of its forehead shone a large, green third eye.

In a lecture titled "The Rising Interest in the Supernatural," Larry McLean, coauthor of *The Early Earth*, compares today's grotesque toys to historical images representing ancient gods:

> These [creatures] that show up in archeology and what we would call mythology were not just figments of the imagination. They were . . . represented as part human and part animal in their characteristics like this bird-human of the Assyrians. [They can be] horse-and-human like centaurs. Or fish-and-human like the god Dagon of the Philistines . . . or part jaguar and part human.
>
> Notice that tongue hanging out over the chin—which is a universal symbol of demonic possession. . . . One of the most popular combinations is human and serpent. . . . It's not surprising that pagan religions worshiped serpents and dragons, for the Bible tells us in Revelation 12 that the old serpent, the dragon, is Satan the devil.[9]

Nor should today's growing popularity of devilish images surprise us. The Bible prophesies that demonic activities will escalate before and during the reign of the Antichrist. Could the multiplication of demonic-looking, alien images be part of Satan's plan to prepare us for these awful future events?

Don't laugh. There is plenty of evidence that a sizable percentage of UFO sightings, alien abductions, crop circles, and other extraterrestrial manifestations fit into the realm of the supernatural. According to John Ankerberg and John Weldon's book *The Facts on UFO's and other Supernatural Phenomena*:

> [F]ew unbiased researchers can logically deny that UFO experiences are of an occult nature. If we catalog the basic characteristics of the occult and compare them to UFO phenomena, we discover an essential similarity. . . .
>
> After 20 years of research, we believe that the demonic theory dovetails extremely well with the totality of UFO phenomena. . . . In fact, we know of no UFO contactee who is not basically a spiritistic medium. In addition, we have read hundreds of articles from the oldest and most respected UFO journal, the *British Flying Saucer Review*, that indicate the psychic and/or non-extraterrestrial aspects of UFOs which, given their actions and messages, indicate probable demonic origin.[10]

These threats have not escaped notice. According to "Above Top Secret: The Worldwide UFO Cover-up" by Timothy Good, "the ubiquitous UFO phenomenon . . . [is] a phenomenon that has caused grave concern at high levels of many of the world's governments, despite their statements to the contrary."[11]

Ankerberg and Weldon arrived at the same conclusion. They found that "in the U.S. alone, tens of millions of dollars have been spent in official UFO investigations by the CIA, FBI, U.S. Army Intelligence, Naval Intelligence, and other organizations." They quote astrophysicist Dr. Jacques Vallee who describes the UFO event as "a bizarre, seductive, and often terrifying phenomenon reported by many witnesses as contact with an alien form of intelligence."[12]

Naturally, many UFO enthusiasts and New Age leaders would disagree. Some began to circulate the far-out notion decades ago: A group of benevolent aliens or ascended masters would suddenly appear on the earth and cleanse it from all who resist its spiritual evolution toward global oneness. At the same time, they would prepare humanity to receive the prophesied New Age "Christ."

Maybe not so far-out after all, at least according to one major New Age figure, Barbara Marx Hubbard. Marx Hubbard believes there will indeed be a cleansing of all those who resist the coming together of all humanity and rejection of its "Christ." She calls this process of cleansing the "Selection Process." Listen to a few quotes by Marx Hubbard as she describes this cleansing. Keep in mind while reading these that Marx Hubbard is not some glassy-eyed spaced-out hippy from the '60s living on an isolated mountainside. As a matter of fact, she has been instrumental in forming a lobby group in Washington D.C. to create a "U.S. Department of Peace." This organization, called The Peace Alliance, works with willing Congress members and other influential figures (such as the late Walter Cronkite) to bring about this Peace plan.[13] From Marx Hubbard's book, *The Revelation*, she quotes from her "Christ":

> Dearly beloved, I approached the crucifixion far more easily than I approach the selection. The crucifixion was done unto my body. The selection will be done unto yours.[14]

> The decisive moment of selection has almost come. The judgment of the quick and the dead is about to be made. The end of this phase of evolution is nearly complete.[15]

> By your acts you shall be judged as to whether you can evolve, or must be "cast into the lake of fire," which is the second death.[16]

> The selection process will exclude all who are exclusive. The selection process assures that only the loving will evolve to the stage of co-creator.[17]

The end is near. The old play is almost over. Suffice it to say, that if you do not choose to evolve into a wholesome, co-creative human, then you shall not.[18]

In former New Age follower Warren B. Smith's book, *False Christ Coming: Does Anybody Care?*, Smith unveils Marx Hubbard's "Selection Process":

Hubbard's "Christ," while describing the "birth experience" and professing his love for all mankind, nevertheless warns that there will be no place in the "New Jerusalem" for those who refuse to see themselves and others as a part of God. He describes, therefore, the necessity of a "selection process" that will select out resistant individuals who "choose" not to evolve. This "selection process" is a "purification" that will be accomplished through "the shock of a fire."[19]

Marx Hubbard likens those who resist this "co-creative stage of evolution," to a "lethal cancer cell in a body: deadly to itself and to the whole."[20] She explains:

The surgeon dare leave no cancer in the body when he closes up the wound after a delicate operation. We dare leave no self-centeredness on Earth after the selection process.[21]

Regardless of how this apocalyptic scenario will play out, be it with the supposed and added element of "aliens" or "ascended masters," or not, these demonic beings will no doubt come as "angel[s] of light" and "ministers of righteousness" (2 Corinthians 11:14-15) illustrating "the beautiful side of evil" rather than the grotesque images of occult idols in order to "deceiveth the whole world" (Revelation 12:9). These "masters" represent a hierarchy of warring demons that match the warning in Ephesians 6:12, which tells us that our battle is not against "flesh and blood" but rather against the "rulers of the darkness of this world" and "against spiritual wickedness in high places."

Different versions of these seductive deceptions have spread around the world through the writings of countless occultists. Their numbers include the infamous Satanist Aleister Crowley as well as the occultic "prophetess" Alice Bailey, whose channeled messages from spirit guide Djwhal Khul inspired United Nations and many education leaders.

But God's Word shows us the truths behind those illusions. Revelation 9:1-11 foresees a day when the Abyss (the bottomless pit where Satan will be cast) will open with a burst of smoke and release an army of powerful deadly creatures onto the earth. They will look like a mixture of man, horse, and locust with wings. They will have stinging "tails like unto scorpions," and their commander will be Satan himself.

> Though children are born with a natural fear of hideous, shocking, and evil-looking creatures, this God-given protection has been dulled by the Western world's mass-media marketing system.

Our God will allow it; for man's evil—as in the days of Noah—and God's eternal justice will call forth His judgment.

Though children are born with a natural fear of hideous, shocking, and evil-looking creatures, this God-given protection has been dulled by the Western world's mass-media marketing system. Children are being conditioned to embrace demonic manifestations, whether they come as beings with superior intelligence from outer space to rescue planet Earth or as evolved mutations from earth itself. Why wouldn't they accept these lies?

Unless we teach them otherwise, today's postmodern anti-biblical beliefs in both physical and cosmic evolution lead most of them to trust in deceptions. Of course—they are told—life had to have evolved on other planets! If there really is a God, He wouldn't have created the whole universe just for earthlings, would He?

Yes, He would. Why shouldn't our God, who sent His own Son to die for us, create such a universe? Why not make it so vast that man's ego would be humbled by such might? Maybe He did it to show us the immeasurable greatness of His magnificent, incomprehensible creative powers and the infinite width, length, height, and depth of His magnificent love. I believe He did.

> O the depth of the riches both of the wisdom and knowledge of God! how unsearchable are his judgments, and his ways past finding out! For who hath known the mind of the Lord? or who hath been his counsellor? . . . For of him, and through him, and to him, are all things: to whom be glory for ever. (Romans 11:33-34, 36)

PAGAN FANTASIES JOIN THE DIGITAL EXPLOSION

WHILE "popular occultism" was embedding its pagan images, fairy stories, and monsters into our modern culture, the world was rapidly adapting to a computerized media. The two seemed made for each other.

"Magic is the science of the imagination, the art of engineering consciousness and discovering the virtual forces that connect the body-mind with the physical world," writes Erik Davis in his article, "Technopagans." Showing the impact of pagan thrills on the cold logical world of computer language, he introduces a pagan leader in computer innovation:

> Mark Pesce is a technopagan, a participant in a small but vital subculture of digital savants who keep one foot in the emerging technosphere and one foot in the wild and woolly world of Paganism. . . . an anarchic, earthy, celebratory spiritual movement that attempts to reboot the magic, myths, and gods of Europe's pre-Christian people. . . .

A startling number of Pagans work and play in technical fields, as sysops, computer programmers, and network engineers. . . .

Over the millennia, alchemists, Kabbalists, and esoteric Christians developed a rich storehouse of mental tools. . . . It's no accident that these 'hermetic' arts are named for Hermes, the Greek trickster god of messages and information. . . .

Using a combination of ceremonial performance, ritual objects, and imagination, Pagans carve out these tightly bounded zones in both physical and psychic space. . . .

[Y]ou find more intimate correspondences between computer culture and Paganism's religion of the imagination. One link is science fiction and fantasy fandom, a world whose role playing, nerd humor, and mythic enthusiasm has bred many a Pagan.[22]

The characters birthed by Tolkien's imagination fit right in. That's why the first generation of dreamweavers and technopagans would masquerade as wizards, hobbits, dwarves, and other Middle Earth characters during the pioneering years of computer conventions. And that's why the emerging world of Dungeons & Dragons adopted Tolkien's orcs, dwarves, trolls, and elves. Tolkien's mystical realms set the stage and built the pattern for North America's future game-makers.

It makes sense. "The makers of D&D were trained in euro magic—all the elements of the medieval craft, same as Tolkien," says Peter Lanz, a former occultist who wrote to us. "As an occult simulation, this system offers a smooth ride into the world of euro magic."

In fact, the most popular role-playing games blend fact and fantasy, myth and history together into a virtual reality that stirs the imagination and implants its dark images in the minds of the players. For example, Warhammer Fantasy Role-Play—like the Tolkien games—is "set in a medieval fantasy world" populated with a vast diversity of orcs, ogres, dwarfs, goblins, wizards, gods, and sorcerers.

"Digital Drugs" Sold on the Internet Induce Altered States of Consciousness

An article titled "A new worry for parents—'digital drugs' sold on the Internet" describes how teens are "getting high" from listening to certain high frequency digital sounds on the Internet. Basically, what is happening is the sounds are being used as a mantra to take listeners into altered states of consciousness, similar to drug use or contemplative/centering prayer (i.e., Eastern meditation). It was the contemplative mystic, Thomas Merton, who compared contemplative meditation to that of an LSD trip.[23] Now, parents have a new worry—their kids getting "high" without drugs. All the more reason for Christian parents to make sure their teens understand the dangers of Eastern-style meditation (e.g., contemplative or centering prayer). The article about "digital drugs" states:

> For decades, parents, doctors and school administrators have worried about the dangers of drugs. In the digital age, they've got a new arena for concern: Sound waves that, some say, affect the brain like a drug—and cost only 99 cents on iTunes and Amazon.com.
>
> Many scientific experts say they're unfamiliar with "digital drugs"—sometimes sold under the brand name I-Dosers—and doubt whether sound patterns could have the same effect as chemical drugs. But some parents—and at least one Oklahoma school system—worry that downloading these sounds could be a teen's first step toward physical drugs.
>
> As proof, they point to YouTube, where hundreds of videos—some of teen "users" getting "high"—have

been posted. On the I-Doser Facebook page, users recommend tracks with comments such as, "Last night I did 'peyote' and 'alter-x' and they really worked." The I-Doser free software is the second most downloaded program in the science category on CNET.com, with 6,500 downloads in a single recent week.*24*

As if all the obvious dangers of the Internet for children are not enough, if youth are now able to "get high" from digital frequencies altering their consciousness, combined with the opportunities to engage in occultic games on the Internet, the impact on the lives of potentially millions of youth could be horrific—especially if the digital drugs help set the stage for turning teens on to actual drugs and deeper forms of mysticism.

THE EFFECT ON CHILDREN

How do television, the media, and the Internet influence our children's view of themselves and their environment? Consider these factors:

• **It replaces other activities.** According to 2012 Nielsen ratings, the average American spends 20% of his day watching television.*25* In another study, eight- to eighteen-year-olds spend an average of over seven hours a day online (which includes cell phones, Internet, gaming devices, and tablets).*26* Family games, reading, conversation, or other forms of social interaction—needed to build caring, responsive, and discriminating individuals—require more initiative and mental energy than many families are willing to exert.

Children cannot test the world they see in the television set. Newspapers and books allow time to stop, ponder, and ask questions. Not television. Since children's ability to evaluate messages can't keep up with TV's rapid action presentations, their learning is often passive and involves automatic acceptance.

- **It produces unreasonable demands and expectations.** Cartoon commercials and ads stimulate children's desires, or the advertisers wouldn't spend millions to persuade them to buy. Young children, unable to differentiate between a show and an ad, receive the exaggerated or deceptive sales pitch with the same trust that they listen to a parent or teacher.

- **It gives a distorted view of the world.** Since children depend heavily on television to fill in gaps in their experience, they tend to accept what it tells them. The younger the child the fewer facts he has for evaluating what he sees and hears. Therefore, the images presented on the screen help shape his perception of his world.

"Children up to age seven understand very little of the plot," says the late Charles Atkin, long time chairman of Michigan State University's Department of Communication. He explained:

> They identify closely with characters . . . and like watching them do things, even though they don't understand the big picture.[27]

In other words, a child might see a burglar break into a home in the first scene, and not connect this crime with the imprisonment shown twenty-five minutes later.

- **It models harmful relationships.** Television programs show adolescents how to relate to the opposite sex and produce a perverted consensus in their peer culture. Sexual promiscuity becomes a normal part of life, while the consequences—unwanted pregnancies, incurable sexually transmitted diseases, the inner torment of out-of-marriage sexual relationships and their usual breakups—rarely receive fair exposure.

- **It models violent behavior.** "Studies have linked violence on TV with aggressive behavior in children and adolescents," says pediatrician Victor Straburger, a consultant to the

American Academy of Pediatrics Subcommittee on Children and Television. "One can't say for sure that a child will start a fire after watching a drama about arson, but the connection appears consistently throughout all kinds of studies."[28]

- **By the time a child reaches the age of eighteen,** he will have witnessed 200,000 acts of violence, including 40,000 murders.[29] Watching hours of painless "fantasy violence," children learn to view violence as a normal and acceptable way to express anger and handle conflicts. Even sexual violence loses its horror. Some are trapped in its deadly grip, as executed serial killer Ted Bundy testified in an interview in 1989 just before his execution:

> The FBI'S own study on serial homicide shows that the most common interest among serial killers is pornography. . . Dangerous impulses are being fueled day in and day out by violence in the media in its various forms, particularly sexualized violence. . . . Some of the violence in the movies that comes into homes today is stuff that they wouldn't show in X-rated adult theatres thirty years ago. This stuff—I'm telling you from personal experience—is the most graphic violence on screen, particularly as it gets into the homes, to children who may be unattended or unaware that they may be a Ted Bundy who has that vulnerability or predisposition to be influenced by that kind of violence.[30]

- **It produces fear.** According to a report from the University of Michigan Health System, children "can come to view the world as a mean and scary place when they take violence and other disturbing themes on TV to be accurate in real life."[31] The report states that:

> » Symptoms of being frightened or upset by TV stories can include bad dreams, anxious feelings, being afraid of being alone, withdrawing from friends, and missing school.

» Fears caused by TV can cause sleep problems in children.[32]

» Scary-looking things like grotesque monsters especially frighten children aged two to seven. Telling them that the images aren't real does not help because kids under age eight can't always tell the difference between fantasy and reality.[33]

No wonder! While violence appears exciting on television, it presents a frightening picture of the world we live in. Children store in their minds vivid images of horrendous possibilities. Families pay a high price for enjoying evil.

- **It clouds discernment of right from wrong.** The biblical attitudes of trust, obedience, and surrender clash with a world where self reigns and values have been turned upside down. Again and again, television presents an ominous reversal: Good is bad, and bad is good. In the Gospel message, confessing sin brings cleansing, and the Cross sets us free. Yet in our "enlightened" society, sin and the Cross are rejected as "negatives" unfit for a new "progressive" world system.

Oprah Winfrey illustrated this game of opposites when she hosted an unlikely pair: Dr. Aquino, a high priest in the satanic temple of Seth, and Christian believer Johanna Michaelsen who wrote *The Beautiful Side of Evil*. About halfway through the program, Oprah turned to Johanna, saying, "Dr. Aquino has told us that the satanism he represents is good, not evil. Is that possible?"

"Well it is," answered Johanna, "if you come from a frame of mind where left is right, bad is good, black is white, in is out, and upside down is right side up—which is the basic approach of satanism. Everything is backwards. So to him, satanism is good and everything else is bad. That's his perspective. However, he is wrong!"[34]

Remember, God warns us about this kind of manipulative make-believe where evil is called good and good is called evil (Isaiah 5:20).

12

GUARDING AGAINST CORRUPTION IN TELEVISION & DIGITAL MEDIA

I will walk within my house with a perfect heart. I will set no wicked thing before mine eyes: I hate the work of them that turn aside; it shall not cleave to me. A froward heart shall depart from me: I will not know a wicked person. (Psalm 101:2-4)

"**PLEASE TURN OFF** the television, David."

"Why can't I see *The Real Ghostbusters*?"

"Because it teaches kids to enjoy the occult, and because it makes man seem like God—able to control the forces of evil."

"All my friends watch it."

"David, you know how I feel about that argument. I don't want you to follow everyone else."

"But when Todd and Troy were my age, you let them see stuff like that. . . ."

"Times have changed. Some of the shows they watched—like *The Munsters* or *The Adams Family*—seemed so remote from reality. But today, kids can experiment with the very things that these cartoons suggest and model. . . . The occult wasn't such an obvious part of our world ten years ago. Today it is blatant. Especially on television."

"You never let me see anything!"

"That's not true. . . ."

I felt my son's frustration—and my own. Longing to offer him something good and fun, I prayed for direction in dealing with him.

That discussion with my son took place many years ago. In time, David learned to discern for himself. It didn't happen overnight; but with prayer, Bible study, practice, and a deepening commitment to follow truth, he developed the habit of seeing and making choices about life from God's perspective.

Step One: Pray

- **Pray for wisdom to know what to watch, and self-control to abstain.** Set a good example.

- **Pray for consistency in maintaining God's standards.** Remember that even if your child knows and agrees with your values, a diet of deception, distortion, and evil will affect his perspective. He cannot enjoy what God hates and remain immune to being "hardened through the deceitfulness of sin" (Hebrews 3:13).

- **Pray that no other hero overshadows the true God in your child's life.** When identifying with T.V. idols, children can lose a sense of need for the God of the Bible. "What's so great about Him?" they wonder. "Does He lift skyscrapers and smash the bad guys with ray guns? Does He zoom through the air or explore outer space?"

We know He who made earth and space can do all these things and more—but from a child's limited perspective, God often seems tame. The biblical stories cannot compete with cartoons and the action-packed stimulation contained therein for which many children have developed an insatiable appetite.

- **Pray for appropriate guidelines for television viewing.**

STEP TWO: AFFIRM GOD'S VALUES TOGETHER

- **Continue family Bible study.**

- **Discuss these questions:** What do you remember best from a movie or television program—the good values or the shocking violence? What do you forget? What could help you remember the good things and overlook evil? If you are watching a show, which suddenly pictures immoral, violent, or occult scenes, do you find it difficult to turn it off? What does that tell you about the subtle appeal to evil?

- **Discuss news reports and other information.** Is all of it true or might there be distortions? Finding the truth in the midst of all the editorializing is work. But work we must, or the media will mold our thinking.

The late scholar Joseph Campbell profoundly affected millions who watched him dialogue with Bill Moyers on public television. Charming and articulate, Campbell viewed Christianity as merely one myth among many. He often validated his conclusions by quoting the Bible. Only those who knew God's Word well enough to discern error—or took time to check each reference—could recognize the distortions in his use of the Bible.

- **Find DVDs that model God's values,** teach Bible stories, or tell a heartwarming story without profanity, immorality, or New Age overtones. Find films that both entertain as well as testify to God's greatness through the lives of His people.

- **List programs or movies seen during the past week.** Discuss the values they taught or demonstrated. Don't just say "This is bad" or "This is good." Be specific. Give reasons. This helps your child to better appreciate and remember what is true and reject what is false.

STEP THREE: TRAIN YOUR CHILD TO DISCERN DECEPTION

Challenge your child to be a scout for God—one who notices every message that wages war against and exalts itself against His truth. Train her to ask herself these questions:

1. Does it picture obscenity, nudity, sex, cruelty, and violence? Watch for the subtle as well as the obvious—images tucked into sweet stories or flashed in front of you in a cartoon.

2. Do one or more of the characters play the role of God? Do some of these gods, such as He-man and Superman, seem greater and more real than God? Or does the story suggest that each person is a god, the designer and creator of his own circumstances? Does it imply each person has power within himself to overcome all obstacles and fulfill his dreams?

3. Does the winning side draw on power not from God? If supernatural power is not from God, it is demonic. Some years ago, this may have seemed less important, but today, as psychic phenomena and demonic power are considered normal, we must guard our children's minds from absorbing this lie and forgetting its danger. Constant exposure tends to bring unquestioning acceptance.

4. Like the graceful, hypnotic dance of a cobra being snake charmed, New Age/New Spirituality is the beautiful, seductive side of evil—and it's deadly!

5. Does good win over evil? Does it show your child that there are consequences for violating God's standards? They may show consequences for violating the world's values, yet reward those who violate God's. For example, one cartoon showed Woody Woodpecker demonstrating all his nasty ways to avenge an offense and get away with it.

6. Do you hear references to New Age phrases such as "higher intelligence," "past lives" (reincarnation), "mind evolution," and "perfection" as can be experienced through magic and counterfeit powers? These are rampant in many space fantasies.

7. Does it emphasize occult power? Are sorcery, spells, clairvoyance, divination, and other psychic formulas presented as helpful tools to successful living? Might it produce curiosity or fascination with the occult and a desire to experiment? These demonic traps are far more deadly than drugs or alcohol. Our God hates these things; how, then, can His children rightly enjoy them?

8. Does it pass the test of Philippians 4:8? "[W]hatsoever things are true . . . honest . . . just . . . pure . . . lovely . . . of good report . . . virtue . . . think on these things" Compile a list of T.V. programs and movies that encourage kindness, helpfulness, morality, and respect for others. Share them with others.

STEP FOUR: JOIN THE BATTLE FOR TRUTH

What kind of examples do we, their parents, set? Do we dare let the power that opposes everything that God is and all that He does, be a source of entertainment for us?

- **Speak up about pornography, sexually explicit scenes, vulgarity, profanity, violence, and the occult.** A silent church is likely to be a compromising church. If we don't hold each other and our leaders accountable, we can all too easily buy into the media message.

- **Write advertisers of objectionable shows.** Since they want to gain, not lose customers, they welcome your opinion. The networks, in turn, respond to complaints from their advertisers.

- **Pray that God would show your family His concerns** so that you can battle in prayer as you watch various shows.

God tells us—children and parents alike—to be "wise as serpents, and harmless as doves" (Matthew 10:16). That means we must be alert to what is happening, see all things from His perspective, resist any compromise with the evil around us, and let God use us to accomplish His purpose.

13

TWISTING THE IMAGINATION THROUGH TOYS & GAMES

> Children project themselves with their imagination into a toy. They give it life, character, abilities and talents and set the surrounding around it. This is how they learn.[1] —
> **Phil Phillips,** *Turmoil in the Toy Box*

TOY STORES ARE safe, happy places. Right? Some are. But most have traded treasured age-appropriate toys for glamour dolls and occult warriors that catapult even young children into the world of adult conflicts.

The macho, magical, and macabre have captivated children for ages. Grimm's Fairy Tales filled my own childhood in Norway with images of wicked, spell-casting witches and three-headed trolls who turned children into stone. The tales were fun, a bit scary but exciting, and obviously unreal.

Today's full-scale acceptance of counterfeit spirituality and the dark forces behind it has made the realm of the mystical become all too grimly real. By itself, a fairytale or toy will hardly shape a child's attitudes. But reinforced by school, movies, music, and television, the combined messages generate tolerance and acceptance of the demonic.

My childhood toys freed my imagination to direct the play. I—not the toymaker—assigned personalities and feelings to my toys and interacted with them according to my understanding of the world around me.

Those traditional toys, if still available, fade in the glamorous light of toys that star in movies, cartoons, and comic books. Complete with built-in personalities, these new playmates both stifle and steer the imagination. G.I. Joe and the Ghostbusters have been outfitted for battle—nothing else. The play naturally moves in that one direction. Phil Phillips, author of *Turmoil in the Toybox*, states:

> When a child watches a cartoon and then plays with a toy connected to that cartoon, he is no longer projecting himself into the toy. Instead, cartoons have programmed the child to play with toys in a certain way.[2]

Whether friendly or scary in appearance, dolls and action figures come to life through a child's imagination. Through their good or evil characteristics, they teach about life and relationships. As the child plays, he acts out his growing (and often distorted) perception of his world, validating and strengthening the message behind the toy. John Dvorak, writing for the *San Francisco Examiner*, offers some interesting insights into the role of toys:

> When trying to understand the mood of the country, its future, and its direction, where do you turn?
>
> Many journalists follow the annals of Congress; others have deep discussion with learned professors. I go to Toys R Us. Here's where the forthcoming generations are molded. Let me tell you, the future die is cast and the image is a sick one. It's not that the toy business hasn't always been fraught with weird fads, tasteless imagery, and warped symbols that have little value. But now it's worse than ever. One is simply overwhelmed by a plethora of toys best described as gruesome, gory, and irresponsible.[3]

A Wonderland of Dreams & Magic

JOIN me on a hair-raising journey through a modern fantasy—and the local toy store. You will meet aliens, demons, ghosts, and goblins. You will see horrendous humanoids, scary supernaturals, haunted humans, and shimmering seductive dolls. You will discover computer and DVD games that equip you with mystical power and pit you against diabolical forces.

Grab a cart, and we'll start by the left wall of the cavernous showroom. Scanning the endless display of unfamiliar games—undoubtedly many good ones—your eyes rest momentarily on Shriefs and Creeks and Eternia—the homeland of the Masters of the Universe. Then, near a stack of Ouija Boards, you spot Therapy, which promises "fascinating fun with a psychological twist." To the true-or-false question, "Playing hard-to-get definitely works," it answers: "False. Males . . . tend to need encouragement. The most popular girls are open with their emotions, not guarded."

Across from the board games stretches the formidable wall of electronic and computer games. Nintendo and Wii sound familiar, so you stop to examine its display. You breathe a sigh of relief at the sight of good old themes like Mickey Mouse, soccer, and baseball. But other pictures jump out at you—strange aliens, shrewd sorcerers, hideous demons, fiery dragons. You quickly move on.

The end wall displays books. You notice a "deluxe" color/activity book called Masters of the Universe. Browsing through its pages you see a story that little children can color: "The Snake Pit—Join He-Man as he rescues Battle Cat from the Snake Men and foils the evil plan of Skeletor!" You scan "Slimy Rescue!" "Laser Messages," "Castle Ghoulies," and "Mirror Magic Mazes."

The four-page posters picture "He-Man in the Blaster-hawk Battle and Skeletor in the Fright Fighter!" Skeletor, the "Lord of Destruction," controls the dark side of the force. His head is a skull, and he carries a ram's head staff, two symbols of death and satanism. You wonder how a little boy could sleep with that awful picture on his wall.

You move down an aisle of guns of every shape and kind, from Galactic Light Blaster to Nickelodeon Super Slimer, which "shoots slime up to 25 feet." A delight to clean up, no doubt.

Turning the corner you almost stumble into the Mad Scientist with lures such as "Doctor Dreadful—Alien Autopsy" or "Aliens—Scorpion Alien with Face Hugger" (that one is for four years old and up).

In the next two aisles, you find armies of action figures you recognize from television cartoons. First, you spot the Teenage Mutant Ninja Turtles, the strange, green humanoid turtles that were introduced in the late 1980s and are still popular. Nickelodeon recently acquired the rights to the TMNT and has created a made for television Ninja Turtles series for kids. Turtles? They look more like muscle men with snake heads.

Next, the Thundercat action figures, which come with Mumm-Ra's Tomb Fortress, where skeletal Mumm-Ra "mystically" transforms into Mumm-ra the Everliving. Two dragon-tailed Man/Beast (mutants) "Statue Guardians" guard the skull-shaped transformation chamber.

You notice you have entered the occult section of the store, for after Sharkoss, Demon of the Deep from "The Other World" waits Mattel's "Masters of the Universe." The blond, handsome He-Man and glamorous She-Rah contrast starkly with the grotesque creatures all around them. The largest boxes contain the skull-shaped "Castle Grayskull," He-Man's home in "Eternia" and the source of his power.

You head for the dolls. "Totally awesome!" shouts dazzling Sasha, one of the Bratz dolls. Does cool mean makeup for little girls? The number of little cosmetic cases suggests it. The pink cases contrast sharply with the Halloween makeup on the same shelf. Instead of a pretty face, try one with gray, ghostly skin, bloody streaks, and ghoulish scars.

You're leaving, and on the way out you glimpse Play-Doh. Ah, there's a good safe toy! But wait, this Play-Doh box wears the title "The Real Ghostbusters—Glow-in-the-Dark Play-Doh."

You don't even have to form your own imagined ghosts and monsters. Play-Doh does it for you!

YOGA, REIKI, AND NEW AGE TOYS

THE New Age has raised its seductive head in the Western world's toy kingdom like never before. Visit a Toys R Us store and here is what you will find:

• Yoga Smarts: a board game for twelve- to fourteen-year-olds. The description: "Challenge your friends, family, and other Yoga enthusiasts with this question and answer game made especially for the Zen at heart!"

• Body Poetry: Yoga Cards: a game for four- to eight-year-olds. The description: Introduce Yoga to your children or students.

• Travel Yoga Mat: all ages.

• Ouija Boards. In 2008, Hasbro, the maker of Ouija Boards, came out with a hot pink Ouija Board just for girls ages 8 and up. Toys R Us was carrying the pink occult game but eventually phased it out because of complaints.

• The Complete Tarot Kit: "This amazing kit gives you everything you need to get started in the art of tarot."

• Fantasma Magic Wishcraft Trio Set: "Includes WishCraft Mystical Tarot Cards, WishCraft Psychic Pendulum and Wish-Craft Magical Wishing Heart."

American Girl Doll Company has joined the mystical New Age ranks too. American Girl Publishing (a division of American Girl) released a book in 2009 titled *Spa Fun*. On the back cover, it tells young readers to try a "Yoga pose." Inside, the chapter called "De-Stress" are sections titled "Balloon Breathes" (instructing its readers to sit cross-legged and practice their deep breathing exercises), "Mini Meditations" (instructing them to sit cross-legged and focus on your breathing), and "Mantras." In "Mantras," it

160

states, "Add a mantra to your meditation. A *mantra* is a sound or a word you repeat to help you focus."[4]

American Girl also has an American Girl Yoga Doll on the market today. Mattel now offers a Barbie Yoga Teacher Doll, which comes with Barbie in a Yoga outfit with a Yoga mat. On Amazon, you can find the Yoga Garden Game for children ages four and up, which has a five star rating on Amazon and received the Parents' Choice Award. Also on Amazon is a Yoga Tool Box for kids, *Little Yoga Coloring Book*, Yoga Plush Bear, *The ABCs of Yoga for Kids*, and numerous other Yoga toys and reading material. There's even a G.I. Joe Street Fighter II Dhalsim Yoga Fighter. Add to this, toys introducing the chakras and Zen, a Séance game for sixteen years and older, a Fairytale Lego set with a witch and a wizard, and a Hello Kitty World Fortune Teller Booth for ages five and up.

> A Reiki teddy bear was being advertised in a New Age magazine. The advertisement read: "This teddy bear can be infused with Reiki energy and given to a child."

In addition to Yoga, New Age practices called energy healing are having an influence with children's toys as well. Reiki, a type of energy healing, supposedly transfers a universal energy from the practitioner to another person. Research analyst Ray Yungen, who has studied the New Age for many years was shocked to discover that a Reiki teddy bear was being advertised in a New Age magazine. The advertisement read: "This teddy bear can be infused with Reiki energy and given to a child."[5]

WHAT DO THEY TEACH?

TOYS can help children learn to solve problems, share ideas, express frustration, use their imagination, develop creativity, and concentrate on a project. But these benefits can be misused. We have seen how counterfeit teaching touches our children through schools, movies, and television. The messages from toys fall into three categories: mind-altering religion, values, and world system, which I discuss below:

• **A counterfeit religion.** The cartoon stories prove that nothing is impossible for them. Humanism (belief in man's infinite capacity) plus New Age power raise these superheroes—and anyone who identifies with them—to spiritual mastery.

Where then is God?

The toy/cartoon connection commands a strong influence. The child bases his play on the story; lacking a strong enough belief-system of his own, he incorporates the fiction into his life. Whether he visualizes himself as G.I. Joe using his power to defeat his enemies or as a Ninja Turtle with super powers to subdue evil villains, a child plays according to Satan's original lie: "You shall not surely die . . . you will be as gods" (Genesis 3:4).

This enticing illusion fires a child's heart with delicious dreams that lure him away from truth. In time, the child outgrows the vision but grasps greedily for the next one that the deceiver dangles. That next vision might come through computer games.

In a world that has lost its awe of God and its wariness of His enemy, why not try? Why not experiment with anything that offers secret knowledge, thrills, and power? Who worries about consequences in a New Age that denies sin, guilt, and an all powerful, almighty God?

• **Counterfeit values.** When I was a child, I spanked my dolls when they "disobeyed." Whether we played "house" indoors, built tree houses in the forest, or dug ice caves outside in the five-foot snow packs, we followed the rules that had already become an accepted part of life. Our playtimes generally affirmed honesty, parental authority, and love.

The cartoons behind today's toys create a radically different kind of atmosphere—where male and, in some cases, female (i.e., Powerpuff Girls) aggression and an all too often overdeveloped vengeance on one's adversary replaces chivalry (as in the case of Dudley-Do-Right of Fractured Fairytales). A world in which cynicism, sarcasm, and dark humor reigns and displaces happy, benign childlike humor. A parallel universe devoid of true-to-life consequences where bad deeds go unpunished, evil is called good, good is called evil, and even doing the "right thing" is often done for all the wrong reasons.

Supermen call for superwomen, and toy shelves abound with slender beauties modeling physical perfection and flashy fashions. Barbie set the trend and others followed. Today's little girls learn the importance of having all of Barbie's fashion accessories: a styling center with makeup (the box shows a little girl hugging her makeup bag), an incredible wardrobe of designer clothes, a townhouse, furniture, a horse, an all-terrain vehicle and, of course, a boyfriend named Ken. If that isn't enough, she can borrow accessories from Bratz fashion dolls and Monster High dolls (that's right, fashionable monster dolls).

In spite of the feminist drive for sexual equality, girls' toys emphasize glamour, glitter, and seductive sensuality, while boys' toys encourage macho violence, ugly monsters, and supernatural power.

POWER RANGERS

KARATE-kicking their way to global fame, the world's hottest super heroes have left the Ninja Turtles behind in the dust. Armed with magic crystals, megazords, and the ancient secrets of martial arts, they claim to be the saviors of the world—ready at the drop of a hat to combat evil aliens and inhuman monsters. Blending body, mind, and animal power into an Eastern form of supernatural empowerment, they are super-fast, super-strong, and super-dedicated. And they are concerned about the environment.

The Power Rangers have built a worldwide army of small but impassioned disciples who share their cause: fighting evil with supernatural power. When the karate heroes transform themselves into high-kicking warriors, they also have an uncanny power to "morph" their young devotees into leaping, wrestling, kicking combatants.

"One simply has to say 'Trini' [a former Ranger's name] and abracadabra, and the little curmudgeons transform before my very eyes into an entire martial-arts army," says Fannie Elliott, a teacher at Kedren Headstart Preschool in Los Angeles. With grunts, groans and cries of "Hi-Yah!" they kick and karate-chop their way around a roomful of potential aliens.

Lori Pino, a teacher in Massachusetts, shared Elliott's concern. "I noticed that with the Power Rangers it was different, there was a real obsession." She tried banning Power Ranger play, but the children simply kept "karate-chopping the air, behind [her] back."

> By the time the child is a teen, unless his parents have instilled Christian values in him, he will have more knowledge of the occult than he will have of God.[6] —Phil Phillips

Obsession with power, violence, and martial arts can prove fatal. One year, Norway, Sweden, and Denmark banned the show for a season after a five-year-old Norwegian girl was kicked unconscious by classmates and died in the snow. Some blamed the Ninja Turtles, which had been broadcasting the skills and thrills of the martial arts longer.

In spite of the bad reports, Power Rangers has remained popular since 1993, and as of 2012, the show has nineteen television seasons with sixteen different series and two theatrical films. While many parents give in to the kicks and screams that follow attempted restrictions, others simply accept the show, hoping that the good outweighs the bad. After all, the Power Rangers demonstrate discipline, teamwork, and the right use of force, don't they? They fight monsters, not humans, so there's no blood. And, since it's just fantasy, the violence won't matter much. . . .

What would you do? Before you decide, ask yourself these two questions. What does the program teach children about reality? Does it train them to look at life from a biblical or an occult perspective?

Since young children soak up images along with words—without much analysis or evaluation, their understanding of the world will be formed by the most fun, forceful, and persistent messages they receive. Children raised on daily diets of biblical truth will recognize and resist occult images. But daily doses of Power Ranger magic with its pulsating rock beat will reduce their resistance to deception. Fantasy or not, the repeated themes and occult context of most contemporary cartoons will train their minds to believe the timeless lies that have always drawn people from truth to lies.

To cool Ranger fever in your home, try asking some leading age-appropriate questions. For example:

◊ What is the source of the Power Rangers' power?

◊ How do they get their supernatural power?

◊ Who gets the credit for winning the battles?

◊ Does someone in the program pretend to be God?

◊ Did you see magic symbols or occult charms?

◊ What does God's Word tell us about these kinds of powers?

God tells us to train our children in the way they should go (Proverbs 22:6). This means helping your child build a biblical view, a mental framework based on God's Word, not the world's distortions. Viewing the world through the filter of truth, your child will accept what God loves, discern what He hates, and enjoy the safety He offers those who follow Him.

How Pokémon & Magic Cards Affect the Minds & Values of Children

Who are the strange little creatures from Japan that came on the world scene in 1996 and remain global superstars? Most kids know the answer well: They are called Pokémon (short for POCKEt MONster and pronounced Poh-keh-mon).

Ash and Pikachu on "loot bag" and napkin. "Gotta catch them all."

"We just sent a letter home today saying Pokémon cards are no longer allowed on campus," said Paula Williams, a second-grade teacher in Danville, California. "The kids know they're supposed to be put away when they come in from recess, but they're often in the middle of a trade, so they don't come in on time. In the more extreme cases, the older kids are getting little kids to trade away valuable cards. . . . It drives a teacher crazy."

It concerns parents even more. "Recently, my children were given a set of Pokémon cards," said DiAnna Brannan, a Seattle mom. "They are very popular with the children at our church and elsewhere. I was instantly suspicious but couldn't discern the problem. We have since been told that they are stepping stones to the 'Magic cards' that have been popular for the last few years, which we do not allow."

She is right. For instance, children exploring some of the most popular Pokémon websites will find links to a selection of occult games and magic. At the site for the Wizards of the Coast (makers of the Pokémon and Magic cards), a grotesque winged creature with a devilish face is plastered over the home page, and a warning is given that there is "blood" and "mild violence." On a Pokémon "Basic Rules" website, it gives this advice:

> Pokémon are incredible creatures that share the world with humans . . . Each Pokémon has its own special fighting abilities. . . . Some grow, or evolve, into even

more powerful creatures. . . . Carry your Pokémon
with you, and you're ready for anything! You've got
the power in your hands, so use it![7]

What if children try to follow this advice? What if they carry
their favorite monsters like magical charms or fetishes in their
pockets, trusting them to bring power in times of need?

Many do. It makes sense to those who watch the television show.
In one episode, Ash, the boy hero, had just captured his fifth little
Pokémon. But that wasn't good enough, said his mentor. He must
catch lots more if he wants to be a Pokémon master. And the more
he catches and trains, the more power he will have for future battles.

So Ash sets out again in search for more of the reclusive,
power-filled, little Pokémon. His first step is to find the "psychic
Pokémon" called Kadabra and snatch it from its telepathic, pink-
eyed trainer, Sabrina.

Or so it would seem to a first-time viewer not familiar with
the contradictory themes. Actually, Ash doesn't try to "catch"
Kadabra. In spite of the prodding to increase his inventory of
Pokémon warriors—and in spite of the constant reminders to
"catch them all"—Ash was merely trying to win a standard battle.
With the ghost Haunter on his side, it should have been a cinch!

But Ash underestimates the power of his opponent. When he
and Sabrina meet for the fight, both hurl their chosen Pokémon
into the air, but only Abra (who becomes Kadabra) evolves into
a super-monster with a magic flash. Haunter hides. "Looks like
your ghost Pokémon got spooked," taunts Sabrina.[8]

Obviously, Ash didn't understand the supernatural powers
he had confronted. Neither do most young Pokémon fans today.
Unless they know God and His warnings, they cannot understand the forces that have captivated children around the world.
And if parents underestimate the psychological strategies behind
its seductive mass marketing ploys, they are likely to dismiss the
Pokémon craze as harmless fun and innocent fantasy. In reality,
the problem is far more complex.

MARKETING A NEW LIFESTYLE

THE Pokémon mania supports a financial conglomerate that knows how to feed the frenzy. The television series is free, but it is the driving force behind the multi-billion dollar business. It also inspires the obsessive games that disrupt schools and families by giving the children—

◊   A seductive vision: to become Pokémon Masters.

◊   A tempting promise: supernatural power.

◊   A new objective: keep collecting Pokémon.

◊   An urgent command: "Gotta catch them all!"

These enticements are drilled into young minds through clever ads, snappy slogans, the "Pokémon rap" at the end of each TV episode, and the theme song at the start of the show:

"I will travel across the land
Searching far and wide
Each Pokémon to understand
The power that's inside.
Gotta catch them all!"

The last line, the Pokémon mantra, fuels the craving for more occult cards, games, toys, gadgets, and comic books. There's no end to the supply, for where the Pokémon world ends there beckons an ever-growing empire of new, more thrilling, occult, and violent products. Each can transport the child into a fantasy world that eventually seems far more normal and exciting than the real world. Here, evil looks good and good is dismissed as boring. Family, relationships, and responsibilities diminish in the wake of the social and media pressures to master the powers unleashed by the massive global entertainment industry.

No wonder children caught up in the Pokémon craze beg

and plead for more games and gadgets. The makers count on it. Since the means often justify the economic ends in the entertainment industry, the Pokémon website is full of tips, explanations, and ads that encourage the urge to splurge—and to express the darker side of human nature.

While children delight in these mysterious realms, concerned parents worry and wonder. What kinds of beliefs and values does the Pokémon world and its links teach? Why the emphasis on evolution, supernatural power, and poisoning your opponent?

CHANGING BELIEFS & VALUES

BARBARA Whitehorse started seeking answers after her son asked a typical question: "Mom, can I get Pokémon cards? A lot of my friends from church have them." As much as she wanted Matthew to have fun with his friends, she gave a loving refusal. Matthew's tutor had already warned her that the Pokémon craze could stir interest in other kinds of occult role-playing games such as Dungeons & Dragons. At the time, she wondered if the tutor had just overreacted to some harmless entertainment. After all, the cute little Pokémon creatures looked nothing like the dark demonic creatures of D&D. But when she learned that a local Christian school had banned them because of their link to the occult, she changed her mind.

Later, during a recent party for Matthew, Barbara heard two of the boys discussing their little pocket monsters. One said, "I'll just use my psychic powers." Already, the world of fantasy had colored his real world. So when some of the kids wanted to watch the afternoon Pokémon cartoon on television, Barbara again had to say "no." It's not easy to be parents these days.

Cecile DiNozzi would agree. Back in 1995, her son's elementary school had found a new, exciting way to teach math. The Pound Ridge Elementary school was using Magic: the Gathering, the role-playing game which, like Dungeons and Dragons, has built a cult following of millions of people of all ages throughout the world.

Mrs. DiNozzi refused to let her son participate in the "Magic Club." But a classmate gave him one of the magic cards, which he showed his mother. It was called "Soul Exchange" and pictured spirits rising from graves. Like most other cards in this ghastly game, it offered a morbid instruction: "Sacrifice a white creature."

"What does 'summon' mean?" he asked his mother after school one day.

"Summon? Why do you ask?"

He told her that during recess on the playground the children would "summon" the forces on the cards they collect by raising sticks into the air and saying, "'Spirits enter me.' They call it 'being possessed.'"[9]

Strange as it may sound to North American ears, demonic possession is no longer confined to faraway places. Today, the government's public schools from coast to coast are teaching students the skills once reserved for the tribal witchdoctor or shaman in distant lands. Children everywhere are learning the pagan formulas for invoking "angelic"[10] or demonic spirits through multicultural education, popular books, movies, and television. It's not surprising that explosive and even deadly instances of untamed violence suddenly erupt from "normal" teens across our land.

> Today, public schools from coast to coast are teaching students the skills once reserved for the tribal witchdoctor or shaman in distant lands.

Occult role-playing games teach the same dangerous lessons. They also add a sense of personal power and authority through personal identification with godlike superheroes. Though the demonic realm hasn't changed, today's technology, media, and multicultural climate makes it so readily accessible and harder than ever to resist its appeal. Consider the following:

Satan is not simply trying to draw people to the dark side of a good versus evil conflict. Actually, he is trying to eradicate the gap between himself and God, between good and evil, altogether.[11]

And have no fellowship with the unfruitful works of darkness, but rather reprove them. (Ephesians 5:11)

AS ABOVE, SO BELOW

"I was taught in ritual magick how to go to different planes of existence outside the physical body," said Peter, a former occultist. "I could create a realm there in which I could practice ritual magick and perfect my magical skills. What I did on the physical plane was what I had practiced on the astral plane through creative visualizations. Through my will and imagination, I made things happen on the physical plane. As above, so below! This ritual magick is a manifestation of the power of your will."[12]

His words reminded me of Starhawk's formula for magic and spells. Starhawk is a prominent voice in modern Wiccan spirituality and founder of the "Covenant of the Goddess." In her book *The Spiral Dance*, she taught her followers that:

> To work magic is to weave the unseen forces into form, to soar beyond sight, to explore the uncharted dream realm of the hidden reality . . . to leap beyond imagination into that space between the worlds where fantasy becomes real; to be at once animal and god . . .

> [Spells and magic] require the combined faculties of relaxation, visualization, concentration, and [mental] projection . . . To cast a spell is to project energy through a symbol.[13]

171

"As above, so below!" These four words summarize the core of magick," explained Peter. But it was new to me, so I did an Internet search. Countless sites came up, linking the occult phrase to beliefs such as theosophy, Kundalini Yoga, the philosophy behind the yin-yang symbol, and Theodynamics. The latter deals with "cosmic or First Force energy and the frequencies supposedly generated by the shape of the pyramid."[14]

A more useful site gave the history and meaning of this simple phrase. But before you read the summary below, let me explain why I share this with you. As you have seen, these old occult teachings—once hidden behind closed doors in secret societies and mystical brotherhoods—have now gone mainstream. Yet, few recognize their dark, occult nature or the forces behind their ancient formulas. For our children's sakes, we cannot afford to be ignorant any longer. To avoid *experiencing* evil, we need to first *discern* evil. So take note of the esoteric concepts in the excerpt below. Many of these have been adapted to Christian counseling, mystical prayer, holistic health, and other familiar practices. They sound good to those who are blind or unwise to the in vogue, yet seductive and beguiling, "wiles of the devil":

> This message [as above, so below] theorizes that man is the counterpart of God on earth; as God is man's counterpart in heaven. Therefore, it is a statement of an ancient belief that man's actions on earth parallel the actions of God in heaven. . . .
>
> To the magician the magical act, that of causing a transformation in a thing or things without any physical contact, is accomplished by an imaginative act accompanied by the will that the wanted change will occur. The magical act and imaginative act becomes one and the same. . . .

To bring about such a change, the magician uses the conception of 'dynamic interconnectedness' . . . Witchcraft strongly imbues the view that all things are independent and interrelated. . . .

The purpose of all rituals in ceremonial magick is to unite the microcosm with the macrocosm to join God, or gods when invoked, with the human consciousness. When such a supreme union is achieved the subject and object becomes one. This is because the magician feels that he is consciously in touch with all elements of the universe, therefore, he can control them. . . . When feeling unison with the universe the magician knows he has reached his Higher or True Self because he has attained mastery of himself and the universe. Thus he . . . receives the power of the superiors and of the inferiors. Therefore, he "hast the glory of the whole world."[15]

This is a devious lie! But it's a message that Satan, masquerading as an "angel of light," has used to deceive people since the beginning of time. Remember what God tells us about this cruel "prince of the power of the air" (Ephesians 2:2):

How art thou fallen from heaven, O Lucifer, son of the morning! how art thou cut down to the ground, which didst weaken the nations! For thou hast said in thine heart, I will ascend into heaven, I will exalt my throne above the stars of God . . . I will ascend above the heights of the clouds; I will be like the most High. (Isaiah 14:12-14)

Though Satan's age-old tactics have served him remarkably well throughout the ages, he takes exquisite pleasure in introducing new twists to satisfy all who are hungry for new occult adventures. The results may well look like Christian miracles to a blinded world. The Bible warns us that many will be deceived. But those who belong to the Lord—"sealed unto the day of redemption" (Ephesians 4:30)—who love God's Word and refuse to participate in this darkness, will be protected and eternally safe in their Lord, Jesus Christ.

[T]hen shall that Wicked be revealed, whom the Lord shall consume with the spirit of his mouth, and shall destroy with the brightness of his coming: Even him, whose coming is after the working of Satan with all power and signs and lying wonders, And with all deceivableness of unrighteousness in them that perish; because they received not the love of the truth, that they might be saved. And for this cause God shall send them strong delusion, that they should believe a lie . . . Therefore, brethren, stand fast, and hold the traditions which ye have been taught.

(2 Thessalonians 2:8-11, 15)

14

PROTECTING YOUR CHILD FROM HARMFUL TOYS & GAMES

WHEN EIGHT-YEAR-OLD Joshua's parents found out what he wanted for Christmas, they felt put on the spot. Joshua only had eyes for the newest rage—Nintendo—along with its most popular game, Super Mario Brothers II. Anything else was "boring."

Joshua's folks had heard disturbing stories about Nintendo addiction—or whatever you call that intense focus that tolerates no interruption. So they didn't relish battling that obsession at bedtime—or any time. A rather pricey toy, Nintendo promised to zap a sizable hole in their budget, and the local stores had already sold out of their holiday allotment of SMB II.

Last year it was simple for Mom and Dad. Joshua just wanted more figures and accessories for his Masters of the Universe toys. The cost was tolerable, and they provided a year's worth of imaginative play. Of course, the gruesomeness of some of the figures caused them uneasiness.

Heidi's parents faced a similar dilemma. Their six-year-old daughter asked for Barbie's Dream House—fully furnished, of course. "They fit together," she explained, "and everybody has them."

Barbie's long-time popularity fails to endear her to Heidi's concerned parents. They often wonder if the doll's curvy figure and flashy clothes might encourage values and sophistication inconsistent with their hopes for Heidi. What kinds of aspirations are built by these symbols of self-centered materialism and the body image issues they instill in young girls at an early age?

If Barbie were the only messenger of image-based hedonistic self-interest, a few more accessories would hardly matter. But pagan decadence beckons children everywhere. "Just throw off all restraints," it shouts, "and let human nature lead the way. Follow your feelings."

It's tough to teach restraint to children who are begging for gratification. Schools and the media have often declared parents the "bad guys." We, as parents, keenly and distinctly feel the confusing values gap and flinch at the thought of being a killjoy once again. Yet we must. God has told us, the parents, to train our children to follow His way, and we can't turn back now. Also, He promises to enable us. Fortified with truth, let's make sure our children have toys that enhance their progress toward God's kind of maturity.

> It's tough to teach restraint to children who are begging for gratification. Schools and the media have often declared parents the "bad guys."

STEP ONE: DEVELOP A SENSITIVITY TO EVIL

A young mother driving a carload of children—including two from her church—posed this question: "Who is the master of the universe?"

"He-Man!" shouted a chorus of voices. The mother grieved as the youngsters praised their idol. Her heart sank further when one boy pulled an ugly figure from his pocket and waved it in the air. "And this is Hordak," he shouted. "He's bad! He fights He-Man!"

Current delight in false gods and demonic creatures may have begun with winsome magicians such as Papa Smurf and Rainbow

Brite. As people welcomed these nonthreatening (in appearance) harbingers of occult forces, they unknowingly opened the door to the grotesque and disturbing realms of the dark occult as well.

At first, we parents closed our eyes to this trend—we didn't want to overreact. Even within the church community, talk about Satan and his dark realm has often been regarded as too negative or heavy-handed. Since we failed to resist, we gradually adapted and then accepted these practices. Now it's time to retrench, take our positions, and fight to regain our discernment and freedom. How do we do this?

> Within the church community, talk about Satan has often been regarded as too negative or heavy-handed. Since we failed to resist, we gradually adapted and then accepted these practices.

- **Continue to read and apply Scriptures.**

- **Share your own observations.** Spark awareness in a young child with comments such as, "That monster looks gross!" or "That creature reminds me of a snake," along with "Did you know that in the Bible, serpents always represent Satan and evil?"

- **To express your feelings to a young child, comment,** "Who would want that evil-looking figure? I don't even like to look at him. Let's find something that makes us feel happy inside."

- **Model wise decision-making.** Tell your child why you wouldn't want to buy certain things.

- **When a child wants something questionable, ask questions** that are prayerfully adapted to your child's age, such as:

  » What does the toy (or game) teach you (about power, about magic, about God, about yourself)? Discuss both the obvious and the subtle with your child.

» Have you seen movies, cartoons, or comic books that made this toy (game) part of a story? What did the story tell you about it? Does the toy (game) remind you of someone who uses magic or supernatural power? Did someone pretend to be God?

» What does it teach about violence or immorality and their consequences?

» Does the toy have any symbols or characteristics that associate it with either the light or dark side of New Age occultism?

Whatever is lovely, gracious, and good originates with God. Satan cannot produce anything new. All he can offer is counterfeits or clever distortions of God's gifts.

STEP TWO: ENCOURAGE YOUR CHILD TO CHOOSE THE GOOD

DEVELOP a mindset that seeks the best, not just the "OK." You have identified and rejected the worst toys. But the rest are not necessarily good either. Discuss these questions to help your child learn to choose only the best. Phrase the questions according to your child's age level.

1. Does it present a true picture of life? In a time when even adults base their lives on counterfeit dreams and false illusions, our children need to learn to tell what is flight of fancy and what is real.

2. How long would the interest last? Fad toys are fun for the moment, but they whet the appetite for every "in" thing, so that decision-making centers on the question, "What will make me feel happy right now?" Determine not to buy that lie. Unfortunately, many quality toy companies have been bought up or squeezed out by giants who can pay the high price for television promotion. The range of major toy lines is narrowing to those that look glamorous on the screen.

3. Will this toy be used for playing alone or with others? A child needs a healthy balance of solitary and social play. Good toys will help her interact both with her imaginary world and with the real world, harmonizing the two. That may require some interaction with you. Perhaps you could agree together to find toys that will help you, the parent, participate in your young child's imaginary world.

4. Does it build godly character? Many toys, hobbies, and games do. Review the biblical principles suggested for evaluating movies and television programs.

STEP THREE: TRAIN YOUR CHILD TO FOLLOW GOD, NOT PEERS

WE want our children to feel good about themselves, be liked by their peers, and not miss out on the fun. But as we realize what their friends choose, we wonder how our children will respond to the peer pressure. How can we prepare them to make wise choices?

• **Counter peer pressure.** Children naturally compare us to the parents of peers, challenging us to match their "generosity." That hurts, since we want them to feel our love for them. We see what they don't realize: that getting the toys they want will not make them feel secure in our love. It's more likely to increase their craving and stir discontent. Also, it teaches them to equate love with material things. If your child is old enough, explain this process to him.

• **Discuss whether "showing off" might be their motive for wanting a toy.** Feeding that feeling produces bondage and increased insecurity. Children as well as adults crave superior luxury items, and toy manufacturers are quick to comply.

• **Be a trendsetter.** Have an abundant supply of ideas and tools to help your child and his friends use their imaginations and develop their own play: dress-up clothes (thrift stores are a good resource), fabrics for making puppets, scrap wood for outdoor structures, a refrigerator carton for making a playhouse, etc.

- **Look to the Bible for guidelines and authority.** God understands our desires to follow the crowd; He feels our struggle to be "in" the world but not "of it" (John 17:16-18). According to age readiness, review Romans 12:1-2 together and then discuss 3 John 11 and Jude 18-20.

- **Self-denial seems out of place in a nation consumed with self-indulgence and self-fulfillment.** But God commanded it, and Jesus demonstrated it. Dare we refuse to acknowledge it? According to the age of your child, discuss Jesus' words in Matthew 16:24 and then allow the Holy Spirit to direct your application.

Don't get me wrong. Far more than earthly parents, God wants His children to be happy and have a good time. But He doesn't want cream puffs to satisfy our hunger and turn us away from the meat of truth. Self-discipline produces the kind of maturity that brings genuine happiness forever, not merely a pleasant moment today.

Our Heavenly Father, who models parenting better than any of us, doesn't major on the superficial. He knows better than to give us all the things we want. For just as most children will choose pop over milk, and chips over carrots, so do we, as adults, often choose that which cannot satisfy. God does not want vain deceits, as He calls them (Colossians 2:8), to mold our appetites, satisfy our hunger, and replace the very best.

It's hard to teach restraint to children who are begging for gratification. Wanting to please rather than overreact, we flinch at the thought of having to continually censor our children's wants, preferences, and desires. Parental authority simply doesn't fit the fast-spreading new views of social equality taught through the media and the schools. Yet, we must obey God. He has told us to raise our children to choose *His* way, and we must rise to the occasion, fight the good fight, and not shrink back.

After hearing God's warning and praying for His wisdom, nine-year-old Alan Brannan decided to throw away all his

Pokémon cards. "My friend did the same," said his mother. "Her twelve-year-old son had been having nightmares. But after a discussion with his parents about the game and its symbols, he was convicted to burn his cards and return his Game Boy game. That night, he slept well for the first time in a month."

"It seemed to us that these cards had some sort of power," continued DiAnna Brannan. "Another nine-year-boy had stolen money from his mother's purse ($7.00) to buy more cards." When questioned, he confessed and said he had heard the devil urging him to do it. The family quickly gathered in prayer, then saw God's answer. Both the boy and his little sister burned their cards, warned their friends, and discovered the joy and freedom that only comes from following their Shepherd.

TRAINING KIDS TO LOVE GOOD MORE THAN EVIL

DON'T play games with the occult! Ouija Boards have always invited oppression, but they are far more likely to invoke unwanted "spirits" today. So it is with the new generation of occult games and DVDs as well.

I became aware of this change back in the nineties when a Canadian psychologist called me. He had read my book *Under the Spell of Mother Earth* and wanted to share some observations with me. In past years, he said, many women would come to scenic Alberta to do a Native American "Spirit Quest" in search of their personal "animal spirit." Few succeeded. But times have changed, and the "spirits" that now answer the summons are numerous as well as oppressive. Treating the scary symptoms as "multiple personality disorders" is no help at all.

Popular occultism is spreading fast, and the "spirit world" has become increasingly more accessible. But few families are equipped to resist it. Contemporary churches offer little or no help. Most simply ignore the danger or endorse the "fun." To avoid offense, the word evil is dropped from their vocabulary.

The primary victims of this blindness end up being our children. Unless we teach them to recognize and resist these dangers, many will come to embrace the darkness.

Those who love and follow God will be repelled by occult myths. And those who love today's popular occultism will run from God's unchanging truths and wise and loving boundaries. For if we are filled with His Spirit and follow His way, we will—by His life in us—"abhor that which is evil: and cleave to that which is good" (Romans 12:9).

> Popular occultism is spreading fast, and the "spirit world" has become increasingly more accessible. But few families are equipped to resist it.

The world cringes when it hears these truths because its fiction and fantasies are too enticing. That's why people find all kinds of arguments to justify their misdirected love.

To prepare your child for daily battles against tempting spiritual counterfeits, consider these three other outlines of vital truths:

The Armor of God—These six truths expose and counter today's most popular deceptions. Even more important, they show us the way to an intimate relationship with God.

The Lord's Prayer—These truths parallel the ones in the armor of God and serve the same purposes.

The Beatitudes—Jesus' message, recorded in Matthew 5, show us a standard for holiness that is far higher than we can achieve, but it comes with the promise that—by His life in us—He will make us all He intends us to be. It ends with the reminder that those who follow Jesus will also share in His suffering. Therefore, our children need to be prepared for persecution. Uncompromising faith and God's unchanging truths have become intolerable in today's postmodern age.

15

IMMORAL & OCCULT SUGGESTIONS IN BOOKS & MAGAZINES

Literature, perhaps more than any other kind of artistic expression, has faithfully chronicled the New Age. A host of fiction and nonfiction works, many already ascribed "classic" status, present the gospel of the 20th century to anyone who can read—or knows someone who can.[1]—**Alice and Stephen Lawhead,** *Pilgrim's Guide to the New Age*

WHILE RELATIVES AND friends cheered their favorite team, two girls huddled in the lower left corner of the stands, oblivious to the thrills of a championship Little League game. They sat bent over a magazine. Only occasionally did they break their silent concentration to point out something special on a page, to giggle, or to share a look of surprise.

Toward the end of the game, the two young teens finally closed the magazine and exposed the title: *Sassy*. Curious about its power to hold their attention, I bought a copy at the local supermarket the next day.

It opened my eyes to a new teen culture. (Or, is the new teen culture being formed by magazines such as *Sassy*?) *Sassy* is now a defunct magazine, but many teen magazines of the same caliber are in publication today: *Seventeen*, *Teen Vogue*, *Twist*, and several others. In addition to gorgeous faces and bodies matched with corresponding beauty tips, these magazines show how to stay physically fit and stay up to date with all the latest styles.

Through compassionate interviews, *Sassy* brought the reader into the hearts of lesbian and gay couples. It encouraged its reader to use contraceptive devices, know the best rock groups, and see the right movies. For example, avoid the low-rated (or near bomb) *Casual Sex*. "After all, what's so funny about watching a couple of L.A. chicks doing what every average sexually active person on Earth is doing?"[2]

Under the column, "Comic Books Are Your Friends," it gave a list of "which comic books are the edgiest: *The Uncanny X-Men, Batman: The Killing Joke, Lone Wolf and Club, ElfQuest,* and *Tales of the Teenage Mutant Ninja Turtles.*[3]

I decided that if this is what girls are reading, I'd better check it out. So I stopped by the local comic book store and read off the list to the salesman. He pointed to his display of the latest hits. My list matched his. Since he had sold the last *Batman: The Killing Joke,* he suggested I substitute with *The Punisher,* and *Mai, the Psychic Girl*—two more top sellers at the time. Because I was beginning to feel uncomfortable in his shop, I quickly bought them all.

"How old are the kids who buy these?" I asked before hurrying out.

"Every age," he answered. "From little kids to adults."

"How can kids afford it?"

"No problem," he smiled. "They've got bucks!"

When I arrived home and began to skim through these contemporary "treasures," I could hardly believe what I saw. Young children read this?! Pornography, cruelty, sadism, violence, and occultism leaped out at me from the pages. In less than five minutes, I had skimmed through all I could take.

WARRIORS — CATS & THE OCCULT

IN the wake of Harry Potter's popularity, a tidal wave of dark, mystical children's books has arisen. Led by Scholastic, publishers across the country have adapted all kinds of occult beliefs and magical rituals to the tastes of young readers. Children everywhere are learning to see paganism and syncretism (i.e., interfaith spirituality) as more "real" and "normal" than true Christianity.

As the boundaries erode between what is truth and what is counterfeit, children are increasingly being exposed to the blatant promotion of paganism. The "new stories" become even more irresistible when cloaked in language that passes for Christian.

Erin Hunter, the official author of the *Warrior* books, is actually the pen name for two women authors: Cherith Baldry and Kate Gary. To popularize their love for cats, folklore, astrology, and sacred sites, Baldrey and Gary (i.e., Hunter) have endowed their furry warriors with human minds and personalities. Cat lovers as young as six and seven can hardly wait for the next series of books to arrive.

The first book, *Into the Wild*, introduces the main hero of the first series: A former "kittypet" named Rusty, who becomes Firepaw when he joins the warriors of the Thunderclan. As he rises within their ranks, Firepaw's name is changed to Fireheart, and finally to Firestar. His tribal religion looks much like the astrology and ancestral worship of ancient human tribes:

> Graypaw didn't take his eyes off the dead cat as he replied, "His spirit may have left to join Star Clan, but the clan will share tongues [verbal fellowship] with Redtail one last time."

> "Star Clan?" Firepaw echoed.

> "It's the tribe of heavenly warriors that watch over all the clan cats. You can see them in Silverpelt. . . . Silverpelt is that thick band of stars you see each night

185

stretching across the sky. Each star is a StarClan warrior. Redtail will be among them tonight."[4]

The all-powerful deity in these stories is StarClan, a growing community of departed warrior cats whose spirits are revived as stars. This collective deity hears the prayers of living cats, strengthens the faithful in their battles, guides them with omens and prophecies, and welcomes them to their starry heights when they die. Notice that the words used to describe the tribe's relationship with StarClan sound much like the biblical words used to describe our relationship with God:

Faith in StarClan: "You'll need the whole of StarClan on your side for this one," answered Graypaw. "Call out if you need a hand."[5]

Thanks to StarClan: "But first, let us give thanks to StarClan for the life of Redtail. Tonight he sits with his fellow warriors among the stars."[6]

Prophecy from StarClan: The Thunderclan leader fixed her clear blue eyes on the medicine cat. "You have never been wrong before, Spottedleaf," she meowed. "If StarClan has spoken, then it must be so."[7]

Safe with StarClan: "Bluestar is injured! . . . Is there anything we can do?" Firepaw asked. "She is in the hands of StarClan now," meowed Tigerclaw.[8]

Prayer answered by StarClan: Firepaw found himself wordlessly begging Star Clan to protect his leader, to send her back to them. Then Bluestar stirred.[9]

Authority through StarClan: "By the powers of StarClan I give you your warrior names. . . . Firepaw, from this moment you will be known as Fireheart.

StarClan honors your bravery."[10]

Prayer to StarClan: Fireheart prayed silently to StarClan.[11]

StarClan will go with you: "The spirits of StarClan will go with you."[12]

The similarities make the pagan suggestions all the more deceptive. This collective "god" offers the cats a similar kind of relationship that God offers His people. We know that this idol can't deliver, but few children know the Bible well enough to discern the deception. Instead, those who identify with the cat warriors will love the forces that guide them. Those forces are designed to seem as real and exciting—if not more so—than the actual power of God.

RE-IMAGINING ANCIENT RITUALS

LONG ago, stone monuments to the "host of heaven" were raised in many parts of the world, the most familiar being Stonehenge—an ancient mystical stone circle in England. A blend of myth, astrology, geometric measurements, and shapes (triangles, rectangles, etc.) determined the placement of its massive "Bluestone" pillars. Moving shadows and rays of light would then guide its pagan celebrations: an ancient form of occult worship that God has always forbidden.

The Warrior cats worship StarClan at a similar ceremonial site called Moonstone. Ponder this dialogue from Book 1:

> "I shall travel to the Moonstone tomorrow," Bluestar (the clan's female leader) announced. "The warriors of Star Clan will give me the strength I need to lead ThunderClan through this dark time."[13]

> "What's the Moonstone?" Firepaw asked Graypaw. "It's a rock deep underground that shines in the dark,"

187

whispered Graypaw. His voice was hoarse with awe. "All Clan leaders have to spend one night at the Moonstone when they are first chosen. There, the spirits of StarClan share with them."[14]

A few pages later, Clan leader Bluestar brings Firepaw to the Moonstone:

"We have entered the cavern of the Moonstone," came Bluestar's soft reply. "Wait here. It will be moonhigh soon." . . . Suddenly, in a flash more blinding than the setting sun, the cave was lit up. Firepaw . . . saw a gleaming rock, which glittered as if it were made from countless dewdrops. The Moonstone! . . . High in the roof was an opening that revealed a narrow triangle of night sky. The moon was casting a beam of light through the hole, down onto the Moonstone, making it sparkle like a star.[15]

Five books later, Firepaw, now a great warrior leader named Firestar, returns to the Moonstone:

Cinderpelt [a medicine cat] stepped forward confidently. . . . "Follow my scent," she told him. "I will lead you to the Moonstone. And from now on, until the ritual is over, neither of us must speak. . . . When we reach the Moonstone, lie down and press your nose to it. . . . StarClan will send you sleep so you may meet with them in dreams."

He closed his eyes, and waited for Star Clan to send him to sleep.

The stars were moving. They . . . began to spiral downward toward the forest . . . toward him. And the cats [who had died] of Star Clan came stalking down the sky. . . . All around Fireheart the hollow of Fourtrees was

lined with their shimmering bodies and blazing eyes. .
. .[S]ome of the starry cats, those sitting closest to him,
were achingly familiar. Bluestar! . . . Spottedleaf—oh,
Spottedleaf! His beloved medicine cat had come back. . . .

A golden tabby cat rose to his paws and strode toward
him. . . . [Lionheart] had been an old cat when Fireheart
knew him, but now he looked young and strong
again. . . . When he was close enough, he stopped and
touched his nose to Fireheart's head. It burned against
him like the hottest flame. . . . "With this life I give
you courage," Lionheart murmured. "Use it well in
defense of your Clan." At once a bolt of energy seared
through Fireheart like lightning.[16]

DIVINATION, OMENS & FULL MOON WORSHIP

THROUGH the ages, witchcraft, divination, and fortune-telling
have included scrying: a magical way of "seeing" future events or
omens in a reflective surface such as a "magic mirror" or a pool of
water. This scene in one of the Warriors books illustrates it well:

As Firestar bent his head to lap from the stream [which
reflected his own image] . . . for a moment the image of
his head disappeared to be replaced by that of a roaring
lion. It was the beast Firestar had heard described in so
many elders' tales, his flame-colored pelt blazing into a
luxuriant mane, his eyes shining with unlimited strength
and power. . . . When he looked up, Spottedleaf [medicine
cat who had died and joined the stars] was facing him
from across the stream. . . . "Take heed of what you have
seen, Firestar," she told him. . . . "Learn what you must
be." . . . Spottedleaf began to fade . . . and her body paled
until Firstar could see the bank of the stream through it.[17]

As in witchcraft and sorcery, *magical work* requires faith in the power of ritual words or affirmations and in the spiritual significance of ritual settings such as a full moon and other traditional "sacred sites."

> Firestar had begun to wonder if the StarClan was going to hide the moon to show that it was not their will for the Gathering to take place. But for now the moon rose high.[18]

> He imagined the spirits of StarClan all around him, sharing the leadership of his Clan. They would be beside him every pawstep until he gave us his last life and went to join them. "Thank you StarClan," he murmured. "Thank you for staying with us. . . . How could I ever have thought that I faced this battle alone?"

> Suddenly he . . . felt the soft touch of Spottedleaf's pelt brushing against his fur. . . . "You are never alone, Firestar. Your Clan will live on, and I will watch over you forever."[19]

"Concentration and visualization are key to all magical practices,"[20] explains Wiccan leader Starhawk in her occult manual, *The Spiral Dance*. They always have been, for Satan's tricks don't change through the centuries. They are merely masked behind the alluring words of changing cultures.

Ancient Israel had seen the wisdom and might of our God in amazing ways, yet they were seduced by the magic and mysteries of their pagan neighbors. So they shut their hearts to the God who loved them and soon succumbed to the tempting lures of Canaanite idolatry. Forgetting God's warnings, they did exactly what they were told not to do. They put their trust in omens as well as idols fashioned from wood or stone, summoned the dead, and worshiped "the host of heaven" (Deuteronomy 17:3).

Unfortunately, in our post-Christian culture, all those practices are becoming part of mainstream awareness and public consciousness. And also, as in those dark days, many still claim and profess to follow God.

Much of what seems innocent and safe enough to our media-saturated minds is abominable to God!

But, some might argue, it's just imaginary fun and fantasy!

No, it's not! Jesus warned us that imagining an evil is as bad as actually doing that evil (Matthew 5:27-28).

When we follow Him, he gives us the strength to resist evil—and to stand firm in Him no matter how great the pressure. "[T]hanks be to God, which giveth us the victory through our Lord Jesus Christ" (1 Corinthians 15:57).

THE UPSIDE-DOWN WORLD OF PULLMAN'S "DARK MATERIALS"

> This will mean the end of the Church . . . the end of all those centuries of darkness! . . . The Dust [psychic elemental particles] will change everything.[21]—from *The Golden Compass*

> The God who dies is the God of the burners of heretics, the hangers of witches . . . [T]hat God deserves to die. The Authority, then, is an ancient IDEA of God, kept alive artificially by those who benefit from his continued existence.[22]—Philip Pullman

MORE than fifteen million copies of Philip Pullman's trilogy, *His Dark Materials*, have been sold. Pullman was a teacher at Westminster College, Oxford, while writing children's books. *The Golden Compass*, book one, won the prestigious Carnegie Medal.

In his mind-bending trilogy, Philip Pullman plunges young readers into occult fantasy worlds that twist God's truths into horrendous lies. Here God is despised as weak and evil, while Satan and his minions become saviors of the worlds. The biblical Fall brings knowledge and freedom, and personal *daemons* (i.e., demons) become the children's closest friends.

Flying witches, talking bears and evolving "Dust" abound in Pullman's *The Dark Materials*. In this confusing cosmos of multiple universes, telepathic seekers seek answers to life's mysteries through divination, Eastern meditation, ancient "wisdom," and ritual magic. These occult practices are essential to the war against God and the despised old Church. There is obviously no room for biblical authority in this world of amoral license.

Lyra, the pre-teen heroine, is a headstrong tomboy raised without parents at an Oxford college in a universe parallel to ours. A proficient liar, she's first seen snooping in a forbidden area with her daemon camouflaged as a moth. From then on, she follows her intuition from one crisis to the next until all remnants of biblical truth and authority have been destroyed. By the end of the series, God is dead. Free-spirited Lyra (still a twelve-year-old) has sexually "come of age" and fulfilled her prophetic assignments in the war on Christianity.

As readers move from book to book, they meet likeable God-haters, experience magical worlds, and discover the strange forces that drive Pullman's occult cosmos. Defying any short, simple synopsis, this mind-changing trilogy appeals more to feelings than to understanding. But those feelings will open hearts to deceptions that produce death and bondage, not life in Christ.

In *The Golden Compass*, the first book in the series, a strange mass of mysterious Dust is discovered during a magnificent display of Aurora Borealis (Northern Lights). But Pullman sees no Creator behind the beauty. Instead, he attributes the amazing Dust to evolving matter driven by intelligent consciousness—an esoteric notion reminiscent of the occult philosophies of Teilhard de Chardin, Willis Harman, ancient Gnostics, and William Blake. The latter, one of Pullman's main sources of inspiration, was captivated by Rosicrucianism, Theosophy, and other occult teachings.[23]

Lyra's choices and circumstances take her to the arctic island Svalbard. She sails northward from England with some valiant gyptians [gypsies] determined to rescue children abducted by the heartless "Church" for experimental purposes. While traveling, she studies her alethiometer ("truth measure") and practices the deep trance-forming concentration needed to receive its mystical guidance. Though she doesn't yet know it, she's being prepared for a greater purpose:

> The witches have talked about this child for centuries past . . . Because they live so close to the place where the veil between the worlds is thin, they hear immortal whispers from time to time, in the voices of those beings who pass between the worlds. And they have spoken of a child such as this, who has a great destiny that can only be fulfilled elsewhere—not in this world, but far beyond. Without this child, we shall all die.[24]

Do you see how this fantasy undermines biblical values? Pullman's crafty tale pulls the readers' minds into an occult context where—through their imagination—they experience life from his occult perspective. In fact, his methods sound just like the transformational tactics in UNESCO's global education plan. These proven methods are designed to:

◊ Give new meanings to old terms
◊ Redefine God and undermine Christianity
◊ Make suggestions that clash with traditional values
◊ Ridicule, rewrite, or reinterpret biblical truth
◊ Immerse readers in tempting occultism and ritual magic
◊ Cloak mysticism in scientific language

Let's examine these methods:

• **Give new meanings to old terms.** In this upside-down universe, the word "daemon" (or demon) refers to a loving, intimate, and normally inseparable companion to its human counterpart. Unlike the demonic deceivers of Satan, these daemons help and encourage their human hosts. Though linked to human souls, they can talk with their hosts and trainers as separate entities.

Next, the word "church" points only to an evil hierarchical dictatorship. The true Church—made up of those who trust and follow Christ—is never mentioned. The proud witch Queen Ruta Skadi describes Pullman's perceived enemy well:

> Let me tell you . . . who it is that we must fight . . . It is the Magisterium, the Church. For all its history . . . it's tried to suppress and control every natural impulse. And when it can't control them, it cuts them out. . . . They cut out the sexual organs. . . . and every church is the same: control, destroy, obliterate every good feeling. So if a war comes, and the church is on one side of it, we must be on the other, no matter what strange allies we find ourselves bound to. . . . Lord Astriel [Lyra's pompous, absentee father] was my lover once, and I would willingly join forces with him, because he hates the Church.[25]

Finally, the biblical "HEAVEN" is presented as a lie. It doesn't exist, according to an apparently homosexual angel, Baruch. Instead, everyone ends up in the "world of the dead"—a miserable "prison camp" established by the evil Authority.[26]

- **Redefine God and undermine Christianity.** Near the end of the third book, *The Amber Spyglass*, Lyra rescues the dead captives in the underworld. Corrupting the young reader's view of Christ, Pullman replaces Jesus, our Redeemer, with this telepathic twelve-year-old girl who could hardly be less like our Lord.

With abysmal audacity, Pullman presents "God" or "Authority" as a feeble old man, slain by a wisp of wind.[27] The following statement by an angel shows Pullman's contempt for him:

> The Authority, God, the Creator, The Lord . . . those were all names he gave himself. He was never the creator. He was an angel like ourselves—the first angel, true, the most powerful. . . . The first angels condensed out of Dust, and the Authority was the first of all. . . . One of those who came later was wiser than he was, and she found out the truth, so he banished her. We serve her still. And the Authority still reigns in the Kingdom, and [archangel] Metatron is his Regent.[28]

In the Gnostic context of multiple gods, the "she" refers to Sophia, the goddess of wisdom. Linked to a "divine spark" in everyone, she encourages self-discovery and gratifying enlightenment rather than truth and obedience. The restraints of authority would only quench the insights and intuition she symbolized. No wonder she was banished! This reminds me of what happened to popular women's author and speaker Sue Monk Kidd (author of *The Secret Life of Bees*). Monk Kidd was once a conservative Southern Baptist Sunday school teacher who began reading books by mystics such as Thomas Merton. Over time, she chronicled her spiritual "journey" through mysticism away from Christianity and into goddess spirituality.[29]

The name Metatron is featured in many occult systems. The Kabbalah and the Tarot view him as a powerful archangel. In Hermetic magic, he is linked to the god Hermes and the mythical Emerald Tablet with its infamous code, "As Above, So Below," which summarizes the occultist's goal of connecting with higher powers in order to command change here below. "As Above, So Below" unlocks the pantheistic/panentheistic view that there is no separation between God and man, Creator and creation, good and evil; but all is the same—God comprises everything, or is in everything as the very substance of everything that is. Quantum spirituality takes the idea one step further by the assumption that the base material all the universe is comprised of is God.[30]

But man's arrogant quests can never dim the power or derail

the plans of our Lord God. Human mockery only demonstrates His never-ending wisdom. For He knows well the nature of man and the battles that would rage through the ages. Therefore, He calls those who trust and follow Him to:

> [E]arnestly contend for the faith which was once delivered unto the saints. For there are certain men crept in unawares, who were before . . . ungodly men, turning the grace of our God into lasciviousness, and denying the only Lord God, and our Lord Jesus Christ. (Jude 3-4)

- **Highlight seductive suggestions that clash with traditional values.** Daemons assume their permanent animal shape when their human partner "comes of age." For twelve-year-old Lyra, that initiation came through sexual intimacy with Will Parry, her close companion and lover near the end of the series. Will's father had been a powerful shaman in another world.

This fits right in with our times, doesn't it? Myths, lies, and counterfeit truth replace truth; that which is of a highly subjective nature replaces morality, and human effort nullifies the Cross. In Pullman's amoral multiverses, all traces of biblical truth must be purged or reinterpreted. For example, Gnostic and other occult philosophies have viewed the serpent as good and the forbidden fruit as enlightening. So did John Milton in his *Paradise Lost*, another source of inspiration for Pullman. Milton, by the way, rejected the biblical view of God the Father and God the Son as illogical (in his book *A Treatise on Christian Doctrine*).

"Something happened when innocence changed into experience," said Lord Asriel. But the results were devastating. To protect us from the consequences of experiential knowledge of evil—the fruit of the forbidden tree in the garden—our wise God warned:

Of every tree of the garden thou mayest freely eat: But of the tree of the knowledge of good and evil, thou shalt not eat of it: for in the day that thou eatest thereof thou shalt surely die. (Genesis 2:16-17)

- **Ridicule, rewrite, or reinterpret biblical Truth.** Near the end of *The Golden Compass*, Lord Asriel condemns the Authority for its despised teachings on original sin: "[I]t's what the Church has taught for thousands of years."[31] Then he reads this false version of Genesis 3:1-7 to Lyra:

[T]he woman said unto the serpent, We may eat of the fruit of the trees of the garden. But of the fruit of the tree which is in the midst of the garden, God hath said, Ye shall not eat of it, neither shalt ye touch it, lest ye die. And the serpent said unto the woman, Ye shall not surely die: For God doth know that in the day ye eat thereof, then your eyes shall be opened, and your daemons shall assume their true forms, and ye shall be as gods, knowing good and evil. And when the woman saw that the tree was good for food, and that it was pleasant to the eyes, and a tree to be desired to reveal the true form of one's daemon, she took of the fruit thereof, and did eat, and gave also unto her husband. . . .

And the eyes of them both were opened. . . . But when the man and the woman knew their own daemons, they knew that a great change had come upon them, for until that moment it had seemed that they were at one with all the creatures of the earth and the air.[32]

Through the centuries, occultists have viewed the horned Pan as an alias for Satan. No wonder Lyra shows her love for Pan, her precious daemon:

Pantalaimon is my special and devoted friend. I don't know you, Death. I know Pan and I love Pan.[33]

But our true Lord reminds us that the time will come when people will not listen to God's Word (2 Timothy 4:3).

• **Immerse readers in tempting occultism and ritual magic.** Magical practices grab the readers' attention and eventually make occultism feel good and normal. Lyra's delight in "reading" her alethiometer may seem harmless, but her success requires the same psychic skills as those used for spell casting and other forms of magic. Notice the resemblance to the meditative practices now welcomed into emerging churches everywhere:

[Lyra] read it every day . . . and she found that she could sink more and more readily into the calm state in which the symbol meanings clarified themselves. . . . "It's almost like talking to someone, only you can't quite hear them, and you feel kind of stupid because they're cleverer than you."[34]

Lyra turned the hands to the [relevant symbols] . . . . Then she sat still, letting her mind hold the three levels of meaning together in focus, and relaxed for the answer, which came almost at once. . . . She blinked once or twice as if she were coming out of a trance.[35]

I got a way of making my mind go blank, and I just see what the pictures mean straightaway.[36]

It's not only the knife that has to cut, it's your own mind. . . . Concentrate. . . . Focus your mind. Think about the knife tip. That's where you are. Now feel with it. Relax . . . You become the tip of the knife.[37]

Dr. Mary Malone, one of Pullman's fictional characters

and a physicist who shares Lyra's fascination with divination, uses I Ching (Chinese divination) and her computer to receive instructions from "those entities she called shadow particles."[38] But they can only be seen "when you make your mind empty," she tells Lyra in the second book, *The Subtle Knife*.[39]

"They told me what to do," she said later.[40]

One of her tasks would be to "play the serpent." She would be the "tempter" who entices Lyra to freely follow her desires and engage in sex.[41]

And, according to a spying priest, "if the child gives in, then Dust and sin will triumph."[42]

- **Cloak mysticism in scientific language.** Pullman's mystical Dust is a perfect example:

Dust came into being when living things became conscious of themselves.[43]

Dust is what makes the alethiometer work. . . . You've heard of electrons, photons, neutrinos, and the rest? They're called elementary particles because you can't break them down any further.[44]

Ascribing subjective consciousness to Dust would make sense to people like Willis Harman who have redefined the meaning of "science." A former Stanford professor, futurist, and founder of the Institute of Noetic Sciences, Harman even spoke at the 1979 "Evangelical" Consultation on the Future sponsored by the Billy Graham Center!

Like Pullman's *Dark Materials* series, Harman's book *Global Mind Change* promotes paganism as evidence for a consciousness-driven evolution:

Down through the centuries a variety of anomalous phenomena, including clairvoyant remote viewing, telepathic communication . . . and other 'psychic' phenomena, had been reported. . . . What was common to all of these anomalous psychic phenomena was that mind seemed to have some effects in the physical world.[45]

(Remember the occult slogan: "As above, so below.")

> Perhaps a species on the long path of evolutionary development is . . . pulled by the kind of teleological force implied in . . . Teilhard de Chardin's *The Phenomenon of Man*. In this kind of explanation, mind is prior to brain, and evolution is characterized both by the organism's freedom to choose and by its inner sense of 'right' direction.[46]

The last sentence summarizes the guidelines for Lyra's success. No one could tell her what to do! As Aleister Crowley said, "Do what thou wilt shall be the whole of the Law."[47] Lyra must be "free" to follow "her own inner sense of right"—no matter how wrong!

That "freedom" meant rejection of authorities such as God, a wise father, or the Ten Commandments. Truth is simply too restrictive in a world trained to follow feelings rather than fact! No wonder Pullman's heroine was raised apart from her parents and with no parental guidance!

Near the end of the trilogy, Mary Malone calls Christianity "a very powerful and convincing mistake."[48] In place of God, she had found unity, "the sense that the whole universe was alive, and that everything was connected to everything else."[49]

This metaphysical unity and rejection of God matches the emerging views of today's change agents. Church leaders, as well as environmentalists and corporate managers, are embracing an illusion of unity through dialogue and systems thinking—which deny the biblical God.[50] Are your children equipped with the facts and truths to counter such lies?

LOVING THE OCCULT

"**WHAT** kinds of books do you like to read?" I asked a ten-year-old.

"Science fiction," she answered.

"What are some of your favorites?"

"The books by Zilpha Keatley Snyder. I just finished *The Headless Cupid*." She recited the story to me.

"That sounds more like psychic fiction than science fiction. What do you think?"

"I guess so. But it's real adventuresome."

"How do you feel when you read stories like *The Headless Cupid*? Spooky and a little scared?"

"It's exciting and fun. I like it."

The children's library has other books by Snyder. "Fifth-and sixth-graders love them!" affirmed the librarian. I checked out *The Witches of Worm*, a story about a demon-possessed kitten who gets a lonely little girl into all sorts of trouble. In the end, the heroine researches witchcraft, learns an occult version of exorcism, and apparently proves man's power to subdue the irascible forces of evil.

Preschoolers also love the scary and magical. Beautiful picture books tell ugly stories about witchcraft, magic, and sorcery. A book for toddlers, *Little Witch's Magic Spells*, even comes with a toy witch.

Elementary children read books like *Bunnicula* by Deborah and James Howe—a tale about a little vampire bunny who mysteriously escapes his cage each night to scavenge in the kitchen and suck the juice out of vegetables. Mom and Dad just can't figure out why vegetables turn white and have fang marks in them.

Worn pages and wrinkled covers prove the popularity of library series like the *Dragontales* and *Endless Quest* books, where the reader is the hero. Both equip youngsters with every kind of occult power.

The latter is published by the producers of Dungeons and Dragons. In Rose Estes' *Dragon of Doom*, you conquer an evil magician with your magical ring, spells, mind-linking with your

201

companions to strengthen the force, entering into trance states, clairvoyance, mental telepathy, and the wisdom of today's "values clarification." Confronting the dreaded Dragon of Doom, you offer this contemporary guideline, which supposedly justifies any action: "[Destroy mankind] because you choose to and not because you have been ordered to do so. It must be your decision."[51]

Libraries and bookstores offer an equally disturbing menu to teenagers. Even sixth and seventh graders devour seductive medleys of science fiction, sex, occult, and psychic adventure—including the adult horrors of Stephen King. These fantasies draw their minds into a demonic dream world where psychic phenomena, sensual highs, and occult terrors become as familiar as things like a starry night or a cloud-filled day.

HARRY POTTER LURES KIDS TO WITCHCRAFT WITH PRAISE FROM CHRISTIAN LEADERS

IN chapter eight, I gave twelve reasons why children should not read and view the Harry Potter books and movies. In this chapter, we'll go into some further detail about how I have come to these conclusions. When you consider that the Harry Potter books have sold over 400 million copies (the films have been equally successful), it is clear to see that Harry Potter has had a significant impact on our Western society. And that certainly warrants seeking a clear understanding of the *nature* of Harry Potter. These two comments from Harry Potter fans are quite revealing:

> I was eager to get to Hogwarts first because I like what they learned there and I want to be a witch.—Gioia B., age 10.[52]

> I like the third book because here [Harry] meets his godfather and Professor Lupin, a really cool guy [This really "cool guy" is a werewolf as well as a wizard, and Harry's godfather is a "shape shifter" who turns himself into a scary black dog].—Harry L., age 7.[53]

What's more, the effect the UK-based Pagan Federation felt as a result of the Harry Potter books speaks volumes:

> The Pagan Federation has appointed a youth officer to deal with a flood of inquiries following the success of the Harry Potter books which describe magic and wizardry.[54]

And an article from the *UK Telegraph*, talking about H.P. creator, J. K. Rowling, reveals that Harry Potter was, at least in part, inspired from Rowling's childhood:

> Dressing up as wizards and witches, concocting fantasy potions and telling stories were just a few of the games Rowling played as a child with Ian Potter.[55]

Might Harry Potter seem as real and true to life as life itself to his young fans around the world? Do children accept Harry's lessons in practical witchcraft as an open door to an occult reality? Many Christian leaders have denied any such danger, but Rowling admits that this happens. In an interview with *Newsweek* magazine, she said:

> I get letters from children addressed to Professor Dumbledore [headmaster at Hogwarts School of Witchcraft and Wizardry, the books' setting], and it's not a joke, begging to be let into Hogwarts, and some of them are really sad. Because they want it to be true so badly they've convinced themselves it's true.[56]

While children everywhere crave supernatural thrills, Great Britain, the birthplace of Harry Potter, has been a wonderland of options for exploring practical witchcraft. And plenty of youth have caught Harry's vision. They want to learn his wizardly ways.

Two British reports on this phenomenon show us the obvi-ous: popular forms of occult entertainment "have fueled a rapidly growing interest in witchcraft among children."[57] Naturally, the island's Pagan Federation is pleased. Though it refuses to admit new members under age 18, "it deals with an average of 100 inquiries a month from youngsters who want to become witches, and claims it has occasionally been 'swamped' with calls,"[58] explaining:

> It is quite probably linked to things like *Harry Potter*, *Sabrina The Teenage Witch* and *Buffy The Vampire Slayer* . . . Every time an article on witchcraft or paganism appears, we had a huge surge in calls, mostly from young girls.[59]

STRANGE COUNSEL FROM CHRISTIAN LEADERS

TYPICAL of our times, a report in *Christianity Today* seems to base its approval of Harry Potter, not on the Bible, but on popular consensus among admired Christian leaders.

"As far as I can tell," writes author Ted Olsen, "while no major Christian leader has come out to condemn J.K. Rowling's series, many have given it the thumbs-up. If our readers know of any major Christian leader who has actually told Christians not to read the books, I'd be happy to know about it; but in my research, even those Christians known for criticizing all that is popular culture have been pretty positive about Potter."[60]

To prove his point, Olsen quotes seven Christian leaders and publications:

1. The late Chuck Colson, in his Breakpoint radio broadcast, commended Harry and his friends for their "courage, loyalty, and a willingness to sacrifice for one another—even at the risk of their lives." Colson dismissed the pagan practices as:

> . . . purely mechanical, as opposed to occultic. That is, Harry and his friends cast spells, read crystal balls, and turn themselves into animals—but they don't make contact with a supernatural world. . . . [It's not] the kind of real-life witchcraft the Bible condemns.[61]

2. *World Magazine* praised *Harry Potter and the Sorcerer's Stone* as:

> . . . a delight—with a surprising bit of depth. . . . Rowling . . . keeps it safe, inoffensive, and non-occult. This is the realm of Gandalf and the Wizard of Id, not witchcraft. There is a fairy-tale order to it all in which, as Chesterton and Tolkien pointed out, magic must have rules, and good does not—cannot—mix with bad.[62]

3. *World Magazine's* second article toned down the enthusiasm: "A reader drawn in would find that the real world of witchcraft is not Harry Potter's world. Neither attractive nor harmless, it is powerful and evil."[63]

4. In the UK *Christianity* magazine, Mark Greene, Director of the London Institute for Contemporary Christianity, wrote a note of regret for not giving it to his god-daughter earlier:

> I wish I'd been the one to introduce her to Harry— fine lad you know, courageous, resourceful, humble, fun, good mind. Comes from good stock, you know. She could do worse, far worse. And, as far as literary companions go, frankly, not much better.[64]

5. *A Christian Century* editorial, "Wizards and Muggles," states:

> Rowling is not the first fantasy writer to be attacked by conservative Christians. Even the explicitly Christian writer Madeleine L'Engle has taken heat for the "magic" elements in *A Wrinkle in Time*. Such critics are right in thinking that fantasy writing is powerful and needs to be taken seriously. But we strongly doubt that it fosters an attachment to evil powers. Harry's world, in any case, is a moral one.[65]

6. Wheaton College professor Alan Jacobs concludes that Harry Potter stories promote:

> . . . a kind of spiritual warfare. . . . A struggle between good and evil. . . . There is in books like this the possibility for serious moral reflection . . . [and] the question of what to do with magic powers is explored in an appropriate and morally serious way.[66]

7. In June 2007, on Rick Warren's original Pastors.com website, under his "Recommended Reading List" was a link to the following statement by evangelical author James Emery White:

> Though the seventh and final installment [of Harry Potter] is yet to be released . . . when it does, it will be well-worth reading. Though some would disagree, I am one to put Rowling's work in the camp of fantasy literature, along with Lewis and Tolkien, with her use of magic more mechanical than occultic. I found her earlier six volumes instant classics of the genre, and the final book will undoubtedly cement this series as among the best written.[67]

Are these Christian leaders right in their assessments of Harry Potter? Maybe they have got it all wrong. Let's take a look at the other side of this issue.

BIBLICAL ANSWERS TO CHRISTIAN LEADERS ON HARRY POTTER

THE mass media's promotion of contrary values has prompted even Christians to replace or distort the pursuit of God with the pursuit of pleasure. God gave us His Word that we might know Him. The Bible reveals His heart, will, and ways. It alone can show us what is truth or error in those seven public responses to the Harry Potter phenomenon.

1. Chuck Colson praised Harry and his friends for their "courage, loyalty, and a willingness to sacrifice . . . for one another—even at the risk of their lives." Those qualities can be found in almost any culture. But, according to the Bible, a brave person is no freer to pursue paganism than a coward is. Harry's occult skills—witchcraft, sorcery, casting spells, spiritism, interpreting omens and "calling up the dead" fit into a category God tells us not to dabble in, even in the least. "For all that do these things are an abomination unto the Lord" (Deuteronomy 18:9-12).

Colson's dismissal of the dangers of delighting in such evils as "purely mechanical," makes no sense from a biblical perspective. He says that "Harry and his friends cast spells, read crystal balls, and turn themselves into animals—but they don't make contact with a supernatural world. . . ." Where then does their power come from? Natural rather than supernatural forces?

Of course not. Rowling doesn't acknowledge the source, but anyone who has researched witchcraft and talked with contemporary pagans will see the alarming parallels between contemporary occultism and Rowling's seductive message to children. (If you find this hard to believe, please read chapters four and eight of my book *A Twist of Faith*.)

2. *World Magazine* made the same error. Calling Harry Potter's world "a delight . . . safe, inoffensive, and non-occult," is a misleading assurance, at best. True, "magic must have rules," but the primary rule of the occult is that Satan doesn't offer free and easy favors for long. He may indulge seekers in a free ride for a while, but as soon as his victims have been captivated and hooked by his lures—all of which are counterfeits of what God offers those who follow Him—he begins to demand his payoff. Suddenly the bright side of evil turns dark indeed. Attempts to resist or turn back usually lead to spiritual terror and demonic oppression.

As *World Magazine* indicated, "good does not—cannot—mix with bad" but not because "good" motives are always "good" even in a pagan context. God's good is corrupted when adapted to a pagan setting. In fact, God doesn't want what He considers good to be linked to or mixed with the occult. He sends us out to pagans to share His love, but we cannot delight in what He calls evil. Remember 2 Corinthians 6:14-17, which tells us to separate ourselves from the things of darkness.

3. *World Magazine's* second article maintained that "the real world of witchcraft is not Harry Potter's world. Neither attractive nor harmless, it is powerful and evil."

Actually, today's pagan movement is attractive to many who are disillusioned by unfriendly churches. It entices "seekers" by showing the "light" side of occultism. Contemporary witches—both men and women—whom I have met are sincere, often compassionate, usually well-educated and frustrated with today's rampant materialism. Few look evil. Instead, they demonstrate God's warning in 2 Corinthians 11:14-15:

> And no marvel; for Satan himself is transformed into an
> angel of light. Therefore it is no great thing if his ministers
> also be transformed as the ministers of righteousness.

The younger generation of pagans shows another side. Many dabble in black magic and the other "dark arts" that are so seductively taught at Hogwart's School of Witchcraft and Wizardry.[68] Apart from the fantasy setting and dramatic demonstrations of magic, there is little difference between Harry's skills and the real world of the occult.

4. Mark Greene's endorsement in the *British Christianity* magazine raises some serious questions. What does he mean by "Harry—fine lad you know. . . . Comes from good stock. . . ." Is he referring to Harry's parents—a witch and a wizard? Is he speaking as director of London Institute for Contemporary Christianity, or is this simply his personal opinion?

One thing is certain. This attitude is driving the current transformation of the Church. It's time for serious Christians to "count the cost" and be ready to stand uncompromisingly strong in the Truth God has given us.

5. *The Christian Century* denies Harry Potter "fosters an attachment to evil powers." It calls Harry's world "a moral one." It's wrong on both points. Just review the testimony from the Pagan Federation, which reaps the fruit from the soaring interest in Witchcraft.

Second, Harry and his friends may show loyalty to each other and courage in the face of danger. But they also lie and steal. Would you call that a moral world?

6. Wheaton College professor Alan Jacobs suggests that the Harry Potter books offer "the possibility for serious moral reflection . . . [and] the question of what to do with magic powers is explored in an appropriate and morally serious way." His words make no sense from a biblical perspective.

Since white magic, like black magic, is "an abomination" to God—and since white magic is far more deceptive and seductive—neither is good. Books written from an occult perspective cannot explore magic powers in "an appropriate and morally serious way"—without redefining the word moral and rejecting the Bible. A context or setting that approves occultism will turn God's values upside down.

7. When James Emery White calls Harry Potter's "use of magic" more "mechanical" than "occultic," he couldn't be further from the truth as I have shown throughout this book. Magic *is* occultic, and there is no way of getting around that. White has done a disservice to many when he says "well worth reading." Rick Warren did a disservice when he placed this link under "Recommended Reading."

The Twilight Vampire "Phenomenon"

In 2005, a book titled *Twilight,* written by Stephanie Meyer, was released, and soon it hit the *New York Times* best-seller list. The book is about a young girl, Bella, who falls in love with a teenage vampire, Edward. Since then, three other novels in the series and a series of five motion pictures (*The Twilight Saga*) based on the book have been released. *Publisher's Weekly* named *Twilight* the Best Children's Book of 2005, and the entire series won the Nickelodeon Kids' Choice Awards in 2009. All five movies have grossed over two billion dollars in worldwide receipts![69]

If my goal was to undermine Christianity, incite rebellion against parents, eradicate biblical values, and spread moral chaos, I would urge teens to read the *Twilight* series. I would prompt them to immerse their minds and emotions in the dark, emotional whirlpool of sensual occultism. And I wouldn't warn them of the consequences.

Of course, my real goal is the opposite: to expose this assault on biblical faith and to equip potential readers with information that enables them to resist the temptation to join the collective journey into the mind-changing realm of the occult. The following points show the raging spiritual war that's sure to intensify in the years ahead:

• **Arousing passion for occultic settings.** Vampires and werewolves are rooted in pagan cultures around the world. The various historical expressions of these mythical creatures were dreaded, blood-thirsty manifestations of evil spirits. Linked to darkness, they were viewed as supernatural creatures of the night. Today's more familiar forms were shaped through folklore, fairytales, and memorable villains such as Count Dracula. Both were re-imagined in more humanized forms through the *Harry Potter* books and Anne Rice's popular *Vampire Chronicles*.

But they're not benign. Bella's passionate love for the mysteriously handsome Edward may be fictional, but the obsession felt by teenage readers who "resonate" with Bella is very real! Young super-fans (Twilighters) identify with her plight, sense her fears, and "feel" her passion. They love the story because it arouses strong, unforgettable emotions—the kind of enchanting thrills that can best be shared within one's peer group, and not with parents.

In the process, they also learn to crave the mystical, paranormal stimuli that belong in the forbidden realm God calls evil.

- **Impact of fantasy and imagination.** Fantasy and imagination can transform beliefs and values more quickly than reality. Many of our readers defend their love for occult entertainment with this standard justification: "I know the difference between reality and fantasy." But it doesn't matter! Believe it or not, persuasive works of fiction and virtual experiences can change young minds and embed lasting memories—leaving indelible, holographic imprints—more effectively than actual real-life experiences!

Popular fantasies, with their boundless and exhilarating thrills and unforgettable images, bypass logical thinking. Their subtle suggestions face little conscious resistance. Designed to stir feelings and produce strong emotional responses, they create new realities in today's "open" minds!

- **Desensitizing of values.** When today's youth love the emotional thrills of popular occultism, they are desensitizing their hearts and minds to its evil. They are turning God's truth upside down. And they—with a little help from the marketing industry—are already turning America's values upside down. It all fits the plans of our globalist leaders and that old serpent in Genesis.

"You can only have a new society," wrote Marilyn Ferguson in *The Aquarian Conspiracy*, "if you change the education of the younger generation."[70]

- **Cognitive dissonance.** *Twilight's* feel-good sensual occultism brings "cognitive dissonance." Committed Christians (in contrast to cultural Christians) face a form of mental and moral confusion when confronted with incompatible values. Since Twilight's worldview clashes with biblical Truth, readers are forced to make a choice: Will they heed home-taught values or the tantalizing messages in books, video games, TV series, and movies.

- **The fruit of compromise.** The consequence of compromise is a new belief system. "These books are so addictive—kind of like drugs," wrote a visitor to my website. "If they can captivate Christians who should know better, just think what they can do to non-Christian readers."

She is right. Like addicts, Twilighters learn to crave more and more of the same genre—or something even more shocking and sensational—as in the taboo-breaking sense. The only belief system I know of that can more than accommodate such sensual and spiritual cravings would be today's New Age/New Spirituality rising out of the channeled messages of occult authors like Neale Donald Walsch, Marianne Williamson, and Barbara Marx Hubbard. Promoting counterfeit gods and practices in the names of "Abraham," "God," and a false "Jesus," they complement the original lies of the serpent.

Driven by winds of change, the faith and values behind America's blessing are fading fast. Filling the vacuum is an amoral, power-seeking, sensual-addicted ideology that clashes with everything we once treasured, upheld, and held fast to in this nation. No wonder we face social and moral anarchy.

- **Redefining evil.** Few Twilighters see their new passion as evil. After all, Edward is a relatively "good" vampire, isn't he? Though he lusts for Bella's blood, he restrains his craving. Other vampires (and some of the werewolves) in the saga are downright murderous, but he's a good guy! Isn't he? Besides, the story has spawned a noble mission.

But it all depends on *who* sets the standards for right and wrong—God or man! While God's standard is like an anchor in a storm, man's values shift with the winds. For the Bible tells us:

> The heart is deceitful above all things, and desperately wicked: who can know it? (Jeremiah 17:9)

- **God's way to peace and victory.** When we choose to follow His ways, He gives us a heart to love Him, spiritual eyes that can know, understand, and love His Word, the comfort of His presence, and a confidence in His constant care—no matter what happens around us. *Twilight's* deceptive thrills are worse than worthless when compared to the wonderful riches our Shepherd promises those who will turn their backs on evil and walk with Him.

A HUMAN SACRIFICE VS. GOD'S SACRIFICE

SINCE the beginning, human nature sought alternatives to God and His guidelines. Spiritual deception gave rise to vast occult belief systems and unceasing manipulation by the forces of darkness. Thus, pagan sacrifices—a devastating corruption of God's perfect plan for His people—became the norm in all parts of the inhabited world. These notes may help explain God's ban on "fellowship with . . . darkness . . . [and] idols," including bloodthirsty vampires.[71]

When the blood is drained from man or mammal, life ends. In the Old Testament sacrificial system (now replaced by the death and resurrection of Jesus Christ), an unblemished lamb died in the place of God's people. Its substitutionary death served as atonement (paid the penalty for sin), bringing redemption. For a limited time, sin had been purged, forgiveness granted, and the sanctified person could joyfully return to being in God's holy presence and in fellowship with Him once again.

In sharp contrast, pagan rituals often involved human sacrifices. The demonic forces behind Moloch, Baal, and other "gods" demanded human blood. A beating heart might be cut right out from a living sacrifice, its blood drained into a bowl and offered to the bloodthirsty "god" by those who hoped for future favors. Others would drink human blood to obtain the strength of their victims. The gruesome Hindu goddess Kali—with her serpent hair, necklace of skulls, and long bloody tongue—reminds us of man's timeless delight in death, cruelty, serpentine symbols, and the dark forces of evil.

213

The cold, pale, bloodthirsty vampires of the past were expressions of those captivating forces. Today's more flattering depictions make them all the more seductive and even likeable.

Human sacrifice, however, is strictly forbidden in the Bible. In fact, God warned His people repeatedly, "be sure that thou eat not the blood: for the blood is the life" (Deuteronomy 12:23). But His people didn't listen. So when they began to imitate the cruel child sacrifices of their pagan neighbors, God "raised up" the armies of Babylon to conquer the land and exile its people.

The sacrificial death of Jesus Christ (God's holy, "unblemished Lamb") differs radically from those pagan sacrifices. He willingly gave His life as our atonement then rose victoriously from death—thus trading the old temporary solution to human depravity for eternal redemption. And as Acts 10:43 promises, "through his name whosoever believeth in him shall receive remission of sins." As believers, we are joined to Him by His Spirit—a glorious gift.

Meanwhile, God is training His people for eternity with Him. He equips us to follow truth in a world that hates His Word and writes its own gospel. Are your children prepared to recognize and resist the counterfeit?

I call heaven and earth to record this day against you, that I have set before you life and death, blessing and cursing: therefore choose life, that both thou and thy seed may live: That thou mayest love the Lord thy God, and that thou mayest obey his voice, and that thou mayest cleave unto him: for he is thy life, and the length of thy days. (Deuteronomy 30:19-20)

16

HOW TO GUARD AGAINST IMMORALITY & THE OCCULT

When children from nine years of age upward are led to believe that [contemporary teen novels] reflect how most people live, then their conduct will certainly be influenced. . . . If more acceptable conduct is desired by society, then society must hold before young people more acceptable conduct.[1]

LITERATURE THAT FAILS to thrill, titillate, or terrorize doesn't get far in today's secular marketplace. Shallow and provocative substitutes for good literature seduce rather than build noble character. Traditionally, the classroom has been a purveyor of character-building books. It still is, but what kind of values does it now build?

When my son was in the eighth grade, his English teacher required her students to read Jay McInerney's *Bright Lights, Big City*. The setting: A nightclub for singles, in the wee hours of the night. The hero: "You."

> You spot a girl at the edge of the dance floor who looks like your last chance for earthly salvation. . . . There she is in her pegged pants, a kind of doo-wop retro ponytail pulled off to the side, as eligible a candidate as you are likely to find this late in the game. The sexual equivalent of fast food.
>
> She shrugs and nods when you ask her to dance. You

like the way she moves, the oiled ellipses of her hips and shoulders. After the second song, she says she's tired. She's at the point of bolting when you ask her if she needs a little pick-me-up.

"You've got some blow?" she says.

"Is Stevie Wonder blind?" you say.

She takes your arm and leads you into the Ladies' [room]. A couple of spoons and she seems to like you just fine, and you are feeling very likable yourself. A couple more. This woman is all nose.

"I love drugs," she says, as you march toward the bar.

"It's something we have in common," you say.

"Have you ever noticed how all the good words start with D? . . . You know. Drugs. Delight. Decadence."

"Debauchery," you say, catching the tune now.

"Dexedrine. . . ."

"Delinquent."[2]

A discussion with my son's teacher resulted in a change in reading assignments. Yet it takes more than an occasional win to slow society's downward spiraling. In *Amusing Ourselves to Death*, mass media critic, the late Neil Postman, compared the chilling prophecies of two authors, George Orwell and Aldous Huxley:

> Orwell feared that the truth would be concealed from us. Huxley feared the truth would be drowned in a sea of irrelevance. Orwell feared we would become a captive

culture. Huxley feared we would become a trivial culture, preoccupied with some equivalent of the feelies, the orgy porgy, and the centrifugal bumblepuppy. . . . In [Orwell's] *1984* . . . people are controlled by inflicting pain. In [Huxley's] *Brave New World*, they are controlled by inflicting pleasure. In short, Orwell feared that what we hate will ruin us. Huxley feared that what we love will ruin us.[3]

Postman suggests that Huxley, not Orwell, was right. I believe that if Huxley was right, Orwell's reality will follow. New Age optimists, who believe man's inherent goodness will lead him on an upward journey to spiritual perfection have, in Huxley's words, "failed to take into account man's almost infinite appetite for distractions."[4]

America still reads, but popular books now aim to entertain, not inform. Thrills sell. Facts don't. A charismatic world leader needs no military weapons, only promises, to take control over a hedonistic and non-thinking people.

I am not a pessimist. Our King has won the war, filled us with Himself, and promised us a glorious future. We don't need to fear anything—other than turning our backs on God.

STEP ONE: PERSONAL PREPARATION

ARE children being taught to read discerningly, or do they accept whatever is in print simply because it is in print?

• **Pray as a family for discernment and wisdom.** Don't let fear of offensive literature keep your family from finding and feasting on wonderful books.

• **Commit yourself to a deeper knowing of the Word of God.** Continue a daily Bible study program together. If children know truth, they will spot the lies.

• **Enjoy books together that demonstrate God's values.** Read-aloud times build in most children a deep love for reading, while they also enable you to direct your children's taste for enriching books. "While the average first-grade student reads from a primer with only 350 words, his listening vocabulary approaches 10,000 words, according to the Council for Basic Education."[5]

When you read aloud to your children, they learn to associate wholesome books with good times.

STEP TWO: BE ALERT TO DECEPTION IN BOOKS

• **A crossless version of Christianity fits the New Age lie that all can be one**—with or without Jesus. It denies man's need for redemption and, in effect, makes man his own savior. "For the preaching of the cross is to them that perish foolishness; but unto us which are saved it is the power of God" (1 Corinthians 1:18).

• **Examine gift books for children.** Some of Audrey and Don Wood's attractive books are filled with enticing New Age magic. Other picture books, like *The Witches Handbook* by Malcolm Bird, treat witchcraft as a game for all to enjoy.

• **Check contemporary children's poetry.** While some poems are superb, others are grotesque and macabre.

• **Check fantasy game books.** They make you the hero—but what beliefs do you follow? What mental pictures will your imagination create? As you make decisions appropriate to the story, will occult forces become part of your thinking? Some titles will tip you off—like *Seas of Blood* and *Castle Death*—but many others sound deceptively innocuous.

• **Be alert to what your child's peers read.** Discuss their influence on your child with him. During the winter of 1989, our son's eighth-grade peers read *Cycle of the Werewolf* by Stephen King, master of occult horror.

- **New kinds of joke books are captivating today's readers.** The object of the humor may be sex, marriage, parents, or God. Some of the illustrations may be pornographic. While we are in dire need of healthy humor, we don't need to laugh at corruption and delight in immorality. God wants us to love, accept, and forgive each other. But He also tells us to discipline and control our own human nature. Discuss these Scriptures with your child: Leviticus 11:44, 20:26; and Matthew 5:6, 8. Review Romans 12:1-2, 9, and Romans 13:14.

STEP THREE: CHECK YOUR LIBRARY

- **Befriend your local librarian.** Learn your library's guidelines and limitations. Know its definition of adult literature and whether or not children can check it out.

Many decision makers deny essential differences that separate childhood from adulthood. Children have neither the knowledge, wisdom, or experience to make adult decisions and carry adult responsibility. Adult movies, television, and books feed children adult-sized mental stimulants that they are unprepared to handle.

- **Scan the books promoted in special displays for children and for young adults (teenagers).** Do they promote anti-Christian religions or poor values? Do biographies promote social philosophies that oppose Christianity? Is the children's section balanced with books that promote other points of view? If not, our libraries become like the media—a political force with incredible power to influence children according to their own bias.

- **Discuss your concerns with the librarian.** Observe the guidelines in chapter two. Suggest solutions. While your local librarians may share your values, the American Library Association denies the need to shield children from certain kinds of adult literature and illustrations.

STEP FOUR: JOIN IN THE BATTLE FOR TRUTH

- **Continue to pray with other Christian families** for God's wisdom and direction.

- **Write those who advertise in offensive magazines.** One voice does make a difference.

- **Keep an up-to-date church library** and encourage other families to support and use it.

- **Let God encourage you with biblical passages that promise victory to those who trust and follow Him.** See Psalm 25:1, 4-5; Exodus 14:13-14; Deuteronomy 1:30; 20:1, 4.

PREPARING CHILDREN FOR SPIRITUAL BATTLE

REMEMBER, this is spiritual warfare. God's enemy fights as hard as ever to win the hearts and loyalties of our children—and he has added all kinds of high-tech tools to his arsenal.

To resist his strategies, they first need to understand them and have in their hearts the Word of God. That's why God told His people long ago to base all conversation—day and night—on His unchanging truth and to teach His truth diligently to our children (see Deuteronomy 6:6-7).

> To prove that our God is far greater than the plethora of alternatives, our lives must demonstrate faith in the midst of difficulties.

Everything we say must reflect the reality of God—His love, His omnipotence, His promises, and His warnings. To prove that our God is far greater than the plethora of alternatives that are out there, our lives must demonstrate faith in the midst of difficulties and His triumph in the midst of turmoil. This is possible, not by our own strength, but by His power and grace. Then, seeing His greatness, children learn to trust His promises.

Likewise, the armor of God (Ephesians 6:10-18) begins and ends with the power of His Word. First, we put on the belt of truth, which holds all the other pieces—His righteousness, peace, faith, and salvation—in place. The last part, "the sword of the Spirit, which is the word of God," is simply His truth and promises memorized, remembered, and affirmed as we face each day's challenges.

This two-edged sword is our main weapon in every battle. It exposes lies and uncovers deceptions while it strengthens our faith and lifts our hearts. The world can't understand it, and many so-called Christians despise it. But to those who love God, it brings the hope, strength, joy, and perseverance needed to walk with Him in peace no matter what happens.

(For the weapons of our warfare are not carnal, but mighty through God to the pulling down of strong holds;) Casting down imaginations, and every high thing that exalteth itself against the knowledge of God, and bringing into captivity every thought to the obedience of Christ. (2 Corinthians 10:4-5)

17

WHEN POPULAR MUSIC BECOMES OBSCENE & IMMORAL

Music engenders mystical experiences . . . Subject to the individual impulses, tastes and delights of consumers and composers, there is much about music that is creative, experiential, and ethereal. But as every genre from military marches to love songs indicate, music possesses a mysterious, if not occult, power to sway the soul. The only question for Christian believers becomes, do their musical preferences, acquisitions, and experiences hinder or facilitate the Holy Spirit's work in their souls?[1]—**Larry DeBruyn**

ADVENTURES INTO THE world of Zen, free sex, and mind-expanding drugs during the '60s paved capricious paths to "higher" consciousness. The long hair of those years was merely a sign of broken boundaries, rebellion against authority, and experimental ways to live—and die.

Music nurtured this liberation. It summoned, taught, inspired, and unified the seekers. Those who sang the same words felt the same rhythms and caught the same visions.

Like New Age spirituality, the music of the New Age has developed through syncretism—a blending of contemporary dreams, ancient paganism, Far Eastern religions, and modern technology.

While there are many varieties of music on the scene today, I would like to draw your attention to two distinct forms of music that have emerged. One, the ambient and "chill-out" sounds labeled "New Age music," which flow from a growing fascination with Eastern-style meditation. The soothing, sometimes ethereal, and at other times, monotonous or monotone tones, relax and often delight. Appealing to man's spiritual yearning for inner peace and harmony with nature, it can be harmless unless accompanied by New Age meditative practices and visualizations. However, the number of CDs now being manufactured to induce trance-like states is soaring.

The other kind—loud, physical rock—unashamedly flaunts counterfeit or occult values, images, rhythms, and verbal expressions. It has captured the hearts and minds of children, teens, and young adults around the world.

On the surface, these two types of music seem as opposite as what they proclaim: inner peace or sensual violence. But they aim in the same direction: union with the "angel of light" who wants to immunize children against truth and persuade them to worship idols.

ANCIENT FORMS OF NEW AGE MUSIC

THE New Age includes the dark as well as the seemingly beautiful. And yet, the mind behind the enticing masks hates the God of the Bible and everything He represents. Thus, New Age music does not just merely include the fluid, hypnotic strains flowing from electric synthesizers, but the full gamut of musical instrumentation and affectation for the purposes of hard selling New Age enticements to today's young people—utilizing and employing the use of meditation, magic, and drugs also to more effectively reach them.

Man's attempts to transcend the boundaries of the physical world through music are intricately interwoven with the history of mankind. While God encouraged His people to worship and enter His presence through songs of praise, Satan—as he always does with God's best gifts—provided a counterfeit. Thus, pagan societies used music as a conduit to help them connect directly to the spirit realm and with other gods. Nevill Drury, who promotes New Age meditation and visualization in his manual, *Music for Inner Space*, points to ancient cultures as models for today:

> [I]n societies where magic and myth define and influence everyday existence man aspires to be like the gods and to imitate them, thereby acquiring mastery of nature. . . . In both primitive societies and ancient culture alike, magical incantations and songs are a source of power.[2]

In India, the ancient Hindu ragas stimulate the imagination. Drury explains that the drone component—"the unchanging basic note or pitch"—sustains the music and "meditatively makes each musical performance an 'inner journey.' One literally travels with the music, lured into new areas of consciousness."[3] Drury continues:

> Repetitive rhythms and mantric musical patterns are used universally to induce trance states. However, we have a choice within the altered state of allowing ourselves to surrender to the music and be "possessed" by its intoxicating rhythms or "ride" the music or drumbeat on our journey to the inner world.[4]

In primitive Africa and South America, the witch doctor functions as a mediator between the tribe and demonic spirits. The sacred drum—credited with magical powers—together with hallucinatory drugs (sorcery) induces trances, which transports him into the spirit world. There he receives guidance.

In the Amazon rainforest, there lived a Yanamamo shaman named Chief Shoefoot. In his testimonial film, *I'll Never Go Back*, Shoefoot, now a born-again Christian, tells how his music- and drug-induced trances put him in touch with horrible and frightening demonic spirits. The music would lull him into these trances, playing a significant role in his making contact with the spirits.[5]

Obo Addy, a drummer and singer from Ghana said, "My father was a medicine man. He told the future and healed the sick. Music invoked the spirits my father possessed."[6] The ceremony often involved the whole tribe. Intoxicated by the drum's beat, the dancers would finally surrender to the persuasive rhythms and enter into a trance. A description of the Macumba (Brazil) spiritists' trance dance ends with this observation: "If I was looking for a mindless joy it was here, in a dance with the brain turned off and the body taking its orders straight from the drum."[7]

Nanci des Gerlaise, author of *Muddy Waters*, is the daughter and granddaughter of Cree medicine men. Now, as a believer in Christ, Nanci warns others about the occultic music in Native Spirituality:

> Now when I hear powwow music, my spirit recoils, and I know without a doubt that it is because there are spiritual forces of darkness at work. Some people, even some Christians, believe there are two different kinds of powwows—one used only for entertaining tourists and the other for traditional competitions. Frankly, it makes no difference to the spirit world which version is used as long as there are drums and chanting.[8]

Musicologists, Manfred Clynes and Janice Walker, explain that "the central nervous system transforms a musical rhythm into a movement pattern." This "rhythmic experience of sound largely is not under control—we are driven by it."[9] Nevill Drury backs this up:

> [The] rhythms which induce trance states are repetitive, energetic, and often loud and overwhelming. They lead the dancer away from the familiar setting of the

everyday world into a disorienting atmosphere pulsing with vibrant rhythms, which usually builds to a climax. . . . in Africa the dancers imitate the movements and footsteps of the possessing spirits.[10]

THE INTOXICATING MESSAGE OF HEAVY METAL ROCK

HARD rock and heavy metal soared to stardom in the late 1960s and early 1970s, even among children. Heavy metal "differs from other forms of rock by its bombastic chords, screaming lead guitars, throat-wrenching vocals, and a demolition derby approach to drumming."[11] Since the birth of heavy metal, several different kinds of metal music have come on the scene. Some of the genres are: Black metal, death metal, doom metal, gothic metal, power metal, speed metal, stoner metal, and thrash metal.[12] As the names suggest, this music exalts wickedness and darkness. Much of this music promotes violence, death, illicit sex, and even rape and Satanism. Many of the songs are sacrilegious, as well as mocking toward God and morality. Album covers often display grotesque pictures smattered with skulls, chains, blood, demons, goat heads in pentagrams, and a mockery of crosses.

Whether the musicians personally practice Satanism or merely play at it for its shock value matters little to the children who absorb the messages. No doubt, the image of a vampire-like Ozzy Osbourne drooling blood and singing about an "X-rated demon that lives in my head"[13] has inspired occult fascination in the hearts of his young worshipers who have moved beyond fear. California pastor Joe Schimmel, producer of the documentary *The Submerging Church,* has done extensive research on rock music and was at one time involved with rock music himself prior to becoming a Christian. He reveals Osbourne's significant influence:

Ozzy was the front man of Black Sabbath who pioneered Heavy Metal in the late '60s and throughout the 1970s. After selling several million albums with

Sabbath, Ozzy was fired and took up a solo career and sold over 70 million albums in the '80s and '90s. Now, in the 21st century, Ozzy is the "star" of MTV's most successful show ever. To be sure, Satan has received a lot of mileage out of Ozzy Osbourne. . . .

Unbelievably, [former] President Bush went out of his way to honor Ozzy Osbourne and his music at the White House Press Correspondents Dinner. Much to the Bush administrations chagrin, Ozzy was said to have almost stolen the show.[14]

It is sad that so many parents, even a president of the United States, cannot see the great harm this occultic music has inflicted upon so many. Given full freedom to indulge natural desires, many young people learn to crave the most shocking, lewd, and brutal entertainment available.

Sadly, and almost unbelievably, there is even a genre of heavy metal called Christian metal, sometimes called White Metal. Popular groups such as The Devil Wears Prada, August Burns Red, Underoath, and As I Lay Dying scream into their microphones in deep grotesque sounding voices while playing heavy metal music. There are dozens of "Christian" metal groups today, and most claim to sing their music as a form of evangelism. If you get the chance, listen to some of this music on YouTube, and see for yourself if you can hear the Gospel being preached in these songs. From the ones I listened to, I sure couldn't. If you decide to check it out though, you may want to pray that God protects your mind from this demonic music.

When Evil Looks Good

WHILE groups such as Metallica, Ozzy Osbourne, and Anthrax are easy to spot for their immoral, occultic, and evil music, Satan knows how to masquerade himself as an "angel of light." Young teens and pre-teens flock to concerts to hear bands their parents believe are moral and good, especially compared to someone like Marilyn Manson.

One group who has slipped under the parental radar is the Backstreet Boys, who "emerged as one of the hottest groups of the 21st century."[15] Joe Schimmel explains:

> Many parents exhale with a sigh of relief when they hear that there are alternatives to the popular and overtly satanic bands on the music scene like Marilyn Manson. One mother was reported to express great joy that there are groups like the Backstreet Boys which she can allow her daughter to listen to. . . . . she appreciated the music of the Backstreet Boys because, "Their focus is on good morals."[16]

But are the Backstreet Boys focusing on good morals? Listen to some of their lyrics, and keep in mind that the average-aged listeners are twelve-years-old girls, and the singers are 24plus-year-old men! The following is from "If You Want it to Be Good (Get Yourself a Bad Boy)":

> If you want it to be good girl, get yourself a bad boy . . . If you want it wild . . . if you really like it hot, Get somebody who hits the spot honey . . . if you like it innovated . . . get yourself a bad boy . . . AND MAMA SHOULDN'T KNOW . . . I wanna show you how. So won't you let me show you right now . . . If you want it to be good girl get yourself a bad boy.[17]

From "Boys Will Be Boys":

> We try to get closer, and you always push me away. You tell me it's much too soon, but I just can't help it. . . . All my senses go right into overdrive. All my defenses are never going to hold, I'm always going to lose control. I hear you singing that you think that we should wait, if I can't hold on anymore. My body is calling for you, so please don't hesitate. No . . . You know I gotta do what I gotta do baby.[18]

Ask yourself, do you really want your young impressionable daughters and granddaughters being serenaded with such songs? Schimmel makes a valid point:

> Groups like the Backstreet Boys are even more dangerous in some ways than groups like Marilyn Manson because most people are intelligent enough not to allow their children or themselves to be influenced by overtly wicked destructive music. Satan is aware of this, which is why he seeks to get in many homes via groups that on the surface seem somewhat tame, but are in fact filled with the poison necessary to damn one's soul. Jesus Christ warned all those who would cause the little one to sin with these sobering words:[19]

And whosoever shall offend one of these little ones that believe in me, it is better for him that a millstone were hanged about his neck, and he were cast into the sea. (Mark 9:42)

WHEN DARKNESS RULES

ONE of *Webster's* definitions for the word muse, the root of music, is "the spirit regarded as inspiring a poet or other article; source of genius or inspiration."[20]

Man has two main sources of inspiration outside of himself: God and Satan. While both communicate their thoughts to willing listeners, the latter is an aggressive liar who desires to inflame rebellion against God. (See 1 Chronicles 21:1; John 3:2, 27; Acts 5:3; 13:10.)

Many popular singers have acknowledged their ties to a supernatural source of inspiration *other* than God. For example, Joni Mitchell admitted being ruled by "a male muse named Art" who opened to her "the shrine of creativity."[21] Angus Young of

AC/DC confessed, "Someone else is steering me. I'm just along for the ride. I become possessed when I'm on stage."[22]

The fact that most rock singers look to themselves, drugs, or alcohol for inspiration, not consciously to Satan or spirit guides, fits the deceiver's plan perfectly. He is a master at using untamed desires for his purposes.

Joe Schimmel has also produced a DVD called *They Sold Their Souls for Rock n' Roll*, which documents how some of today's top Rock n' Roll performers have literally sold their souls to the devil in exchange for musical talent and fame.[23]

As Christian parents, we must do *everything we can* to protect our children from wicked influences. Let us also pray for those who are delivering Satanic music to millions of young people. God tells us not to give up on those who are caught in deception. Instead He encourages us to speak the truth in love so that "they may recover themselves out of the snare of the devil, who are taken captive by him at his will" (2 Timothy 2:26).

WHAT DO CHILDREN LEARN?

> Music is a lot like alcohol and drugs. It can be very deceiving and destructive when misused and can distort one's emotions, reasoning, judgment, perspective, and behavior. Peer pressure only makes it worse. Music, with or without lyrics, can be a very powerful force in our lives. That is why instrumentals alone can bring a tear to an eye or screams from a crowd before a single word is ever sung. Likewise, other emotions can easily be stirred by lyric-free melodies and rhythms resulting in joy, happiness, excitement, anger, bitterness, depression, and rage. To say that music without lyrics is amoral is like saying music without lyrics is dispassionate. It's absurd.[24]—Paul Proctor (former country musician)

ACCORDING to a 2010 study, children between the ages of eight and eighteen spend an average of nearly two and a half hours a day listening to music or some form of audio.[25] That's over 10,000 hours of music during their pre-teen and teen years. And with the rapid growth of computer technology, where one can listen to music on iPods, iPads, laptops, touch phones, and cell phones, that number is sure to grow.

And music isn't getting any nicer either. Dr. Joseph Stuessy, author of *Rock and Roll: Its History and Stylistic Development* and Director of the School of Music at the University of Texas, contends: "There is a new element in the music, a meanness of spirit—outright hatred—that was not present in the early days of rock."[26] People are more likely to remember a musical message than words spoken alone. When you add the fact that repetition internalizes the message, the sum spells DANGER.

Most hard rock and heavy metal bands—whether listened to through YouTube, iPods, CDs, radio, MTV, or concerts—drum the following anti-Christian messages into children's minds:

◊ Spurn Jesus Christ.

◊ Fuel the imagination with promiscuity, perversion, and violence.

◊ Indulge in drug and alcohol abuse.

◊ Experience the thrills of the dark occult.

◊ Envision a one-world government.

BONO, A "ROLE-MODEL" FOR OUR YOUTH?

FEW entertainers have more effectively confused young minds and corrupted the Gospel than Bono, the ultra-famous star of the Irish rock band, U2. Playing the devil, twisting God's Word, and mocking genuine Christianity, Bono has tragically led many Christian youth into the dangerous world of occult music.

Bono's great leap forward came in the early nineties, when he claimed the persona of MacPhisto: "the devil."[27] With his red horns, whitened face, bright red lipstick, black hair, and golden suit, his message grew more outrageous. But the celebration of evil—joined to an enticing illusion of "good"—enlarged the crowds and helped popularize the emerging, unrestrained "Christianity" that's becoming a norm today.

Back in 1989, he was asked in a *Mother Jones* interview, "Do you still believe that Jesus is the way? Doesn't that biblical injunction deny that followers of other religions can enter paradise?" Bono answered:

> I don't accept that. I don't accept that fundamentalist concept. I believe, what is it? "The way is as narrow as the eye of the needle," and all that. But I think that's just to keep the fundamentalists out. . . . (laughs) I never really accepted the whole "born again" tag.[28]

U2's 2005 tour was aimed at joining all religions into a unified global spirituality. To emphasize the coming solidarity, the word "COEXIST" was featured on a giant screen. The capital "C" pointed to the Islamic crescent, the "X" symbolized the Jewish Star of David, and the "T" was a reminder of the Christian cross. Bono led massive crowds in a vibrant chant: "Jesus, Jew, Mohammed—It's True!"[29]

Not everyone approved. Singer/songwriter Tara Leigh Cobble said, "He repeated the words like a mantra, and some people even began to repeat it with him. I suddenly wanted to crawl out of my skin. . . . Was Bono, my supposed brother in Christ, preaching some kind of universalism?"[30]

"I felt like I was witnessing an antichrist," said her friend.[31]

In one song, "God's Country," Bono belts out the words, "I stand with the sons of Cain."[32] The Bible tells us that Cain "was of that wicked one, and slew his brother" (1 John 3:12), not exactly someone who a Christian would want to be found standing in agreement with.

Are Christian leaders speaking up and warning others about Bono? No, on the contrary, reveals one Christian journalist:

One of the leaders being promoted today by those purporting to be officiating the way for our young people—to include Bill Hybels, Brian McLaren, Rick Warren, and Rob Bell—is "Christian" Rock star Bono of U2, whom many emergents view as their "prophet" and the main icon of their movement. In Bono's rendition of Psalm 23, he alters the entire thrust and message of this beautiful psalm to something that sounds nothing less than blasphemous. For example . . . he alters the wording to say "I have cursed thy rod and staff. They no longer comfort me."[33]

And in the summer of 2005, Rick Warren attended the Live 8 Concert with Bono where he was made the official pastor at the event.[34] Rick Warren did not issue a warning at the event about Bono, leaving the impression on thousands of young people's minds that Bono is OK.

A 2009 article titled "Evangelical Movement at 'Head-Snapping' Moment, Says Scholar," states that "[a]cross the nation, young evangelicals are naming Rick Warren or Bono as their role model for social engagement."[35] I find it troubling to read something like that, observing how Bono portrays himself and how Rick Warren doesn't show discernment or wisdom.

Parents, grandparents, youth workers, pastors, and teachers need to take heed. The music our young people are listening to, much of it by professing Christians, is leading the way toward a mass deception, and youth are its primary victims.

But these speak evil of those things which they know not: but what they know naturally, as brute beasts, in those things they corrupt themselves. Woe unto them! for they have gone in the way of Cain, and ran greedily after the error of Balaam for reward . . . to whom is reserved the blackness of darkness for ever. (Jude 10-11, 13)

"Contemplative" Music For Children

As our culture increasingly embraces the New Age and mystical practices, meditative music (much different than rock n' roll), specifically created to provide an atmosphere for meditation is becoming more and more popular, and parents need to be on the alert. The emerging church has introduced "sensory worship" using candles, dimmed lights, and soft repetitive music. This "vintage" Christianity has been introduced into thousands of youth groups across North America. Roger Oakland, author of *Faith Undone,* explains:

> Stimulating images that provide spiritual experiences are an essential element of the emerging church . . . many are bewildered as to why their churches are darkening their sanctuaries and setting up prayer stations with candles, incense, and icons.[36]

Mark Yaconelli, a leader in the contemplative prayer movement, teaches youth leaders how to bring their young protégés into the "silence." He states in his book *Contemplative Youth Ministry: Practicing the Presence of Jesus:*

> The environment can be a help or hindrance when leading kids in contemplative prayer. Set a mood that's conducive to silence. Turn out the lights and light a candle. Go outside under the stars. Play some music that helps youth settle down. Make sure there's plenty of space. Better yet, ask the youth to set up the room for contemplative prayer. I find that youth are very receptive to contemplative prayer, especially when led by adults who are experienced in prayer and can lead it with a sense of "lightness."[37]

In an interview with *Christianity Today,* contemplative advocate John Michael Talbot compares this contemplative music to New Age music:

There is an aspect of music, of sacred music, that can speak the unspeakable . . . The only other style of music that attempts to go to the deeper place of the silence that is music is New Age music.[38]

John Michael Talbot says he "began practicing meditation, specifically breath prayer . . . Tai Chi and yoga."[39]

While Christian contemplative music specifically for children has not become popular yet within the evangelical church, there is plenty of music designed to help children meditate in New Age, Catholic, and mainstream (Episcopal, Orthodox, etc.) circles. One CD, *Children's Yoga Songs and Meditations* plays songs repeating various mantras such as "Om," "Sa Ta Na Ma" (a form of Kirtin Kriya yoga), and other Hindu and Buddhist chants. On one Christian CD titled *Open Our Hearts—Christian Meditation for Children,* the description reads:

Each track on this CD is designed to lead the children through a period of meditation from beginning to end. The meditators listen to the music and scripture, join in the song and the mantra and continue repeating this sacred word silently throughout the timed silence which begins after the sounding of three chimes. Similarly, the chimes sound again to signal the end of the meditation.[40]

Contemplative music certainly doesn't have the loud blasting sounds of heavy metal, but it is every bit as dangerous, if not more so. Teaching children to meditate leads them to a panentheistic, interspiritual spirituality that has no room for the Cross or the Gospel.

18

WHAT CAN PARENTS DO ABOUT SEDUCTIVE MIND-CHANGING MUSIC?

THE REAL HEROES of today are the parents, trying to raise their children in an environment that seems to have grown more and more hostile to family life. Music and the media flood their children's world with the glorification of drugs, violence, perversity, the New Spirituality—and there's nothing they can do about it, they're told, because of the First Amendment. . . .

There was a time when much of America and Canada was Christian (or at least largely influenced by Judeo/Christian values), and most people were not involved with the occult. Today, in both countries, occultism has moved into the forefront of our society. As rebellion against God intensifies, and as Christians continue to flirt with the world (and the occult) thus quenching God's Spirit, demonic forces rush in. Many believe that the very drumbeat that mesmerizes children is also beating out a worldwide summons to the powers of darkness.

While some may reject that theory, all can agree that music possesses the power to influence and change people. That is why, in the Psalms alone, we are encouraged more than sixty times to sing unto the Lord. Singing shapes, affirms, and strengthens what we believe. It expresses the depths of our souls. Words that enter in on the wings of music tend to light, nest, and imprint themselves on our minds—and later, flit back into our thoughts whether or not we consciously willed them to.

We can battle the contemporary decadence in music by training our children to listen to God's thoughts, to enjoy music and songs that build faith, and to base their actions on God's truth.

STEP ONE: LISTEN TO GOD, NOT THE WORLD

- **Renew your mind with truth (Romans 12:2).** Continue daily Bible study—not just to gain facts or engage in mental ascent, but to know and hear God's heart and have Him write His words upon your heart. He will speak to those who love and follow Him (John 10:3-5; 14:21-27). Read the following Scriptures, looking for God's messages. Discuss His guidelines for they apply to music as well as other kinds of influence.

    » What is God's attitude toward evil? Psalm 97:10-11; Proverbs 6:16-19; 15:9, 26; 21:4.

    » What are the consequences of dabbling with evil? Proverbs 1:29-33; 21:16.

    » How does God want me to respond to evil? Romans 13:11-14; 1 Peter 5:6-9; Psalms 1; 141:3-4; Proverbs 2.

    » How does He want me to live each day? Ephesians 4:17-32; 5:3-21.

- **Avoid compromising suggestions and situations.** God says, "Flee also youthful lusts" (2 Timothy 2:22). This is not easy when an entire society, culture, or nation craves immorality and violence.

- **Count on what Jesus accomplished on the Cross.** When He declared, "It is Finished!," He completed His atoning work on the Cross. Through His finished work, He not only defeated sin, but He provided a way (grace) for us to live a life that is pleasing to Him. "[R]eckon ye also yourselves to be dead indeed unto sin, but alive unto God through Jesus Christ our Lord. . . . Neither yield ye your members as instruments of unrighteousness unto sin: but yield yourselves unto God . . . and your members as instruments of righteousness unto God" (Romans 6:11, 13).

• **Trust and follow the Holy Spirit.** When children turn from moral absolutes to moral relativism, they become uncomfortable in God's presence. Those who have developed an appetite for immorality hide from Him. Feeling judged by His holiness, they have two choices: run, or repent and receive His loving forgiveness. Most refuse to break their bondage to their sensual lifestyle. The apostle Paul wrote to the Galatian Christians who lived in a pagan society:

> Walk in the Spirit, and ye shall not fulfil the lust of the flesh. For the flesh lusteth against the Spirit, and the Spirit against the flesh: and these are contrary the one to the other: so that ye cannot do the things that ye would. . . .

> [T]he works of the flesh are manifest, which are these; Adultery, fornication, uncleanness, lasciviousness, Idolatry, witchcraft, hatred . . . wrath, strife, seditions, heresies, Envyings, murders, drunkenness . . . and such like . . . they which do such things shall not inherit the kingdom of God. But the fruit of the Spirit is love, joy, peace, longsuffering, gentleness, goodness, faith, Meekness, temperance. (Galatians 5:16-17, 19-23)

When we place our faith in Him and what He accomplished for us and not what we can do, the Holy Spirit is faithful to provide strength, wisdom, and guidance to see us through any situation or temptation we might face.

STEP TWO: HELP YOUR CHILD CHOOSE ENRICHING MUSIC

WHAT is good music? This subjective question has no simple answer in these days of diverse selections and divisive preferences. While *you* may love classical or Christian praise music and hymns, most teenagers today do not. If your child has developed an appetite for thrash metal, you may have to start the weaning process by moving a step at a time.

- **Ask God to lead you to His choices for your family.**

- **Listen to the music your child likes.** Develop an atmosphere of love, mutual respect, and acceptance. Be open, understanding, and supportive. Discuss the message of the lyrics. Ask questions such as: "Do you agree with those lyrics? Do your friends? What happens in your mind when you keep hearing the same message over and over?"

- **Study and buy music together.** Examine CD covers and inserts, and read the titles. Discuss different groups. Talk about the values, attitudes, behavior, and dress promoted by Lady Gaga, Usher, and other music idols.

So-called New Age music didn't seem to impress the youth culture until 1988, when Enya's hit album *Watermark* blended it with a mellow form of rock. Since the door is open to new variations, watch for hypnotic and meditative sounds intended to produce altered states of consciousness. Listen for lyrics that teach New Age spirituality. But remember, New Age music is a broad umbrella that may even include meditative (contemplative) "Christian music." As God said in 1 John 4:1, "try [test] the spirits."

- **Include your child in choosing music for your home.** Tell why you like certain kinds of music; share the benefits you receive. Explain that biblical truth set to music delights God and builds faith and spiritual strength in us. Ask yourselves these questions:

  » Does it honor or dishonor God?

239

» Does it encourage me to trust and follow Him?

» Does it communicate the power of God, of man, or of Satan?

» Does it focus my mind on the glory of God or the rebellious forces of Satan? (Philippians 4:8; Colossians 3:1-3)

» Does it encourage adherence to or rebellion against God's values?

» Does it produce a craving for a form of music rather than for God?

» In concert, do listeners worship God or the musician/singer? (Deuteronomy 5:7-8)

• **Consider how your music lines up with your personal goals.** Ask questions such as: Do I want to be close to God? To please Him? To enjoy His peace and protection? What happens when I listen to songs that oppose truth?

Look at Paul's goal in Philippians 3:7-10. If you choose the same goal—to know Jesus, share His suffering, and live by His resurrection life—rejection and exclusion for your obedience to Christ become stepping-stones to triumph.

• **Set limits.** While you cannot monitor what your child hears and sees at a friend's house, you can say no to certain kinds of music in your home. Explain your concerns. Many children welcome parental boundaries as their excuse to say no to peers.

• **Guard against trying to please your children** by providing "Christianized" versions of pagan delights. For example, adding biblical words to a raging heavy metal beat most likely makes mockery, not wholesome music. Don't be like ancient Israel, which craved the corrupt practices of their heathen neighbors. Adding idolatry to traditional worship, they became spiritually blind and morally corrupt. Enemies invaded their land, when "every man [did] whatsoever is right in his own eyes" (Deuteronomy 12:8).

STEP THREE: JOIN GROUP EFFORTS TOWARD CONSTRUCTIVE CHANGE

- **Agree with other parents on setting limits** when it comes to destructive forms of music.

- **Ask the youth leader of your church** to teach about contemporary music.

- **Pray together for God's guidance and victory.** God cares about your child's spiritual health even more than you do. Remember, while He calls us to join Him in His battles, the final outcome is certain: He has won the war. Continue to thank Him!

When foreign armies attacked Jerusalem, King Jehoshaphat trusted God, called the people together, acknowledged God's superior power, and praised Him for His total sufficiency. God responded with tremendous encouragement that lifted hearts and built faith—which He still does today for His children. "[F]ear not, nor be dismayed; to morrow go out against them: for the Lord will be with you" (2 Chronicles 20:17).

Do you remember the rest? Jehoshaphat organized musicians to lead the procession of soldiers into battle. Then as the people sang and praised God, He accomplished the victory on their behalf. (See 2 Chronicles 20:1-22.)

Make a joyful noise unto the Lord, all ye lands. Serve the Lord with gladness: come before his presence with singing. Know ye that the Lord he is God: it is he that hath made us, and not we ourselves; we are his people, and the sheep of his pasture. (Psalm 100: 1-3)

19

MYSTICAL NEW AGE THRILLS ENTICING CHILDREN

> And he caused his children to pass through the fire in the valley of the son of Hinnom: also he observed times, and used enchantments, and used witchcraft, and dealt with a familiar spirit, and with wizards: he wrought much evil in the sight of the Lord. (2 Chronicles 33:6)

"SOFTENING UP" FOR OCCULT REVIVAL—HERMETIC MAGIC & HEGEL'S DIALECTIC PROCESS

WHY WOULD OUR country, so richly blessed by God, embrace the occult? What caused this drastic change in values? How could it have happened so seemingly fast?!

Actually, the entire Western world had already been "softened up" by the 1960s when the rising rebellion against God erupted into public view. The century-old pursuit of social solidarity based on Georg Hegel's occult philosophy and consensus process had been an effective tool for change.

Hegel's 19th century pattern for "group thinking" denied God's absolute truths and trained people to adapt to "continual change" and group consensus. By the year 2000, it had been embraced by schools, corporations, community organizations, mainline churches, and political structures throughout America. Through the global media, people around the world have caught Hegel's vision of spiritual synthesis—an enticing blend of spiritual illusions and practices that appeal to our capricious human nature.

Hegel studied alchemy, Kabbalah (Jewish mysticism), and theosophy, which were all influenced by the heretical teachings of Gnosticism. He "read widely on Mesmerism, psychic phenomena, dowsing, precognition, and sorcery. He publicly associated himself with known occultists . . . and aligned himself, informally, with 'Hermetic' societies such as the Freemasons and the Rosicrucians" and embraced their symbolic systems of sacred circles, mystical triangles and astrological signs.[1]

Considering Hegel's occult connections, it's not surprising that his teachings would undermine biblical faith and all opposing facts. Nor is it strange that the postmodern (or some now say *pseudo-modern*) generation has been, by and large, inoculated and indoctrinated against genuine Christianity. After all, Hegel's revolutionary dialectic process was the center-piece and hallmark of Soviet brainwashing. It effectively purged God's unchanging truths and filled the vacuum with evolving "truths" and enticing dreams.

While Communist leaders embraced Hegel's process, they ignored his occult beliefs. In contrast, the Western world began to restore those pagan roots long before revolutionary baby-boomers began proclaiming and shouting out their demands for sensual freedom and earth-centered spirituality. In other words, the '60s didn't initiate this radical change; the turmoil of the '60s was the result of the psycho-social program of "re-learning" which had begun to transform America decades earlier.

As the old moral and spiritual boundaries were torn down, the mainstream media preached tolerance and acceptance of all kinds of forbidden thrills. Before long, occult secrets emerged from their centuries-old closets and claimed their place in mainstream entertainment.

We who trust God need to recognize our enemy, resist his tempting strategies, and know the truths that counter these deadly deceptions. The very safety of our children depends on it.

Yoga

There's no arguing it, children in public schools are learning Yoga. According to Yoga instructor, Mark Blanchard, of Progressive Power Yoga, he taught children at Colfax Elementary School in California. On his blog, he wrote: "I will be introducing Yoga to all of the kids at the school as I donate a full Yoga program."[2] Blanchard has been featured in many magazines such as *Family Circle* and *Seventeen* and has trained many actors and actresses (like Jennifer Lopez and Drew Barrymore).[3] Blanchard plans to "bring Progressive Power Yoga to as many places as [he] can around the states (as well as the globe)."[4]

Part of Blanchard's plans include working with Mini Yogis Yoga for Kids. On the Mini Yogis website, they list not only Blanchard's company but many other organizations as well, many of which are schools like Happy Land Preschool in Culver City and St. Monica's Elementary School in Santa Monica[5] (both in California).

Yoga for kids is on the rise, and if your child attends public school, you may want to check to see if teachers there are teaching him or her Yoga. A program called YogaEd provides Yoga classes under the heading of "health/wellness" programs for schools. These programs take place in several states including California, Colorado, New York, Washington and Washington, D.C.[6]

In an article titled "Yoga Causes Controversy in Public Schools," veteran apologist Dave Hunt is referenced and quoted:

> Dave Hunt, who has traveled to India to study yoga's roots and interview gurus, called the practice "a vital part of the largest missionary program in the world" for Hinduism. The Bend, [Oregon] author of *Yoga and the Body of Christ: What Position Should Christians Hold?* said that, like other religions, the practice has no place in public schools.
>
> "It's pretty simple: Yoga is a religious practice in Hinduism. It's the way to reach enlightenment. To

bring it to the west and bill it as a scientific practice for fitness is dishonest," said Hunt.[7]

Parents whose children are in Christian schools may need to be concerned too. More and more churches and Christian organizations are opening their doors to the practice of Yoga. And the biggest Christian publisher, Thomas Nelson, published a book titled *Yoga for Christians* in 2006. It's just a matter of time before kids in Christian schools will be learning Yoga and the "art" of meditation.

It is tragic to know that countless public school children are being taught practices that are rooted in Eastern mysticism and will learn how to say "Namaste" (the god in me greets the god in you) before they learn they can have a relationship with God through Jesus Christ without going into altered states of consciousness through meditation. And it is equally tragic that many Christians will not even be able to help them because they are learning similar practices through their own "Spiritual Formation" (i.e, contemplative spirituality) programs in their churches.

SESAME STREET WILL TEACH YOUR CHILDREN YOGA

FOR parents or grandparents who once thought it harmless to let their little children or grandchildren watch an hour of Sesame Street once a day, a word of caution is needed. While many Christian parents have noticed the liberal slant of the popular T.V. show and kept their children away from the show turning to Mr. Rogers instead, many others have allowed Sesame Street into their homes feeling that the underlying New Age, liberal message was subtle enough to bypass the hearts and minds of little eyes and ears.

But a *New York Times* article titled "Same Street, Different World: 'Sesame' Turns 40" shows that Sesame Street is now promoting Yoga to children. The article states:

> The pedagogy hasn't changed, but the look and tone of "Sesame Street" have evolved . . . Now there are green spaces, tofu and Yoga.

> This season has an Om sensibility. "My mom takes me to Yoga class, I love doing Yoga," a little girl in pigtails says in [a Sesame Street] episode. . . She is narrating a short film that shows a pixieish teacher and her pupils folding into the downward dog position. After class her mother arrives with a plastic water bottle. "She says it's important to drink water when you exercise," the girl explains. "When I grow up I want to be a Yoga teacher."[8]

While warning a four-year-old not to participate in any Yoga exercises they might see on Sesame Street can make parents feel they have done their job in protecting their kids, it isn't likely that four- or five-year-olds will understand the dangers when Big Bird tells them how much fun it is or when they see their favorite personality on Sesame Street telling a room full of kids to do the Yoga exercises.

RETHINKING HALLOWEEN—A REVIVAL OF EARTH-CENTERED SPIRITUALITY

MOST pagan communities adapt Halloween to their own liking. Across America, Wiccan priests and priestesses—teachers, engineers, and other well-meaning and often well-educated professionals who would never appear in a black pointed hat—are creating rituals that give new meaning to the seasonal Celtic celebrations such as the summer and winter solstices, Halloween, and Beltane (the sensual springtime fertility feast).

Starhawk has taught her Wiccan rituals to "Christian" as well as secular and pagan groups on college and university campuses across the country. In *The Spiral Dance*, she describes one such Halloween celebration:

246

Before leaving home for the ritual, each covener sets out a plate with cakes and drink and a lighted candle as an offering to their own beloved dead. . . .

The circle gathers, does a breathing meditation, and the Priestess says, "This is the night when the veil is thin that divides the worlds. It is the New Year in the time of the year's death, when the harvest is gathered and the fields lie fallow. . . . The gates of life and death are opening; the Sun Child is conceived . . . We meet in time, out of time, everywhere and nowhere, here and there, to greet the Lord of Death who is Lord of Life, and the Triple Goddess who is the circle of rebirth."

Purify, cast the circle and invoke the Goddess and God. . . .

The Priestess says, "Here is the circle of rebirth . . . through me all may be born again. Everything passes, changes. Seed becomes fruit; fruit becomes seed. In birth, we die; on death, we feed. Know Me, and be free from all fear. For My womb is the cauldron of rebirth, in Me, the circle is ever turning.[9]

Notice that Starhawk refers to "the Lord of Death" but doesn't name or define him. Others have named him. They call him Samhain, the God of the Dead, who gave his name to the harvest celebration. But there is little documentation to prove his reported influence and fearsome power. At the same time, the historical record does show some of the sobering details of the celebration:

October 31 was the eve of the new year in both Celtic and anglo-Saxon times and one of the ancient fire festivals. It was connected with . . . the practice of divinations and its association with the dead, whose souls were supposed to revisit their homes on this day. Since November ushers in the darkest and most barren

247

half of the year, the autumnal festival acquired sinister significance, with ghosts, witches, hobgoblins, fairies and demons of all kinds roaming abroad. . . . The crops as well as the flocks and herds had to be protected from demonic influences that were rife at the turn of the year. It was the time to placate the supernatural powers controlling the processes of nature. Coupled with this were fire rites, divinations, funerary practices and masquerades. . . .

It was on Halloween that the general assembly, or open-air parliament (Freig), was held at Tara in Celtic Ireland, celebrated once in every three years with special solemnities lasting for two weeks. . . . The proceedings opened with sacrifices to the gods at Tlachtgha in County Meath, the victims being consumed by fire.[10]

Which gods were appeased by these sacrifices? We know that the Celts—like the Greeks, Romans, Mayans, Scandinavians, and other earth-centered religions of the last two millennia—sought favors from a wide range of nature gods and goddesses. This pantheon of supernatural beings usually included a ruthless god (or goddess) of the dead whose standard domain was the underworld. Considering the Celts' fear of nasty ghosts or spirits from the underworld during the Samhain celebration, one might suspect that the powerful Druids, the spiritual rulers and political advisors, did indeed encourage sacrifices to the God of the Dead.

An online version of the *Encyclopedia Britannica* includes a few more details:

Huge bonfires were set on hilltops to frighten away evil spirits. . . . The souls of the dead were supposed to revisit their homes on this day. . . . It was the time to placate the supernatural powers controlling the processes of nature.

In addition, Halloween was thought to be the most favorable time for divinations concerning marriage, luck, health, and death. It was the only day on which the help of the devil was invoked for such purposes.[11]

THE DARK SIDE OF SAMHAIN

THE family-centered blend of old Mexican traditions and Catholic teachings sheds its resemblance to Halloween when you look at the grisly roots of the popular holiday. *Ancient Wisdom and Secret Sects* (Time-Life Books) refers to Roman records that describe how the Celts:

> . . . constructed huge, human-shaped wicker cages, crammed them with victims, then set the twigs ablaze.

> Although convicted criminals were usually the ones offered to the gods. . . . innocent victims were substituted if malefactors were in short supply. Some sources claim the Druids even sacrificed their fellow members if the need to do so arose.[12]

The classical author Diodorus Siculus also reported scenes of human sacrifice. "When they attempt divination upon important matters they practice a strange and incredible custom, for they kill a man by a knife-stab in the region above his midriff." After the sacrificial victim fell dead "they foretell the future by the convulsions of his limbs and the pouring of his blood."[13]

The 1984 discovery of a sacrificial victim in Cheshire, England, helps validate the reality of ritualistic human sacrifice. The well-preserved young man had apparently belonged to an elite social class in the second century B.C. After two sharp blows to the head, he had been strangled. Then, like the countless sacrifices to Aztec and Mayan gods, his body had been drained of the human blood needed to please and appease their god(s).[14]

The roots grow darker yet. In his *National Geographic* report on "The Celts," Merle Severy, writes:

> According to the Dinshenchas, a medieval collection of 'the lore of prominent places,' firstborn children were sacrificed before a great idol to ensure fertility of cattle and crops. Samhain eve was a night of dread and danger. At this juncture of the old year and the new, our world and the otherworld opened up to each other. The dead returned, ghosts and demons were abroad, and the future could be seen. . . .
>
> Behind such Halloween games as bobbing for apples lie Celtic divination arts to discern who would marry, thrive, or die in the coming year. Behind the masks and mischief, the jack-o' lanterns and food offerings, lurk the fear of malevolent spirits and the rites to propitiate them.[15]
>
> Page 601 gives additional insight: "Tacitus tells us of the bloodstained Druid altars of Anglesey in Wales. Caesar describes mass human sacrifice in Gaul: 'Some of the tribes make colossal wickerwork figures, the limbs of which are filled with living men; these images are then set alight and the victims perish in a sea of flame.'"[16]

It is clear to see that while Halloween clashes with God's guidelines—it fits the world, its best-selling entertainment, and our human nature very well.

That's why the mastermind behind this spiritual war has kept employing the same tactics throughout the ages. Satan's main strategy has always been to tempt people to love what God hates, prompt them to pursue his enticing path, and deceive them into thinking that his "new" way is as good, or even better, than the *old* ways God has shown us. Since his strategies don't change, God's warning is as relevant now as it was in King Solomon's days:

> There is a way which seemeth right unto a man, but the end thereof are the ways of death. (Proverbs 14:12)

In a different context—apart from the Halloween setting—some of Halloween's symbols would be neutral. Many are simply parts of nature. After all, God made pumpkins, spiders, bats, and black cats. These are good gifts from Him and given for our blessing. But they take on new meanings when humans twist their God-given purpose to be representative of practices and observances contrary to God's Word.

The occult images of Halloween desensitize people to evil and prompt the masses to embrace the new global paradigm. God's people in the Old Testament didn't hesitate long before they conformed God's teaching to the pagan practices of their neighbors. The same kind of compromise is still changing the spiritual climate of churches today.

This politically correct "cooperation" or ecumenism threatens the faith of Christian adults as well as children. A young man, who grew up in a "Christian home" and attended church regularly, told me a sobering story. At the time, his mother was sick and dying, and he had expected her to look forward to eternity with Jesus. Instead, He was shocked to hear her say, "I wonder what I will be in my next life." Distressed, he asked, "How did she turn from faith in God to belief in reincarnation?"

The answer is simple. We live at a time when popular culture, peer pressure, and public training in the consensus (dialectic) process are pushing masses toward a global blending of all the religions. Halloween promoters may never mention reincarnation or Satan, but their efforts have desensitized the masses to a spiritual mix that promotes both. They succeed by taking the darkest images of the occult and packaging them as the most enticing celebration of the year.

God warned us it would happen—again and again—for neither human nature nor Satan's tactics change much throughout the course of human history.

A "New Age" For the Girl Scouts

For nearly one hundred years, since 1912, the Girl Scouts of the USA has existed. By 1920, over 70,000 girls had joined; and there are currently about 3.6 million Girl Scouts and an alumnae of more than fifty million women. The founder, Juliette "Daisy" Gordon Low, believed in developing girls "physically, mentally, and spiritually."[17] While there have been many wholesome and practical aspects of the Girl Scouts in the past (teaching cooking, sewing, and outdoor skills), today the Girl Scouts has become a place where potentially millions of girls will be introduced to New Age spirituality. Although the organization discourages the use of Christian emphasis in its meetings, it seems to show no reluctance when it comes to New Age spirituality.

For instance, on a twelve-page brochure for their 2010 annual National Council Sessions, it states, "Channel your inner being. Be one with your mind, body, and soul. Yoga for everyone!"[18] And on their website it states: "Doxology is not an appropriate Girl Scout event song, as it is easily identified as a Christian church song."[19]

As to their push for Yoga in young girls' lives, references to Yoga can be found in Girl Scout literature and activities, such as the Spring-Summer 2007 issue of *Leader Magazine* (the official GSUSA publication) where it tells of a Charleston, West Virginia Girl Scout chapter participating in Yoga.[20] And then there is a program called Fit's Inn where "[g]irls try sports and dance, and even learn Yoga."[21] Yoga is also mentioned in a report titled "A Report from the Girl Scout Research Institute" in a favorable way.[22] In a 2003 article on the group's main website, the subheading reads, "Volunteering—From Yoga to PR,"[23] and another article titled "Become the Best You Can Be" encourages learning "how to meditate" and practicing Yoga.[24]

While these references and promotions of Yoga are disturbing to say the least, they pale in comparison to a partnership between GSUSA and a group called "the Ashland Initiative," which will take Girl Scouts to a whole new level of New Age spirituality! The Girl Scouts are now incorporating the Ashland Initiative's Coming Into Your Own program, saying the program's aim "is to create a team of adult champions who will model a search for integrated leadership that springs from a deep sense of self-knowledge."[25] The Ashland Institute (located in Ashland, Oregon) is a group that teaches Attunement (metaphysical energy healing) described as "Creative Energy Practice," which "Deepen[s] connection with the Source of Life."[26]

The Coming Into Your Own is a "personal development program for women" who are going through "transition."[27] An opening quote in the program brochure is from homosexual poet May Sarton (1912-1995).[28] A 75-page online book about the Coming Into Your Own program reveals the New Age nature behind the program.[29]

Another partner of the Ashland Institute is The Fetzer Institute, where a broad assortment of mystical, New Age/New Spirituality resources is offered.[30] Panentheistic mystics such as Thomas Merton, the Dalai Lama, and David Steindl-Rast are among those promoted.[31] The Ashland Institute lists resources for their participants—the majority of which are other New Age groups such as Collective Wisdom Initiative, Co-Intelligent Institute, The Millionth Circle (to "shift planetary consciousness"), and The World Cafe.[32]

The Girl Scouts' partnership with the Ashland Initiative will help create leaders within the GSUSA who will take the New Spirituality agenda to countless girls, and instead of just teaching girls sewing, outdoor skills, and cooking, they will introduce them to meditation and the divinity within—the basic message of the New Age. This is further evidence that today's world has become a mystical New Age society; and much of this has been accomplished by directing efforts toward children.

MEDITATION IN THE CLASSROOM

IT isn't just Halloween, youth organizations such as Girl Scouts, and Yoga on *Sesame Street* where children are being introduced to Eastern-style meditation. Across North America, public school classrooms are opening their doors to welcome mystical meditation.

An article in *The Capitol Times* titled "Kid Contemplatives: UW Neuroscientist's Project Aims to Give Middle-Schoolers Tools of 'Mindfulness' and Meditation" tells about a pilot project done with middle school students that studied the effects of "contemplation in the classroom."[33] The article states:

> Middle school students are being targeted because early adolescence is a time of heightened vulnerability due to body and brain changes. . . .

> Centering prayer, meditation, breath work, chanting, sitting in silence, extended concentration on an object and focusing on positive thoughts and images are examples of contemplative exercises that can be taught.[34]

Neuroscientist Richard Davidson, who was the chair for the project, wants to use his research in meditative practices by studying the brains of Buddhist monks, in the classroom. Davidson, named by *Time* magazine as one of the world's 100 most influential people in 2006, and others like him are making inroads into meditation becoming the norm in schoolroom settings.

In *The Capitol Times* article, contemplative activist and Catholic priest Thomas Keating is quoted as saying that meditation in the classroom is "not a religious issue" and that "sitting in silence for twenty minutes, twice a day, 'gradually introduces us to our deeper self.'"[35] But the article contradicts Keating's view that meditation is not religious:

Like Buddhist meditation, centering prayer for Christians is an age-old religious practice that has experienced a revival in contemporary times.[36]

And as this article reveals, children are being targeted with meditation:

"Most people without a special (contemplative) practice tend to be pushed around by external events," Keating contends. In classrooms, "the younger the child, the easier it is" to teach contemplation because young participants typically aren't impeded by as much emotional baggage.[37]

As one researcher of the New Age explains:

The field of education presents an ideal setting for transformation. In virtually every area of education and instruction, from kindergarten to universities, from weekend workshops to family counseling sessions, the Ancient Wisdom is being taught either up front or covertly. This is largely happening because teachers, principals, and other administrators in particular have become involved in metaphysics.[38]

While not every public school has introduced meditation in their classrooms yet, more and more schools are implementing Yoga and other forms of Eastern-style meditation practices into students' lives.

As I have tried to show in this book, children truly are being bombarded by New Age spirituality at every turn, and it is happening on a level that is nothing short of epidemic. Unless parents take a pro-active approach to vigilantly protect their children from this onslaught, there is little chance they will escape from being affected and drawn into this global-wide spiritual deception.

20

HOW TO GUARD AGAINST MYSTICAL NEW AGE THRILLS

WHAT THEN HAVE our children learned? Which Scriptures will help them to stand firm on God's solid truths and "continue in" them, no matter what battles they face?

In Ephesians 6, God tells us to "[p]ut on the whole armour of God" so that we can "stand against the wiles of the devil" (vs. 11). We are reminded that our battle is not against "flesh and blood" but rather "against principalities, against powers, against the rulers of the darkness of this world, against spiritual wickedness in high places" (vs. 12). And if we take upon ourselves this armor of God, we "may be able to withstand in the evil day, and having done all," we will be able to stand (vs. 13).

STEP ONE: HELP YOUR CHILDREN PUT ON THE ARMOR OF GOD

USE the outline from chapter two to help your children put on this special armor. Make sure they know the Scriptures behind each part, so that their faith and understanding will be based on God's Word. Then pray through the pieces of the armor, simplifying each part to fit the ages of your children. Talk about the opposite viewpoints and how they are contrary to the God's Word and when followed, lead to spiritual deception: the Belt of TRUTH, the Breastplate of RIGHTEOUSNESS, the Sandals of the preparation of the GOSPEL, the Shield of FAITH, the Helmet of SALVATION, and the Sword of the SPIRIT, His WORD.

- **Belt of TRUTH:** His almightiness, love, wisdom, and holiness. (Deuteronomy 4:39; Psalm 18:1-3) **Opposite:** Pantheistic, monistic, polytheistic gods and goddesses.

- **Breastplate of RIGHTEOUSNESS:** Jesus Christ and His blood, which cleanses us from sin. The cross which frees us from bondage to selfish nature. **Opposite:** Confidence in the natural goodness, connectedness, and sacredness of all life.

- **Sandals of the preparation of the GOSPEL of peace:** Our peace with God comes from being justified by faith through our Lord Jesus Christ (Romans 5:1). **Opposite:** Peace through occult practices and union with a cosmic force or nature spirits.

- **Shield of FAITH:** Our continual trust in God, His Word, and His promises. **Opposite:** Trust in Self, inner wisdom, dreams, visions, gods, goddesses, cosmic force, coincidences, etc.

- **Helmet of SALVATION:** God's promises of daily and eternal salvation in Jesus Christ. **Opposite:** Evolving spiritually by growing in consciousness and connectedness.

- **Sword of the Spirit, His WORD:** The power of God's Word to counter deception and triumph over spiritual foes. **Opposite:** The power of thoughts, words, and affirmations to change reality and direct spiritual forces.

STEP TWO: MONITOR YOUR CHILD'S SCHOOL & ORGANIZATIONS — YOU CAN DO SOMETHING

IN a public elementary school in Aspen, Colorado, Christian parents protested when they learned that the school was going to start teaching the students Yoga. The parents argued that:

> [Y]oga's Hindu roots conflicted with Christian teachings and that using it in school might violate the separation of church and state.[1]

In Encinitas, California, parents went to school district trustees when they learned that a Yoga program was coming to the school. They explained to officials that by bringing in Yoga, they were introducing the children to Hinduism:

"Yoga practices and poses are not merely exercise; they're religious practices," said Marsha Qualls, who has a student at Olivenhain Pioneer Elementary School, calling the techniques "a kind of prayer."[2]

Because of these concerned parents, school officials decided to at least wait on the Yoga program until further investigation. The point here is that you can do something to protect your children. Whether your children are in public or private school, keep an eye on new programs coming into the school, and when you find out about New Age/New Spirituality based programs, speak up.

STEP THREE: TEACH YOUR CHILDREN ABOUT THE SPIRITUAL ANCHOR IN A TIME OF CHANGE

Let that therefore abide in you, which ye have heard from the beginning. If that which ye have heard from the beginning shall remain in you, ye also shall continue in the Son, and in the Father. (1 John 2:24)

IN a busy world, which has so many demands that can rob us of our quiet times with God in His Word, we run the risk of not knowing His will, understanding His truths, or delighting in His promises. Instead, we can become like ships without anchors, drifting along with changing currents. Like the captain of the Titanic, we can become blind to danger and presumptuous in our quest for success.

The world no longer needs the lonely lighthouse that once led ships through dark nights and coastal reefs. Nor does it want God's absolute truths. To many, the Bible seems as obsolete as that old lighthouse—and far more dangerous to their vision of global peace.

But to those who know Him, His Word shines far brighter than any man-made beacon—lighting our path, keeping us safe, and fixing our hearts on the goal ahead. The Bible says it well, "Which hope we have as an anchor of the soul, both sure and stedfast, and which entereth into that within the veil" (Hebrews 6:19).

What, then, can we do to anchor our children in His unchanging Word? Consider these suggestions:

◊ Pray. For Jesus said, "without me ye can do nothing" (John 15:5).

◊ Understand the nature and tactics of Satan.

◊ Do a Bible study on verses that contrast the New Age version of man (that man is divine and equal to God) and the Bible's description of man (that his heart is sinful, and he needs a Savior).

◊ Memorize some of God's important promises.

◊ Read *The Invisible War* and help your children understand what it means to put on God's armor.

> Be sober, be vigilant; because your adversary the devil,
> as a roaring lion, walketh about, seeking whom he may
> devour. (1 Peter 5:8)

STEP FOUR: USE THIS TEST FOR "CHRISTIAN" MEDIA

TODAY, we are faced with new challenges in protecting our kids from the media available to them. It used to be that we only had to worry about books and movies from the *secular* media, but now we need to also weigh the things children and teens are exposed to by Christian publishers and film producers.

Media labeled as "Christian" can be even more dangerous for children in two ways: First of all, heretofore when we purchased

Christian media, we would expect that these materials could be trusted, but by the day, this is becoming less the case. Secondly, the deception is more subtle. Former New Age follower Warren B. Smith often points out that what makes deception most effective is when you have what is false mixed into a lot of truth.

Oftentimes, you may see the Bible quoted extensively with small portions of false doctrine injected into it; or Bible stories may be utilized where subtle twists are injected into the story that parallels the true account yet alters its meaning and significance.

As parents, teachers, or guardians, the responsibility is now more squarely on our shoulders to review even Christian media presented to our children. Below is a list of things to look for in previewing a "Christian" movie or book. You can use this checklist when you are trying to decide whether something is suitable or not for your child. If your child is age appropriate, go over these points with him or her.

◊ 1) What does it tell you about God?

◊ 2) Is God's holy Word used out of context?

◊ 3) What does it teach about the invisible forces of evil?

◊ 4) Does it demonstrate faith? (What kind? In whom or what?)

◊ 5) Might the imagined scenes stir interest in occultic powers?

◊ 6) Do the heroes in the story use magic?

◊ 7) What does it teach about life and death?

◊ 8) Is there a Christ-like person in the story?

◊ 9) Why would it be called "redemptive"?

◊ 10) What does it teach about good and evil, right and wrong?

21

BECOMING AWARE
OF SPIRITUAL DECEPTION
IN THE CHURCH

Postmodern, or "progressive" culture is a change-or-
be-changed world. The word is out: Reinvent yourself
for the 21st century or die.[1]—**Leonard Sweet,** emerging
church leader

MYSTICAL OCCULTISM AND spiritual deception have always
been around. But what used to be a trickle in the Western world
has now become a tsunami as I believe I have documented in
this book. Even many churches are welcoming the mysteries
that secret societies and Taoist alchemists once hid so well. Most
Westerners raised in a "safe" Christian culture tend to discount
the source of these powers. In fact, many Christians don't really
believe there is such a thing as an esoteric realm and very rarely
think about the topic of spiritual deception. North American
Christians have conveniently shut their eyes to occult realities
that were once marginal because of the influence of Christianity—but now those dark realities are exploding with a vengeance.
And sadly, children are the ones who are being affected the most
by this breach in biblical integrity.

I have tried to show how the New Age/New Spirituality
has affected and is altering our children's lives. I have shown
how children are being bombarded with occultism and New
Age philosophies that are totally contrary to the Word of God
and God's plans for our children.

Countless distortions of God's Word have led to a flood of spiritual deception in the Christian church today. After all, today's more experiential, permissive, and "feel good" lessons are far more compatible with "church growth" and seeker friendly" than the Bible itself. Few realize that the new teaching is made even more deceptive because it is cloaked in the least offensive Christian terminology. And children's lessons are prepared to please the new generation and make sure they return the next week—bringing their friends.

Shaping the Global "Christian" Youth

Kids can change the world . . . right now! So, how do you as an adult inspire these world changers? First, world changers need MENTORS to inspire them. . . . Honor and celebrate the uniqueness of each child. Ask relationship-building questions.[2]—KIDMO

"[T]HE whole world lieth in wickedness," we are told in 1 John 5:19. And leaders in today's world are undermining God's Word just as much as those who despised Christ and His disciples two millennia ago. The fact that their tools and tactics are more sophisticated these days gives us plenty of reasons to heed God's repeated warnings: Be watchful! Pray! Don't be deceived!

The guiding vision of contemporary world leaders was summarized by Professor Raymond Houghton back in 1970. As you ponder his words, remember that the key strategies used in secular schools are now embraced by churches around the world:

[A]bsolute behavior control is imminent. . . . The critical point of behavior control, in effect, is sneaking up on mankind without his self-conscious realization that a crisis is at hand. Man will . . . never self-consciously know that it has happened.[3]

262

The main targets of these change agents have been our children, our youth, and our biblical faith. Have these revolutionaries succeeded? Yes! We are now immersed in the fruit of their labor: a postmodern world that rejects the truth and moral foundations that once shaped faith and freedom.

Like our secular guides, today's emerging, sensual-driven church guides keep sounding the trumpet for continual change. And their captive restless audience—dulled by decades of "progressive education" and corrupt entertainment—is fast falling in line behind the most popular pied pipers.

Little holds them back from the tempting snares that tug at their hearts these days. The greatest obstacle to deception has always been God's unchanging Word. But that wall of resistance is crumbling fast. Today's transformational leaders know their pleasure-loving followers would rather dialogue *about* "biblical principles" in popular movies than study or memorize Scriptures. And such facilitated dialogue is central to this revolution. As Professor Benjamin Bloom ("Father of Outcome-Based Education") wrote back in 1971:

> [A] large part of what we call "good teaching" is the teacher's ability to attain affective objectives through challenging the students' fixed beliefs and getting them to discuss issues.[4]

Bloom was building on the revolutionary foundation laid by Julian Huxley, first head of UNESCO. In his 1946 treatise of the UN agenda, "UNESCO: Its purpose and Its Philosophy," Huxley wrote:

> That task is to help the emergence of a single world culture. . . . And it is necessary, for at the moment two opposing philosophies of life confront each other from the West and from the East. . . . [Can] these opposites be reconciled, this antithesis be resolved in a higher synthesis? . . .

In pursuing this aim, we must eschew [shun] dogma

> [doctrine]—whether it be theological dogma or Marxist dogma . . . East and West will not agree on a basis for the future if they merely hurl at each other the fixed ideas of the past. . . . If we are to achieve progress, we must learn to uncrystallize our dogmas.[5]

Could pastors and other Christian leaders be willing to "uncrystallize" their biblical foundations? Faced with the world's tempting incentives, today's pragmatic leaders are selling their souls for the latest marketing models. For example, "the leading Christian curriculum for kids," and one of the most popular Sunday School programs out there today is the costly KIDMO (which was birthed at Rick Warren's Saddleback Church). Its website emphasizes a unifying "mission," not biblical literacy:

> In order to equip mentors to inspire world changers, your kids need a MISSION. . . . It creates clarity, causes action, and changes perspective.[6]

Changing perspectives is key to this transformation. As Professor Houghton warned decades ago, you won't even "know that it has happened." Compromise becomes the norm as blinded shepherds of God's flocks pursue the latest strategies for "success." The steps below are vital to their unbiblical mission:

◊ Replace solid biblical teaching with feel-good storytelling.

◊ Reinvent our righteous and holy God as a permissive buddy who applauds your goodness.

◊ Keep affirming God's love and understanding; forget His holy standard and judgment.

◊ Trade Bible study (too didactic and divisive) for facilitated group dialogue.

◊ Stress human deeds, not God's doctrine.

◊   Contextualize the Gospel and emphasize unity in diversity.

◊   Tolerate everything except old-fashioned parents, fundamental Christianity, and other obstacles to change.

SQUEEZING PARENTS OUT OF THE PICTURE

WHERE do parents fit into this picture? Mike Yaconelli, the late celebrated founder of the popular emerging church organization Youth Specialties, gave us a clue in his article, "The Problem of Parents":

> What's the biggest obstacle to effective youth ministry? Parents. . . . Why are young people stressed out? Parents. Why are young people obsessed with education, good grades, SAT scores . . . ? Parents. . . . Who supports our ministries until their child has a negative experience, or is disciplined, or is injured, or doesn't like youth group, or the music, or their counselor, or a new sponsor, or the way the youth group is being run? Parents.[7]

Responsible concerned parents have distressed secular change agents as well. That's why Professor John Goodlad, who worked with UNESCO in the 1970s, warned fellow educators that:

> [M]ost youth still hold the same values as their parents. . . . If we do not alter this pattern, if we don't resocialize . . . our society may decay.[8]

> Enlightened social engineering is required to face situations that demand global action now. . . . Parents and the general public must be reached also. Otherwise, children and youth enrolled in globally oriented programs may find themselves in conflict with values assumed in the home.[9]

Megan, a visitor to our website, shows us the results of this anti-parent ideology. "I ran across an article by Mike Yaconelli from Youth Specialties about a week ago," she wrote, "and I was floored by his open disdain for parents and traditional church leadership. But it served to bring to mind my own rebellion, and I began to wonder if his disdain and my experiences in youth group weren't really all that far apart." She continued:

> I began attending a mega-church . . . which has recently strayed into the Emergent Church scene (though they wouldn't admit it). Within one year of attending that church, I was in the beginning stages of rebellion against my parents and against the foundation of God's Word that was instilled in me as a young girl. Two years after becoming an *active* member of the youth group (and in its leadership), I was in full rebellion against everything my parents had taught me as a child.
>
> I thought I was righteous. I thought I was the one who had it right. I thought my parents were legalistic (I HATED the writings of Paul). I thought my parents had too many expectations for me. I thought they weren't really concerned about spreading the Gospel as much as I was. I thought I was on fire for Christ. But I thought wrong . . . and had God not delivered me from that rebellion, I would be lost. Just another product of a youth group much like Mike Yaconelli envisions for every youth group. God help us![10]

I wonder how many children raised in Christian homes have had their faith turned upside down by well-intentioned but misguided youth leaders who have bought into the notion that their "new" kind of Christianity has more to offer kids than the children's own parents.

We parents need to make sure we understand the innerworkings of the New Age/New Spirituality and have a good grasp on avenues of spiritual deception that have come into the church.

And on that foundation, we find out who is teaching our children and what those teachers believe.

SPIRITUAL FORMATION OR SPIRITUAL DECEPTION?

> The Spiritual Formation movement is widely promoted at colleges and seminaries as the latest and the greatest way to become a spiritual leader. It teaches people that this is how they can become more intimate with God and truly hear His voice. Even Christian leaders with longstanding reputations of teaching God's word seem to be succumbing.[11]—**Roger Oakland**

SPIRITUAL Formation has become a widely used term that was introduced to the evangelical church in the 1970s, primarily through a Thomas Merton disciple named Richard Foster and his longstanding, best-selling book, *Celebration of Discipline*. Today, there are few venues in the church that have not been influenced by the Merton/Foster model of Spiritual Formation.

While at first glance the Spiritual Formation movement seems profitable and spiritual at best, harmless and benign at worst, that is only because it has been disguised with Christian language and out-of-context Scriptures all the while making grandiose claims that through Spiritual Formation, you can *really* know God.

In a nutshell, Spiritual Formation teaches that in order for someone to have an intimate relationship with God, he or she needs to practice certain "spiritual disciplines" that will help one to become more Christ-like. Sounds good so far, right?

What many people don't really know, however, is that the driving force behind the Spiritual Formation movement is a mystical prayer technique called contemplative or centering prayer. The Spiritual Formation leaders, such as Richard Foster, Henri Nouwen, and Brennan Manning, have told their followers for years that we must get rid of distractions in our minds or else we cannot hear the voice of God.

In order to reach a state of silence or stillness (where the mind is basically put into neutral), a word or phrase is repeated (or the breath is focused on) and a meditative (altered) state can then be achieved. But while contemplative advocates insist that this is not the same thing as Eastern-style meditation because their intent is different (they repeat *Jesus Jesus*, not *om om*), the results are the same as practicing Transcendental Meditation (TM) and demonic realms are experienced in this silence. One meditation writer explains:

> The meditation of advanced occultists is identical with the prayer of advanced mystics; it is no accident that both traditions use the same word for the highest reaches of their respective activities: contemplation [samadhi in yoga].[12]

That's a little background of the Spiritual Formation (i.e., contemplative prayer) movement. Although the dangers of this mystical spirituality should be obvious to most Christians, it appears this is not the case, and children have not been exempt from the impact. Evangelical youth groups, children's organizations, Sunday School curriculum, books, and so forth are introducing contemplative spirituality (i.e., Spiritual Formation) to children.

For instance, in a book titled, *Perspectives on Children's Spiritual Formation*, Greg Carlson and John Crupper (executive leaders of the Awana's children organization at the time the book was written) praise Richard Foster's contemplative-promoting book *Streams of Living Water*. Carlson and Crupper also say that the contemplative "tradition" is an important contribution to Christians:

> In his excellent overview, *Streams of Living Water*, Richard Foster outlines six different spiritual traditions that are present within the Christian faith. They are the contemplative tradition, the holiness tradition, the charismatic tradition, the social justice tradition, the

evangelical tradition, and the incarnational tradition. Each of these has *played an important part* in the larger history of the Christian church. . . . Each of these traditions has made *significant contributions to Christian spirituality* and each has weaknesses when isolated from other traditions.[13] (Emphasis added.)

When Carlson and Crupper say "weaknesses," they mean they don't have a problem with contemplative as long as it is used in conjunction with other spiritual practices or "traditions." They say that each of these models can learn from the other.[14] Clearly, this gives the green light on contemplative. Carlson and Crupper add:

[W]e would see many of the techniques [from the Contemplative-Model] of teaching as valuable tools for learning . . . the ideas of repetition and routine . . . are important; and we affirm them.[15]

Perspectives on Children's Spiritual Formation identifies some of these "techniques" and "tools" as lectio divina, centering prayer, labyrinths, the Jesus Prayer, and breath prayers, all of which are part of contemplative spirituality.

Incidentally, in one section of the book, it favorably references the Catholic mystic Thomas Merton, who once said that he "intend[ed] to become as good a Buddhist"[16] as he could and that he "was impregnated with Sufism."[17] Merton never hid his admiration for Eastern-style meditation or his panentheistic beliefs (that God was in all humanity). For Awana leadership to co-author a book that speaks highly of Thomas Merton, shows little discernment or understanding.

Even though Carlson and Crupper are no longer in executive leadership roles with Awana, the book is still on the market today. Plus, Awana is referred to several times in the book so someone reading it would believe that Awana itself has given an OK to contemplative.

While it is troubling to see this kind of pass on contemplative spirituality by Awana leadership, calling it a "significant contribution" that has "played an important part" in the church, I believe there are many local Awana leaders who are not compromising their teachings and are staying true to God's Word. Perhaps they will be the ones to help Awana stay on the right path.

One Christian group that has pushed contemplative spirituality onto children is NavPress. In one issue of their *PrayKids!* publication, an article titled, "Contemplative Prayer" states:

> Contemplative prayer is a form of meditative prayer that focuses on communing with God. Although sometimes confused with its Eastern (and non-Christian) counterpart, true Christian meditation has been practiced since Bible times.
>
> This issue of *PrayKids!* helps kids learn to slow down their fast-paced lives long enough to experience a meaningful relational encounter with their Heavenly Father.[18]

In one feature article in *Pray!*, "Empowering Kids to Pray," Brad Jersak is referenced in relation to kids and prayer. Jersak's book, *Stricken by God* (endorsed by emergent church figure Brian McLaren) is a compilation of essays by various authors including Eastern-style meditation proponents Richard Rohr and Marcus Borg. Borg rejects basic foundational tenets of Christian doctrine (such as the virgin birth of Christ and the atonement),[19] and Rohr is a panentheistic Catholic priest who embraces interspirituality and mysticism.

Considering that NavPress, the publishing arm of the Navigators, has a publication for children specifically to teach children contemplative prayer illustrates how integrated the New Spirituality has become within Christianity. Children in the church are being targeted. This is tragic—church is supposed to be one of the safest places for our children.

And it doesn't get better as they get older. Unaware parents who are anticipating their children attending "good" Christian colleges when they are old enough may be very surprised and rudely awakened to find that Spiritual Formation has now entered almost every accredited Christian college, seminary, and university. Lighthouse Trails (the publisher of this book) has been following this trend for over eleven years now and has discovered that some of the top accreditation associations for Christian schools are requiring Spiritual Formation programs to be implemented in schools now before they can be accredited![20] Students in Christian colleges are now being required to study the works of Henri Nouwen and Richard Foster and to take practicum courses in contemplative and centering prayer where they may be required to practice contemplative prayer for a passing grade.

Pray for discernment and guidance, and use the ideas on how to protect your children from spiritual deception that I have laid out in this book to make sure your child is equipped and "armored" to face what is now so prevalent in evangelical/Protestant Christianity.

TRAINING TOMORROW'S WORLD CHANGERS

CONTRARY to biblical guidelines, the church and the world now share a common goal: to train today's youth to lead tomorrow's pluralistic world. Both the church and the world are handpicking their most promising leaders—those who avidly pursue the "right" vision and the evolving global mission. I have even met some of them at United Nations conferences and Mikhail Gorbachev's State of the World Forums. Those "chosen" teens from diverse nations were led through the dialectic process to synthesize opposing views and embrace an evolving, preplanned consensus. They were trained to think, speak, and act as citizens of a collective global village.

Many of those "chosen" youth believed in God but doubted the Bible. They believed in personal truths but rejected God's absolute Truth. They believed in a Christ but not in our Savior.

271

They loved the creation but denied the Creator. As Harvard student Bill Burke-White reported during Gorbachev's 1996 Forum:

> We have spent this week re-imagining and re-envisioning the world we have inherited. . . . Just a few short steps from your meeting rooms this week there is a community of youth who were born into the global village. . . . This is a community that will not tolerate the continued ecological devastation of the sacred landscape of our home . . . [and] that has no tolerance for dogmatism and fundamentalism.

> This community needs to learn about the new paradigm or to unlearn the old—we were born into an awakening Earth. . . . Imagine, if you will, a world which has realized the Youth summit's vision of building a Global Youth Alliance, a planet-wide conversation, an interlinking, a networking of the many youth organizations that share these heart-felt visions.[21]

"Unlearning the old" ways is key to the global transformation. And its pied pipers are "V for vendetta" determined to break the old ties and restraints, whatever it takes. Like the Phoenix rising up from its own ashes, the new world must rise above the old beliefs and values. Their arguments sound good and noble—almost Christian—to those who never learned to love God's true and living Word. Notice the logical progression from untrue assumptions (#1) to mainstream deceptions (#3):

1. Global peace demands global oneness. Therefore all must follow the global guidelines to unity.

2. Global unity demands collective thinking. Therefore all must participate in small group dialogue.

3. Dialogue and consensus require respect for diversity and synthesis of opposites. Therefore resisters and their divisive Truth must be silenced.

This transformation is kicking into high gear. Those who simply go with the flow of this "revolution" will find acceptance, while those who passionately pursue "progress" will probably become tomorrow's leaders. But concerned resisters will be forced to come face to face with having to make some incredibly hard choices.

Remember these exhortations from God's Word, bury them in your heart, and teach them to your children. Pray that they will also bury the Word deep within their own hearts:

> If ye were of the world, the world would love his own: but because ye are not of the world, but I have chosen you out of the world, therefore the world hateth you. If they have persecuted me, they will also persecute you . . . because they know not him that sent me. (John 15:19-21)

> But none of these things move me, neither count I my life dear unto myself, so that I might finish my course with joy, and the ministry, which I have received of the Lord Jesus, to testify the gospel of the grace of God. (Acts 20:24)

PUTTING "CHRISTIAN" FICTION TO THE TEST

> In recent years, fiction aimed at Christians has exploded in the marketplace. Reading it used to be a more or less reliable escape. But nowadays popular authors in that marketplace are emphasizing more and more of those disturbing elements that once were relegated to pagan, occult, or secular novels.[22]—**Richard and Linda Nathan,** authors, researchers of the New Age

You can see that deception comes in all shapes and sizes. While there is certainly some worthy Christian fiction for children and youth, much of it classified as "Christian" is not. *Shadowmancer,* written by Anglican minister Graham Peter (G.P.) Taylor, is an allegorical novel for teens about the battle between good and evil.

It has been translated into 48 languages and was on the *New York Times* best-sellers list. In reading *Shadowmancer*, I discovered that while the "good" may win the spiritual battle in the story, I believe for many readers, the "evil" will implant stronger memories.

Though marketed to ages twelve and up, *Shadowmancer* is readily available to younger fans. In fact, the likeable Reverend Taylor is described as a "best-selling children's author."[23] Naturally, many parents may wonder what kind of message this "tale of sorcery and fantasy" communicates to their children. Is it a redemptive story, or does it fuel today's growing fascination with occult thrills, magical forces, and corrupt spiritual masters?

What about its "Christian themes"?[24] Do they justify the dark and scary scenes that make it so popular among adults as well as teens? Or do they—like the counterfeit truths taught by various adaptations of Christianity—make deception all the more believable? And, is it right to expose our children to the forbidden fruit of dark forces that have such addictive appeal to human nature? As one reader said:

> I decided on reading *Shadowmancer* because of the hype that it was receiving in Christian circles. Being the Christian that I am, I was very excited about a book that combined a spiritual otherworldly subject matter with an adventure story set in a very exotic and fascinating world of 1800 England.[25]

In this fast-paced story, three brave teenagers conquer overwhelming occult forces because they supposedly trust the biblical God! Here's a glimpse of the thrilling battle from its publisher's perspective:

> Vicar Obadiah Demurral isn't satisfied running the affairs of his village—he foolishly wants to control the world. And if his plan works, he will obtain a weapon so powerful that all of creation will fall down at his feet. . . .

> Who will stand against him? Raphah, a young man on
> a godly mission, has come a long distance to reclaim
> the ancient relic Demurral has stolen—dangerously
> volatile in the wrong hands—but he can't do it alone.[26]

Published in the U.S. by Charisma House (Strang Communications), *Shadowmancer* gained a quick entrance into Christian bookstores and websites.

Some argue that this "Christian version" of Harry Potter brings the Gospel to children who wouldn't think of opening a Bible. Wouldn't such outreach justify its scary images? Can't the good overshadow the evil? Besides, it's just fiction! Can't an author freely adjust truth and historical facts to fit his story?

Well, possibly. But can such a story be trusted as a Christian book? A "Christian book" can't deviate from the truth. It can't reinvent God and spiritual warfare without misleading readers and distorting their understanding of our Lord and His Word. In light of today's tendency to blend "soft" seeker-friendly Christian messages with multicultural pragmatism—those misconceptions may never be corrected. As Christian researcher and author Mike Oppenheimer warns:

> We are watching a metamorphosis take place inside the
> church at large. Some call it a movement of positive
> alternatives to doing church; others see it as a trend.
> What we see is many moving from a biblical emphasis
> to anecdotal storytelling and experimenting with new
> methods invented by men.[27]

As biblical literacy fades, we see the rising tolerance toward occult philosophies, pagan practices, gender diversity, illicit sex, and twisted truths in churches as well as culture. Books that popularize Christianity by adapting it to tantalizing tales only fuel this process.

In this compromising atmosphere, it's not easy to provide convincing reasons to mistrust a book that has some good points.

Take some time and use the questions at the end of chapter 19 to see how *Shadowmancer* (or any "Christian" book or film) lines up with the Word of God and His truths.

Remember, just because something is called "Christian" doesn't mean it has biblical integrity and Christian values. We parents cannot assume; rather we must test, pray, and use our God-given wisdom to effectively protect our children.

As the Bible warns us:

> For the time will come when they will not endure sound doctrine; but after their own lusts shall they heap to themselves teachers, having itching ears; And they shall turn away their ears from the truth, and shall be turned unto fables. But watch thou in all things. (2 Timothy 4:3-5)

"Progressive" Christianity—A Glimpse into the Next Generation

Today's "progressive" emerging churches have little love for the old certainties that have grounded genuine Christians in God's revealed truth for almost 2000 years. They say those precious guidelines don't fit the new dialectic and collective ways of thinking. Today's entertainment-driven Christians prefer "feel good" assurances stripped of unwanted references to sin, guilt, or moral boundaries.

In other words, the old delight in a personal relationship with Jesus Christ as Savior and Lord is being replaced with a new emphasis on one's relationship to the group or "collective." Many flock to the "emerging" or "postmodern" churches that have expanded their positive message far beyond the old biblical "box."

Consequently, many churches simply ignore the reality of our omnipotent, all-powerful Savior and King. Such almighty power and authority simply doesn't fit our times. Too many self-proclaiming Christians are happy to trade His eternal Word for ever-changing truths that match the permissive god of their subjective imagination. "We're on a journey," they say, "So nothing can be set in stone." Always changing, always transforming!

With biblical doctrine set aside, there is no longer a sure anchor for discernment, leaving parents "tossed to and fro, and carried about with every wind of doctrine" (Ephesians 4:14) and their children without a foundation for their lives. Meanwhile, pastors, teachers, and popular Christian leaders keep writing books that promote rebellion against Him. For example, popular author and pastor Brian McLaren has openly rejected, even mocked, the major tenets of the Christian faith. In a 2006 radio interview, he told listeners that the doctrine of Hell is "false advertising for God."[28] To him and many others, there is no need for the Cross as a substitutionary death and an atonement for sin.

McLaren's award-winning book, *A New Kind of Christian*, is written as a semi-fictional dialogue, so that readers can experience the thrill of questioning old truths and discovering new truth through the dialectic process. Notice how the introduction touts the postmodern worldview while raising doubts about biblical faith:

> I realize, as I read and reread the Bible, that many passages don't fit any of the theological systems I have inherited or adapted. Sure, they can be squeezed in, but after a while my theology looks like a high school class trip's luggage—shoestrings hanging out here, zippers splitting apart there. . . .
>
> I read what other people who are having similar experiences are saying, including people writing outside of the religious context—like this from [Buddhist sympathizer] Peter Senge: "In any case, our Industrial Age management. . . . our Industrial Age way of living will not continue. . . . It's not sustainable in ecological terms, and it's not sustainable in human terms. It will change. The only question is how. . . ."

I meet people along the way who model for me, each in a different way, what a new kind of Christian might look like. They differ in many ways, but they generally agree that *the old show is over*, the modern jig is up, and *it's time for something radically new*.[29] (Emphasis added.)

McLaren sounds strikingly similar to New Age teacher Barbara Marx Hubbard when she says, "The old play is almost over" (see page 142). Hubbard believes there will be a "selection process" that will somehow eliminate those who are slowing down the New Age (Age of Enlightenment) plan. Could Brian McLaren's emerging church fall into lockstep with New Agers who believe biblical "dogmatic" Christians are the world's enemy? Very possibly. The New Age and the emerging church both promote a false exalted view of man and a diminished view of Christ's atonement.

Many evangelical leaders helped to bring Brian McLaren's dream for a "radically new" Christianity to the forefront.

Rick Warren was one of those who recommended McLaren on his original pastors.com website.[30] And in emerging figure Dan Kimball's book, *The Emerging Church*, Rick Warren and Brian McLaren shared the spot of writing forewords for the book, giving the impression that they were in unison regarding the emerging church. Bill Hybels of Willow Creek often included McLaren in his leadership conferences.

While these Christian leaders later distanced themselves from Brian McLaren, the indispensible role they played in helping to launch him into fame was undoubtedly significant. In the year 2000, practically no one had heard of Brian McLaren; by 2005, *Time* magazine named him one of the top 25 most influential evangelicals in America![31] That influence continues to this day.

How does all this relate to our children? Brian McLaren gives us a glimpse in his book, *Finding Our Way Again: the Return of the Ancient Practices.* He explains that the emerging church must infiltrate the very "institutions that rejected it,"[32] saying:

> [O]ver time, what they reject will find or create safe
> space outside their borders and become a resource so
> that many if not most of *the grandchildren of today's
> fundamentalists* will learn and grow and move on
> from the *misguided* battles of their forebears [biblical
> believers].[33] (emphasis added)

In other words, what Brian McLaren is predicting is that
our children and grandchildren will move away from the biblical
truths we have instilled in them. Rick Warren once said that the
older traditional Christians will have to leave the churches or die
because they won't change,[34] thus the emphasis in the emerging
church is on the youth.

What's alarming is that Brian McLaren's vision of infiltration
is working. McLaren expresses his high hopes:

> At the center, safe space happens. A learning community
> forms. New possibilities emerge. A new day dawns. If
> the guardians of our fragmented religious institutions
> forbid their members to meet in the center, the
> members will not be able to comply. They will simply
> go undercover [talking about emerging figures] and
> arrange secret liaisons . . . Eventually, the shared
> resources, vitality, and new possibilities that unfold . . .
> will penetrate and reinvigorate . . . Trying to stop [this
> is] a losing game.[35]

There is an agenda that is after the minds of our children and
grandchildren! And it is disguised in seemingly Christian vernacular.

Our children and grandchildren stand in the wake of this
spreading deception. If they are not prepared and equipped to
follow God and take a stand, they may yield their hearts to this
process with little or no resistance.

Never before have our children been surrounded by so many
spiritual counterfeits, seductive suggestions, and occult imagery

279

and precepts. And never before has the Christian community been *less* prepared to resist a spiritual assault on the bride of Christ.

It's up to us as parents and grandparents to teach our children and grandchildren to stand strong against these deceptions, put on the whole armor of God (remember chapter two), and walk by the light God has given us through His Word. We can't trust church personnel, Sunday school teachers, or youth pastors to fulfill *our* God-given assignment. But when we do trust God and when we prepare our own hearts, teach His Word, and train our children to follow His narrow way, we will experience a kind of fellowship in our families that far exceeds the fleeting, deceptive fun that the world offers.

During the last three centuries, while there have always been some who were involved in the occult, North Americans have, for the most part, enjoyed relative freedom from the occult forces that have tormented so many other parts of the world. The pilgrims and a significant number of other believers trusted God and played a huge role in helping to build a foundation on biblical and moral standards. And God protected this land, so that few were exposed to words and actions that led to the occult.

Today's emerging world system has called for an unbiblical peace (a global peace that does not include Christ) and a pre-scribed form of solidarity that has little tolerance for Christians who refuse to compromise. Yet, if we continue in the faith and in trusting Jesus Christ, our Savior and Lord, He promises never to leave us, and He will surely meet all our needs according to His will. Those who resist the world's tempting lies in His name will be safe in Him—now and forever!

If we remain firm in our faith, we offer the next generation (our children and grandchildren) a heritage they can carry forth into the future. We need to pass the torch of faith and truth on to them. When Paul and Silas were asked by the jailer, "What must I do to be saved?" they replied, "Believe on the Lord Jesus Christ, and thou shalt be saved, and thy house" (Acts 16:30-31). And although this was not an unequivocal statement that we can automatically pass our faith onto our children, Christian parents need to realize and be encouraged by the fact that our faith, if it is firmly rooted in the Gospel and His Word, has the potential of having a profound effect on the next generation. So, while wolves in sheep's clothing have come out of the woodwork from both the secular and the professing Christian realms and have invaded the fold, let us be all the more diligent in our efforts to pave the way for our children's future—a future where they can be well-equipped with spiritual armor to face the various trials and testings of their faith and tribulations that are to come.

This world system denies the message of the Cross and gravitates more and more toward an interreligious global body. That is becoming more apparent and self-evident with each passing day for now laws have been put into place demanding that even the name of Jesus be banned from all kinds of public places. But we must remain vigilant and steadfast in the faith once delivered to the saints! What Jesus prayed to His Father almost 2000 years ago is now His message for us:

I pray not that thou shouldest take them out of the world, but that thou shouldest keep them from the evil. They are not of the world, even as I am not of the world. Sanctify them through thy truth: thy word is truth. As thou hast sent me into the world, even so have I also sent them into the world.—Jesus (John 17:15-18)

AFTERWORD:
THE FIRST &
FINAL DECEPTION

ALEISTER CROWLEY WAS called "the most evil man in the world." This founder of the Hermetic Order of the Golden Dawn defined magic as "the science and art of causing change to occur at will."[1]

Whose will?

Not God's! The following occult statement describes one of the most devious traps set by the evil one since the beginning of time:

> [U]nless you make yourself equal to God, you cannot understand God: for the like is not intelligible save to the like. . . . Believe that nothing is impossible for you. . . . Mount higher than the highest height; descend lower than the lowest depth. Draw into yourself all sensations of everything created, fire and water, dry and moist, imagining that you are everywhere, on earth, in the sea, in the sky.[2]

Remember what the serpent said to Eve in the garden after tempting her to eat the forbidden fruit:

> Ye shall not surely die: For God doth know that in the day ye eat thereof, then your eyes shall be opened, and ye shall be as gods, knowing good and evil. (Genesis 3:4-5)

It was a devious lie! Instead of making her like God, her sin banished her from His presence. By "knowing . . . evil" experientially, she became an unholy creature who could no longer walk in the presence of our holy God! Satan's lofty promise was actually a deadly trap!

Yet it supports what children are taught in schools, youth organizations, and many churches. In this fantasy world, it makes sense for opposing sides—good and evil—to join hands in perfect harmony. Like the dialectic process that "frees" group members from biblical authority and values, Satan's devious message promotes an arrogance that matches the Old Testament description of Lucifer who said in his heart: "I will ascend into heaven, I will exalt my throne above the stars of God. . . . I will be like the Most High" (Isaiah 14:13-14).

If we choose "other gods" and yield to Satan's temptations, we will surely face consequences. Ponder these warnings:

> [They] walked in the counsels and in the imagination of their evil heart. (Jeremiah 7:24)

> But every man is tempted, when he is drawn away of his own lust, and enticed. Then when lust hath conceived, it bringeth forth sin: and sin, when it is finished, bringeth forth death. (James 1:14-15)

> And as it was in the days of [Noah], so shall it be also in the days of the Son of man. (Luke 17:26)

And what was it like "in the days of Noah"?

> And God saw that the wickedness of man was great in the earth, and that every imagination of the thoughts of his heart was only evil continually. . . . The earth also was corrupt before God, and the earth was filled with violence. (Genesis 6:5, 11)

A vivid memory that happened several years ago sticks in my mind like it was yesterday—I was walking down a sidewalk when suddenly I was standing in front of an assortment of Ghostbusters, Teenage Mutant Ninja Turtles, Supernaturals—an exotic collection of action figures and accessories lay scattered on the ground outside a Boston apartment. Four-year-old Jimmy, their proud owner, smiled a welcome as I stopped to watch him play.

"Which do you like best?" I asked.

"Rock-N-Roll Michaelangelo," he answered, pointing to one of the black-belted Ninja Turtles.

As we discussed Michaelangelo and the two snakes he carried as weapons, I noticed an interesting book cover.

"May I see your book?"

"Sure. It's *Nanny Noony and the Magic Spell.*"

I opened it and read a few paragraphs. "It looks like Nanny Noony put a hex on the farm," I said.

"But she didn't really do it," protested Jimmy. "She's a good witch. She just makes potions to undo bad hexes."

Jimmy's mother, who had been listening, asked me a few questions. When she learned that I was writing about the New Age, she announced that she was a Christian. But she liked spirit-guide Seth's messages better than the Bible.

She went inside and returned with three paperbacks. "Here's what I believe," she said, handing them to me. Penned by the late trance-channeler Jane Roberts, they were filled with messages from the prolific Seth, who first "spoke" to his human medium through a Ouija Board.

Soon I was sitting in her living room surrounded by New Age literature: Seth material, a magazine called *Mothering*, two books about Edgar Cayce's channeled revelations, and *The Aquarian Gospel of the Christ.* The last of these, written like a Bible but presenting distortions of God's truth, fills Jesus' "missing years" with New Age "insights"—at the feet of "higher Masters" in India, Persia, and Egypt.

What messages do these and other spirit guides like Ramtha (who has about 35,000 followers), Lazaris, Carl Jung's Philemon, and thousands of Higher Selves bring? *You can be God! Just believe in your divinity, create your own reality, and build a new world of light and love.*

Jimmy's home is tragically representative of the growing number of households, including the homes of many professing Christians, who have opened their doors to counterfeit gods. While millions have studied Seth's teachings, thousands of amateur spiritists have learned to channel their own spirit guides. The reports of terrifying encounters with evil spirits fade in the optimism of infinite possibilities.

Unfortunately, what we are experiencing today is a synthesis of the "I am God" ideology and accelerating occult activity. In fact, the two are inextricably linked together in that they have the same source—the demonic realm. Aleister Crowley, who promoted the ancient occult maxim "as above, so below" (i.e., man and creation are equal to God and the heavenly realms), also mobilized the youth of the hippie era with his own maxim, "Do what thou wilt" as being the whole of the law.

This maxim was then propagated to the mass youth of the sixties with the expression, "Do your own thing." Today, we have a similar onslaught from Hell that is destined to be even more devastating to children and teens as they attempt to incorporate their notion of divinity within by practicing "divine powers," all the while being caught in the web of self, pride, deceit, and occult manifestations.

As this new edition of my book was being prepared for press, on December 14th, 2012 a horrific event took place in America. A young tormented demonized man walked into an elementary school in Connecticut and shot and killed twenty children, six adults, then himself. It shocked and shook the nation. Less than twenty-four hours after the event, President Barak Obama, and others in government, raised the gun control issue, believing that if there is enough gun control, such atrocities wouldn't happen.

Tragically, what most do not realize is that we have turned this country into an esoteric New Age society, and the "fruit" of it is rearing its ugly grotesque face more now than ever. And these violent crimes committed by young people are only going to increase, especially if most people don't realize what the true source of such incredible violence is.

What should Christian families do? Should we hide ourselves and our loved ones from the world's charms and ills, or should we shine our light, work while it is day, and speak the truth in love and in boldness?

Of course, even if we wanted to, we really couldn't hide. And though we heed God's call to pray, study His Word, love one another in Christ, and reach out to the lost, we still can't stop today's rapid spread of evil. Yet Christian families can make a huge difference in the lives of untold numbers of seekers, if we let God use us to spread His light in a world growing darker by the minute.

We need to show our children how to be in the world but not of the world. We can be God's ambassadors in an increasingly corrupt land, but we cannot allow its darkness to quench His light in us. We can demonstrate God's concern for the poor, but we can't compromise with a counterfeit social gospel and New Age solutions.

Let us pray that He fill us with His wisdom, compassion, patience, and love. And may God bless you as you work to accomplish His will at home with your own children and grandchildren.

As ye have therefore received Christ Jesus the Lord, so walk ye in him: Rooted and built up in him, and stablished in the faith, as ye have been taught, abounding therein with thanksgiving. (Colossians 2:6-7)

APPENDIX

LEADING YOUR CHILD TO
RECEIVE JESUS AS SAVIOR AND LORD

Jesus answered, Verily, verily, I say unto thee, Except a man be born of water and of the Spirit, he cannot enter into the kingdom of God. That which is born of the flesh is flesh; and that which is born of the Spirit is spirit. Marvel not that I said unto thee, Ye must be born again. (John 3:5-7)

HOW DO WE lead our children into a lasting and true relationship with Jesus Christ?

• Pray that God will prepare their hearts. Spiritual rebirth is God's work, not ours (John 6:44). We merely cooperate with God's process for we are co-laborers with God.

• **Lay a foundation.** Include Jesus in your conversations. Let your children hear you talk to Him. Pray with them. Talk about how He helps you each day. Make comments like, "Jesus understands. He is sad when you are sad. Let's ask Jesus what He wants us to do."

• **Wait for God's timing.** While you watch for signs of openness, be ready for an opportune moment. Perhaps it will come at a time of special need for comfort and strength. Or when a child shows you by his questions that he genuinely wants to know and follow God.

Explain the basic saving truths. Lead your child through the following steps, and then ask if he wants to pray to receive Jesus. If he says no, tell him he can pray that prayer anytime on his own with the same wonderful results. If your child wants to pray alone, suggest that he come and tell you afterward. Don't forget the date. Keep it as a most special birthday. Here are some key points to share with your child:

- **God loves you.** He wants you to be part of His special family. He wants you to live with Him in His invisible kingdom. "Suffer little children to come unto me, and forbid them not: for of such is the kingdom of God" (Luke 18:16).

- **By yourself, you can't come to God.** God is holy and perfect and can't let any sin into His kingdom. Sin separates us from Him (Isaiah 59:2). "For all have sinned, and come short of the glory of God" (Romans 3:23). Think about the different kinds of sin like selfishness, envy, lying, wanting your own way. Can you be completely free from them? No, you can't, despite how hard you try.

- **Jesus made a way for you.** He said, "I am the way. . . . no man cometh unto the Father, but by me" (John 14:6). He died on the Cross, taking the punishment for your sins. "For God so loved the world, that he gave his only begotten Son, that whosoever believeth in him should not perish, but have everlasting life" (John 3:16).

- **You must invite Jesus to come and live in you.** "But as many as received him, to them gave he power to become the sons of God, even to them that believe on his name" (John 1:12). With His perfect life inside, you may live and walk with God forever.

Tell your child that his prayer must include confession (understanding and admitting he or she is a sinner), repentance (turn from the direction one is heading, and follow Jesus), faith (trust that Jesus Christ died and rose again to give man eternal life in Him), and the invitation.

Pray something like this: "Dear Jesus, I know I am a sinner, and I have sinned against You. I don't deserve to be Your child. But I believe You died for me to pay for my sins, and you have forgiven me. Please come into my heart. I want you to be Lord and Savior of my life. Thank you."

ACKNOWLEDGEMENTS

What a wonderful Lord we serve!

I thank Him for opening my heart to Him and revealing the forces of darkness that are permeating today's schools, media, popular entertainment, and even churches—thus training countless children to love alluring deceptions more than His unchanging Truth.

I thank Him for the wise and discerning work of the editors at Lighthouse Trails Publishing.

I thank Him for my kind and patient husband who has supported me in this venture.

And I thank Him most of all for the joy of fellowship we share through our Savior and King—our best Friend and beloved Shepherd—today, tomorrow, and forever.

ENDNOTES

Chapter 1—Children At Risk!

1. Patricia Leigh Brown, "In the Classroom, a New Focus on Quieting the Mind" (*The New York Times*, June 16, 2007, http://www.nytimes.com/2007/06/16/us/16mindful.html?pagewanted=all&_r=1&).

2. This conclusion was shared at a Christian Writers Conference, which I attended in the early nineties, soon after my books *Your Child and the New Age* and *Under the Spell of Mother Earth* had been published. Both books were selling briskly, but others who shared my concerns would have little opportunity to share their messages through Christian publishers. Apparently they found little interest among Christians for such warnings. Robin Evans, "Spiritual awakenings: "Young Children Learn the Rituals of Their Parents' Religions (*San Jose Mercury*, February 2, 2005, http://www.rcevans.me/kidsFaith.html).

3. Lori Anderson, "Indigo: The Color of Money" (http://selectsmart.com/twyman.html).

4. Amazon's IMDB movie site: http://www.imdb.com/title/tt0379322.

5. Wendy H. Chapman, "What's an Indigo Child?" (Metagifted, http://www.metagifted.org/topics/metagifted/indigo).

6. "Independent film, 'Indigo' premieres in two local screenings," (*Bozeman Daily Chronicle*, January 27, 2005, http://www.bozemandailychronicle.com/go/article_764a2f6e-c406-5dca-a150-70b1184c114d.html). Excerpt: "More than 90,000 people will view 'Indigo' during the two-day event. For the 60 million Americans who consider themselves 'spiritual' but not necessarily 'religious,' a new genre of film is rapidly emerging—films with heart and soul—called 'spiritual cinema.'"

7. Sharon Jayson, "Does the Science Fly?" (*USA Today*, May

31, 2005, http://usatoday30.usatoday.com/news/religion/2005-05-31-indigo-kids_x.htm).

8. Patricia Leigh Brown, "In the Classroom, a New Focus on Quieting the Mind," op. cit.

9. Ibid.

Chapter 3—Schools & the War on Christianity

1. Information together with copies of a letter and a memorandum to Ken Roberts from the principal were distributed by Beverly LaHaye, Concerned Women of America, January 1989.

2. Therese Iknoian, "Teachers' Lesson in Self-Esteem" (*San Jose Mercury News*, October 12, 1988).

3. Told by a parent in Palo Alto, California.

4. The term "beautiful side of evil" is from Johanna Michaelsen's book by the same name (Harvest House Publishers, 1982), currently out of print, but used copies can be purchased on the Internet.

5. John Dunphy, "A Religion for a New Age" (*The Humanist*, January/ February 1983), p. 26.

6. "The Humanist Manifesto I" (1933)—the first public declaration of the views and objectives of humanism—rejected God and His values, but affirmed humanist faith in the power and evolution of man. (See: http://www.americanhumanist.org/Humanism/Humanist_Manifesto_I.) "The Humanist Manifesto II" (1973) reaffirmed and amplified this man-centered, relativistic, utopian belief-system.

7. Bill Sidebottom, "This Teacher's Union Agenda Has Little to Do with Education" (*Citizen*, September 1988), pp. 10—11.

8. Paul C. Vitz, *Censorship—Evidence of Bias in Our Children's Textbooks* (Ann Arbor, MI: Servant Books, 1986), pp. 3—4, 18—19.

9. Ibid.

10. Mel and Norma Gabler, *What Are They Teaching Our Children?* (Wheaton, IL: Victor Books, 1985), p. 38.

11. Geoffrey Botkin, *The Guiding Hand* (American Portrait Films, 1992).

12. Ibid. Quoting Ellen Gilchrist, author of *In the Land of Dreamy Dreams*, quoted by a student.

13. Kurt Lewin, "Group Decision and Social Change" at: www.

crossroad.to/Quotes/brainwashing/kurt-lewin-change.htm.

14. *The Guiding Hand,* op. cit.

15. Ibid.

16. Ibid.

17. Ibid.

18. David Krathwohl, Benjamin Bloom, Bertram Massia, *Taxonomy of Educational Objectives, The Classification of Educational Goals, Affective Goals* (New York, NY: David McKay Publishers, 1956), p. 55.

19. Ibid., p. 88.

20. *The Guiding Hand*, op. cit.

21. "Obama Would Curtail Summer Vacation" (*Associated Press*, http://www.nbcnews.com/id/33044676.

22. All of the quotes in these numbers sections are from *The Guiding Hand*, op. cit.

23. Berit Kjos, "The Transformation of America" (http://www. crossroad.to/charts/paradigm-shift.htm).

24. *The Guiding Hand*, op. cit.

25. "3rd Caltrain Teen Suicide Spurs Action" (August 24, 2009, http://cbs5.com/local/caltrain.teenager.suicide.2.1141695.html). or use this: Sarah Netter, "Teen Train Suicide Cluster Shakes Affluent California Town" (*ABC News*, October 21, 2009, http:// abcnews.go.com/US/palo-alto-struggles-rash-teen-train-suicides/ story?id=8881813).

26. Dick Stutphen, "Infiltrating the New Age into Society" (*What Is?*, magazine, Summer 1986, Vol. 1, No. 1), p. 14.

27. Deborah Rozman, *Meditating with Children* (Boulder Creek, CA: University of the Trees Press, 1975), p. v.

28. Ibid.

29. Ibid., p. 32.

30. Ibid., p. 96.

31. Ibid., p. 42.

32. Ibid., p. 115.

33. Ibid., p. 146.

34. Shirley Correll, "Quieting Reflex and Guided Imagery: Education for the New Age" (Pro-Family Forum Alert, September 1985), p. 5.

35. Mel and Norma Gabler, *What Are They Teaching Our Children?*, op. cit. p. 39, citing *People of the World, Teacher Tactics, Scott Foresman Spectra Program* (Scott Foresman and Company, 1975), p. 50.

36. Told by a high school student in Mountain View, California.

37. Ibid.

38. Mary Ann Collins, "Is This America?" (Kjos Ministries, October 24, 2007, http://www.crossroad.to/articles2/007/america-4.htm), part 4; information from David Limbaugh, *Persecution: How Liberals Are Waging War against Christianity* (Washington, DC: Regnery Press, 2003), pp. 84-85.

39. Ibid, information from Limbaugh, pp. 81-82.

40. Nanci des Gerlaise, *Muddy Waters* (Eureka, MT: Lighthouse Trails Publishing, 2012, 2nd Expanded Edition), p. 82.

Chapter 4: What Can Parents Do About the War on Christianity?

1. Cyndie Huntington and Nita Scoggan, *Combat Handbook for Parents with Children in Public Schools* (Manassas, VA: Royalty Publishing Company, 1988), pp. 9-10.

2. Protection of Pupils Rights—the Hatch Amendment (http://www.learn-usa.com/relevant_to_et/pr002.htm).

3. Family Educational Rights and Privacy Act (FERPA) (http://www2.ed.gov/policy/gen/guid/fpco/ferpa/index.html).

4. Patrick Crough, *Seducers Among Our Children* (Eureka, MT: Lighthouse Trails Publishing, 2012), p. 195.

Chapter 5: Schools & the Promotion of Corrupting Values

1. Phyllis Schlafly, *Child Abuse in the Classroom* (Westchester, IL: Crossway Books, 1988), p. 195.

2. Ibid., p. 146.

3. Margaret Sanger, *The Pivot of Civilization* (New York, NY: Brentano's Publishers, 1922), p. 271.

4. Humanist Manifesto II (http://www.americanhumanist.org/Humanism/Humanist_Manifesto_II).

5. William Glasser, M.D., *Schools Without Failure* (New York, NY: Harper & Row, 1969), back cover.

6. Ibid., p. 161.

7. Sidney B. Simon, Leland W. Howe, and Howard Kirschenbaum, *Values Clarification—A Handbook of Practical Strategies for Teach-*

ers and Students (New York, NY: Hart Publishing Co., 1972), p. 38.

8. Ibid., pp. 39, 41—46.

9. Ibid., pp. 49, 54.

10. Phyllis Schlafly, *Child Abuse in the Classroom,* op. cit., p. 57.

11. Ibid., pp. 45—46.

12. Richard A. Baer, Jr., "Teaching Values in the Schools: Clarification or Indoctrination?" American Education (January 1982, https://confluence.cornell.edu/download/attachments/11542/Teaching_Values_in_the_Schools.pdf?version=1&modificationDate=1338225531000), p. 11.

13. Phyllis Schlafly, *Child Abuse in the Classroom,* op. cit., pp. 156—157.

14. Ibid., p. 126.

15. Ibid., pp. 83—84.

16. Ibid., p. 27.

17. Ibid., p. 34.

18. Ibid., p. 137.

19. Dr. Robert Shnonds, *As the Twig Is Bent* (Costa Mesa, CA: Citizens for Excellence in Education, 1984), p. 40; citing Sidney Simon, "Sexuality in School" (Colloquy, May 1970).

20. Simon, Howe, and Kirschenbaum, *Values Clarification—A Handbook of Practical Strategies for Teachers and Students*, op. cit., p. 119.

21. Richard A. Baer, Jr., "Teaching Values in the Schools: Clarification or Indoctrination?," op. cit., p. 21.

22. Ibid.

23. Compiled and edited by SIECUS, *Sexuality and Man* (New York NY: Charles Scribner's Sons, 1970), p. 130 by Lester Kirkendall.

24. Ruth Bell, *Changing Bodies, Changing Lives* (New York, NY: Random House, 1980), p. 94, cited in Jane Chastain's *I'd Speak Out on the Issues If I Only Knew What to Say* (Regal Books, 1987).

25. Ibid., p. 114.

26. Ibid., p. 121.

27. Ibid., p. 87.

28. Elizabeth Winship, Frank Caparulo, and Vivian K. Harlin, *Masculinity and Femininity* (Boston, MA: Houghton Mifflin Co., 1978, revised edition), p. 63.

29. Ibid., p. 57

30. Marilyn Ferguson, *Aquarian Conspiracy,* op. cit., p. 398.

Chapter 6: How to Guard Your Child Against Corrupting Values

1. Richard A. Baer, Jr., "Teaching Values in the Schools: Clarification or Indoctrination?," op. cit., p. 18.

Chapter 7: Schools & New Age Globalism

1. Adolf Hitler speech at the Reichsparteitag, 1935 (can listen on www.youtube.com).

2. Carl Teichrib, "Education for a New World" (Kjos Ministries website, http://www.crossroad.to/articles2/forcing-change/12/8-education.htm).

3. Robert Muller, *New Genesis: Shaping a Global Spirituality* (New York, NY: Doubleday and Co., 1982), p. 49.

4. "Muller's Plan for a World Spiritual Renaissance & Education" (Herescope Blog, Discernment Research Group, October 30, 2005, http://herescope.blogspot.com/2005/10/mullers-plan-for-world-spiritual.html).

5. Mel and Norma Gabler, *What Are They Teaching Our Children?,* op. cit., pp. 47-48, citing from *Search for Freedom: America and Its People* (The Macmillan Company, 1973), pp. 7, 348, 384—390, 403, 412.

6. Ibid., citing from *Many Peoples, One Nation* (Random House, Inc., 1973), p. 88. Adapted from a speech by Frederick Douglass and presented to students in the present tense without refutation.

7. Ibid., citing from *A Global History* (Allyn and Bacon, Inc., 1970), Units Four-Nine.

8. Ibid., citing from *A Global History of Man* (Allyn and Bacon, Inc., 1979), p. 444; from an address by the editor of *This Week* magazine (Spring 1962).

9. Humanist Manifesto II, op. cit.

10. Dr. James Kennedy, *Train Up a Child* (Fort Lauderdale, FL: Coral Ridge Ministries, sermon delivered on June 2, 1985), p. 7, citing a 1992 handbook from the NEA.

11. Kathleen Hayes and Samantha Smith, *Grave New World*

(Golden, CO: New Awareness Consultants, 1986), p. 18.

12. Raymond English, *Teaching International Politics in High School* (University Press of America, 1989), p. 7, citing William Bennett from his essay: "America, the World and Our Schools" (presented at the Ethics and Public Policy Center Conference, Washington, D.C., December 5, 1986).

13. Ibid.

14. Andre Ryerson, "The Scandal of 'Peace Education'" (*Commentary,* June 1986), pp. 38-41.

15. Raymond English, *Teaching International Politics in High School, op. cit.,* pp. 8, 10, *citing William* Bennett.

16. Ken Keyes, Jr., *The Hundredth Monkey* (St. Mary, KY: Vision Books, 1982), pp. 13-18.

17. Ibid.

18. John Randolph Price, *The Planetary Commission* (Austin, TX: The Quartus Foundation for Spiritual Research, Inc., 1984), pp. 68-69.

19. Raymond English, *Teaching International Politics in High School, op. cit.,* p. 9, *citing William* Bennett.

20. "An Emerging Coalition: Political and Religious Leaders Come Together," A Special Report (North Bay, ON: *The Omega Letter*, November 1988), p. 2, citing Robert Runcie.

21. Ibid., p. 3.

22. Warren B. Smith, *False Christ Coming: Does Anybody Care?* (Magalia, CA: Mountain Stream Press, 2011), p. 47, quoting Benjamin Creme in *The Reappearance of the Christ and the Masters of Wisdom* (North Hollywood, CA: The Tara Press, 1980), p. 30.

23. URI Kids Activities: "Individual Spiritual Growth—Create Your Own Religion" (http://www.uri.org/kids/act_indiv_createrelig.htm).

24. Paul de Parrie and Mary Pride, *Unholy Sacrifices of the New Age* (Westchester, IL: Crossway Books, 1988), p. 76, citing Samuel Blumenfeld, "Blumenfeld Education Letter" (February 1987).

25. Ibid., p. 75, citing Samuel Blumenfeld, op. cit.

26. Ibid., p. 75 citing Richard Mitchell, *The Leaning Tower of Babel* (Boston, MA: Little, Brown and Company, 1984).

27. Ibid.

28. Phyllis Schlafly, *Child Abuse in the Classroom*, op. cit., p. 308.

29. *Education Reporter* (March 1988), p. 1.

30. Gregg L. Cunningham, "Blowing the Whistle on 'Global Education,'" prepared for Thomas G. Tancredo, Regional Representative, U.S. Department of Education, Denver, Colorado, 1986, p. 22, citing George Otero and Zoanne Harris in *Death: A Part of Life* (Denver: Center for Teaching International Relations, 1981), p. 39.

31. Ibid., p. 47.

32. Corinne McLaughlin and Gordon Davidson, *Spiritual Politics* (New York, NY: Ballantine Books, 1994), p. 147.

Chapter 8: What Can Parents Do About New Age Globalism?

1. Robert Muller, "World Core Curriculum," taken from *The Joyful Child* by Peggy Jenkins (Santa Rosa, CA: Aslan Publishing, 1996), p. 238.

2. Brian D. Ray, Ph.D, "Homeschool Population Report 2010" (January 3, 2011, http://www.nheri.org/research/nheri-news/homeschool-population-report-2010.html).

3. Julie Lawrence, "Number of Homeschoolers Growing Nationwide" (*Education News*, May 21, 2012, http://www.educationnews.org/parenting/number-of-homeschoolers-growing-nationwide).

4. A few online resources for homeschooling include: 1) HSLDA—Home School Legal Defense Association: http://www.hslda.org; 2) Abeka, homeschooling and Christian school curriculum: http://www.abeka.com; and 3) BJU Press Homeschooling: http://www.bjupresshomeschool.com. There are many other homeschool resources on the Internet, but please always use discernment when choosing materials—the New Age/New Spirituality has had influence in this area too.

Chapter 9: The Mind-Changing Visual Messages in Movies

1. Ray Yungen, *For Many Shall Come in My Name* (Eureka, MT: Lighthouse Trails Publishing, 2nd ed., 2007), p. 89.

2. See "The Story of Atlantis," *Encyclopedia Britannica* online. Excerpts: "Atlantis was the domain of Poseidon, god of the sea.

When Poseidon fell in love with a mortal woman, Cleito, he created a dwelling at the top of a hill near the middle of the island and surrounded the dwelling with rings of water and land to protect her. . . . At the top of the central hill, a temple was built to honor Poseidon which housed a giant gold statue of Poseidon riding a chariot pulled by winged horses. . . . For generations the Atlanteans lived simple, virtuous lives. But slowly they began to change. Greed and power began to corrupt them. When Zeus saw the immorality of the Atlanteans he gathered the other gods to determine a suitable punishment."

3. *Mystic Places* (Alexandria, VA: Time-Life Books, 1987), p. 28.

4. Norma Milanovich and Shirley McCune, *The Light Shall Set You Free* (Albuquerque, NM: Athena Publishing, 1996), pp. 38, 104.

5. Corinne McLaughlin and Gordon Davidson, *Spiritual Politics, op. cit.,* p. 257. See also "Bush, Gorbachev, Shultz and Soviet Education," scroll to 6th paragraph: http://www.crossroad.to/text/articles/Bush4-99.html. She mentions her involvement with the EPA, DOE, Pentagon, and PCSD during a workshop Berit Kjos attended during a 1995 commemoration of the United Nations' 50th anniversary titled Celebrating the Spirit.

6. Ibid.

7. Marilyn Ferguson, *The Aquarian Conspiracy*, op. cit., p. 49.

8. Mountain View High School newspaper on October 12, 1988.

9. Patrick Buchanan, "Hollywood's War on Christianity" (*San Jose Mercury News*, July 28, 1988).

10. Ibid.

11. David Ansen, "The Raider of Lost Art," (*Newsweek*, May 23, 1988), p. 70.

12. From Avatar-forums.com.

13. *Avatar: The Na'vi Quest*, adapted from the movie by Nicole Pitesa, (Harper Festival, 2009), pp. 1, 57. This small book provides some details not explained in the movie.

14. Ibid., p. 39. The above book answers that question: The Na'vi were meat-eating hunters, but they had to understand the pantheistic oneness before they could take life. When Jake kills a hexapede, he prays: "I see you, brother, and thank you. Your spirit goes with Eywa, your body stays behind to become part of the people."

15. Ibid.

16. Mike at Avatar-forums.com.

17. Tracy McVeigh, "Teachers Warn of Occult Dangers in Potter Movie Magic" (*The Observer,* November 3, 2001, http://www.guardian.co.uk/uk/2001/nov/04/books.theharrypotterfilms), citing Peter Smith, former general secretary of the Association of Teachers and Lecturers in the UK.

18. Samay Gheewala, "Psychic Eye Flourishes as New Agers Seek Goods, Services" (*Mountain View Voice,* CA, July 26, 2002, http://www.mv-voice.com/morgue/2002/2002_07_26.psychic.html).

19. Also read: Berit Kjos' "Harry Potter and Dungeons & Dragons: Like Two Peas in a Pod?" (Kjos Ministries, http://www.crossroad.to/text/articles/D&D&Harry.htm).

20. Naomi R. Goldenberg, *Changing of the Gods: Feminism & the End of Traditional Religions* (Boston, MA: Beacon Press, 1979), p. 3.

Chapter 11: Shameless Corruption Through Television & Digital Media

1. Marlin often invited me to be a guest on his radio show, and we often discussed television's power to manipulate. This quote is cited in many documents without any reference, but it summarizes one of his main warnings to families. He also sent me to various UN conferences as a reporter for his radio show, which provided insights into plans for global manipulation and indoctrination.

2. Paula Patyk, *Parental Adviser* (Knoxville, TN: Whittle Communications, 1987), p. 2.

3. Wilson Bryan Key (1925-2008), *Subliminal Seduction* (Prentice Hall Trade; First Edition), p. 69.

4. NBC TV, Saturday morning, March 25, 1989.

5. Marlin Maddoux, *American Betrayed* (Lafayette, LA: Huntington House, Inc., 1984), pp. 39—40.

6. Timothy Sexton, "The Effects of Horror Movies on Children" (EHow, http://www.ehow.com/about_5030719_effects-horror-movies-children.html#ixzz2GaBMeV00). The study was done by the National Institute of Mental Health (NIMH).

7. Peter Lalonde, *The Omega Letter*, October 1988, p. 16.

8. Stefan Kanfer, "In All Seasons, Toys Are Us" (*Time* magazine,

June 24, 2001), citing Ralph Shaffer, former director of new-product development at General Mills Toy Group who worked with Bernard Loomis who conceived the idea of sets of action figures "with lots of characters and a story tying them together." Promoted through television, these toys required little personal imagination since they came with built in myths and pre-designed personalities. Read the interesting history by David Owen in "Where Toys Come From" (*The Atlantic Monthly*, http://www.theatlantic.com/past/docs/issues/86oct/owen.htm, October 1986).

9. Larry McLean, from tape of lecture titled, "The Rising Interest in the Supernatural" given at the Seventh Mid-America Prophecy Conference, Oklahoma City, July 27, 1988.

10. John Ankerberg and John Weldon, *The Facts on UFOs and Other Supernatural Phenomena* (Eugene, OR: Harvest House Publishers, 1992), pp. 14-15.

11. Ibid., p. 6, citing Timothy Good, *Above Top Secret: The Worldwide UFO Cover-up* (New York, NY: Morrow, 1988), p. 12.

12. Ibid., pp. 5, 18.

13. For detailed information on Barbara Marx Hubbard's Peace Plan, please read Mike Oppenheimer's article titled "The Plan" online at: http://www.letusreason.org/NAM20.htm.

14. Barbara Marx Hubbard, *The Revelation* (Belvedere Tiburon, CA: Nataraj Publishing, 2nd ed., 1995), p. 197.

15. Ibid., p. 189.

16. Ibid., p. 254.

17. Ibid., p. 303.

18. Ibid., p. 195.

19. Warren B. Smith, *False Christ Coming: Does Anybody Care?*, op. cit., p. 28.

20. Barbara Marx Hubbard, *The Revelation*, op. cit., p. 255.

21. Ibid., p. 240.

22. Erik Davis, "Techopagans" (*Wired*, July 1995: http://www.techgnosis.com/index_technopagans.html).

23. An interview with Matthew Fox, http://web.archive.org/web/20060425035122/nineoclockservice.tripod.com/mattiefx.htm.

24. "'Digital Drugs' Sold on the Internet Induce Altered States of Consciousness" (*Press of Atlantic City*, June 29, 2010: http://www.

pressofatlanticcity.com/life/article_05dfa9fb-9361-5733-960e-c982a59ec419.html).

25. Nielsen ratings, accessed December 2012: http://www.nielsen.com/us/en/measurement/television-measurement.html.

26. Dr. Kim Mason, "Social Media Responsibility and Digital Footprint: Protecting Kids Against High-Tech Troubles" (University of New Orleans, 2012, http://www.stmcougars.net/uploaded/About_STM/Parent_Links/Mason_Parents_Social_Media_Digital_Citizens_Handout_2012.pdf).

27. Michalene Busico, "TV or Not TV" (*San Jose Mercury News*, December 13, 1988), citing Charles Atkin.

28. Paula Patyk, *Parental Adviser*, op. cit., p. 2, citing Victor Straburger.

29. Aletha Huston, et al., *Big World, Small Screen: The Role of Television in American Society* (Lincoln, NE: University of Nebraska Press, 1992).

30. The interview that took place on January 23, 1989 with Ted Bundy and James Dobson can be viewed on YouTube at: http://www.youtube.com/watch?v=dYAxfdj5_hY.

31. Kyla Boyse, RN. Reviewed by Brad Bushman, Ph.D., "Television and Children" (University of Michigan Health System: http://www.med.umich.edu/yourchild/topics/tv.htm), updated 2010.

32. Ibid., citing Joanne Cantor, *Mommy, I'm Scared: How TV and Movies Frighten Children and What We Can Do to Protect Them* (San Diego, CA: Harcourt Brace, 1998).

33. Ibid., Kyla Boyse, op. cit.

34. Oprah Winfrey with Johanna Michaelsen and Dr. Aquino, February 1988.

Chapter 13—Twisting the Imagination Through Toys & Games

1. Phil Phillips, *Turmoil in the Toy Box* (Lancaster, PA: Starburst Publishers, 1st Printing, May 1986), p. 17.

2. *Ibid.*, p. 35.

3. John Dvorak, "Notes and Quotes" (*Frontpage, A Publication of Today, the Bible and You,* July 1988), p. 5.

4. "Spa Fun" (*American Girl* magazine, Spiral Edition, September 1, 2009).

5. Ray Yungen, *For Many Shall Come in My Name,* op.cit, p. 170.

6. Phil Phillips, *Turmoil in the Toy Box,* op. cit., p. 25.

7. Pokémon TCG Basic Rules: http://www.pojo.com/pokemon/rules/oldbasicrules.html.

8. "Haunter versus Kadabra," aired on May 20, 1999.

9. Transcribed from a recorded interview with Cecile DiNozzi in Pound Ridge, New York.

10. For practical understanding of these occult dangers, read chapters four and eight in *A Twist of Faith* by Berit Kjos (Green Forest, AR: New Leaf Press, 1997, order directly from http://www.crossroad.to/text/1-books.htm, from online outlets such as Amazon, or from the publisher: http://www.newleafpublishinggroup.com).

11. Ray Yungen, *A Time of Departing* (Eureka, MT: Lighthouse Trails Publishing Company, 2nd ed., 2006), p. 101.

12. Not his real name. Because he was deeply involved in the occult before his conversion, we prefer not to include his real name. Instead we are calling him Peter Lanz. His words were written in a personal letter.

13. Starhawk, *The Spiral Dance* (New York, NY: Harper & Row, 1979), p. 62.

14. Theodynamics at http://www.theodynamics.com/theo/volume2/chapter10.html.

15. "As Above, So Below" (http://www.themystica.com/mystica/articles/a/below_above.html).

Chapter 15: Immoral & Occult Suggestions in Books & Magazines

1. Alice and Stephen Lawhead, *Pilgrim's Guide to the New Age* (Lion Publishing, 1986), p. 83.

2. "Watch It" (*Sassy* magazine, July 1988), p. 22.

3. Christina Kelly, "What Now?" (*Sassy*, July 1988), p. 14.

4. Erin Hunter, *Warriors 1—Into the Wild* (Avon Books, 2004), p. 45.

5. Ibid., p. 102.

6. Ibid., p. 51.

7. Ibid., pp. 4-5.

8. Ibid., p. 187.

9. Ibid.

10. Ibid., p. 270.

11. Erin Hunter, *Warriors 6—The Darkest Hour* (Avon Books, 2004), p. 33.

12. Ibid., p. 305.

13. *Erin Hunter, Warriors 1—Into the Wild,* op. cit., pp. 160-161.

14. Ibid., p. 161.

15. Ibid., p. 177.

16. Erin Hunter, *Warriors 6—The Darkest Hour*, op. cit., pp. 39, 43-47.

17. Ibid., pp. 149-150.

18. Ibid., p. 131.

19. Ibid., p. 341.

20. Starhawk, *The Spiral Dance*, op. cit., p. 62.

21. Philip Pullman, *The Golden Compass* (New York, NY: Random House Children's Books, 1995), p. 394.

22. Philip Pullman's answers to Questions about Science and Religion at www.geocities.com/the_golden_compass/rvreligion.html.

23. See the following: http://www.crossroad.to/Books/BraveNewSchools/5-Earth.htm#cosmicevolution, http://www.crossroad.to/Quotes/occult/gnostic-apostle-thomas.htm, http://www.crossroad.to/Excerpts/books/lilith.htm#Swedenborg, and http://www.crossroad.to/Quotes/occult/theosophy.htm.

24. Philip Pullman, *The Golden Compass*, op. cit., p. 176.

25. Philip Pullman, *The Subtle Knife* (New York, NY: Random House Children's Books, 1997), pp. 50-55.

26. Philip Pullman, *The Amber Spyglass* (New York, NY: Random House Children's Books, 2000), p. 33.

27. Ibid., p. 410.

28. Ibid., p. 31.

29. To learn about Sue Monk Kidd's change from evangelical Christianity to goddess spirituality, go to: http://www.lighthousetrailsresearch.com/suemonkkidd.htm.

30. In Warren B. Smith and Bob DeWaay's DVD lecture series, *Quantum Lie: God is NOT in Everything*, they describe what is meant by "Quantum Spirituality." (To view preview clips of these lectures,

visit, www.youtube.com/joiful77.

31. Philip Pullman, *The Golden Compass*, op. cit., p. 373.

32. Philip Pullman, *The Amber Spyglass, pp. 371-372.*

33. Ibid.

34. Philip Pullman, *The Golden Compass*, op. cit., p. 238.

35. Ibid., p. 174.

36. Philip Pullman, *The Subtle Knife*, op. cit., p. 95.

37. Ibid., pp. 182-183.

38. Philip Pullman, *The Amber Spyglass*, op. cit., p. 80.

39. Philip Pullman, *The Subtle Knife*, op. cit., p. 92.

40. Philip Pullman, *The Amber Spyglass*, op. cit., p. 440.

41. Ibid., p. 80.

42. Ibid., p. 68.

43. Ibid., p. 451.

44. Philip Pullman, *The Golden Compass*, op. cit., p. 370.

45. Willis Harman, Ph.D., *Global Mind Change* (New York, NY: Warner Books, 1988), pp.13, 55. See also http://www.crossroad.to/Quotes/globalism/julian-huxley.htm#teilhard.

46. Ibid.

47. For more on Alister Crowley, read Joe Schimmel's article, "Twilight, Harry Potter, The Wizard of Oz and the Wiccan Revival"(http://www.goodfight.org/a_co_twilight_harrypotter.html).

48. Philip Pullman, *The Amber Spyglass*, op. cit., p. 449.

49. Ibid.

50. http://www.crossroad.to/articles2/Gore.html, http://www.crossroad.to/Quotes/management/blanchard.htm, http://www.crossroad.to/Excerpts/community/system-theory.htm.

51. Rose Estes, *Dragon of Doom, A Dungeons & Dragons Adventure Book* (Lake Geneva, WI: TSR, Inc., 1983), p. 84.

52. "What Readers Think About Goblet?" (*San Francisco Chronicle*, July 26, 2000).

53. "Harry's Biggest Fans" (*San Francisco Chronicle*, July 26, 2000, http://www.sfgate.com/books/article/Harry-s-Biggest-Fans-Young-reviewers-explain-3237960.php).

54. Andy Norfolk, quoted in "Potter Fans Turning to Witchcraft," (*This is London* magazine, August 4, 2000).

55. Danielle Demetriou, "Harry Potter and the Source of Inspiration" (*The Telegraph*, July 1, 2000, http://www.telegraph.co.uk/news/uknews/1345980/Harry-Potter-and-the-source-of-inspiration.html).

56. Malcolm Jones, "The Return of Harry Potter!" (*Newsweek*, online edition, July 1, 2000, http://www.thedailybeast.com/newsweek/2000/07/09/the-return-of-harry-potter.html).

57. "TV shows fuel children's interest in witchcraft" (August 4, 2000, http://web.archive.org/web/20010606132941/http://ananova.com/entertainment/story/television_children-entertainment-religion-paganism_926320.html).

58. Andy Norfolk, quoted in "Potter Fans Turning to Witchcraft," op. cit.

59. Ibid.

60. Ted Olsen, "Positive About Potter" (*Christianity Today*, December 6, 1999, http://www.christianitytoday.com/ct/1999/december6/12.0a.html).

61. Chuck Colson, "Witches and Wizards—The Harry Potter Phenomenon" (Breakpoint, November 2, 1999, http://www.breakpoint.org/commentaries/4635-witches-and-wizards).

62. Roy Maynard, "Books: Kiddy Lit" (*World Magazine*, May 29, 1999, http://www.worldmag.com/1999/05/books_kiddy_lit).

63. Ann McCain and Susan Olasky, "More Clay Than Potter" (*World Magazine,* October 30, 1999, http://www.worldmag.com/1999/10/more_clay_than_potter).

64. This particular quote is not online; however, a more recent article by Mark Greene reiterates his support for Harry Potter: "Harry Potter & the Magic of Love" (*Christian Today*, August 3, 2011, http://in.christiantoday.com/articles/harry-potter-the-magic-of-love-warning-contains-plot-spoiler/6516.htm). In referring to *Harry Potter and the Death Hallows*, Greene states: "True love, Rowling teaches us, comes in many forms. And she has thereby given us, it seems to me, one of the richest explorations of love ever offered in children's fiction."

65. "Wizards and Muggles" (*Christian Century*, December 1, 1999, http://www.christiancentury.org/article/2011-07/wizards-and-muggles).

66. Alan Jacobs, "On Why Harry Potter's Magic Shouldn't Trouble Christians" (September/October 1999, Mars Hill Audio Journal, Vol. 40, http://web.archive.org/web/19991127183930/http://www.marshillaudio.org/catalog/current_tape.shtml).

67. James Emery White, on Pastors.com (June 2007); no longer online. Lighthouse Trails confirmed that this took place.

68. Andy Norfolk, quoted in "Potter Fans Turning to Witchcraft," op. cit.

69. Statistics taken from Wikipedia: http://en.wikipedia.org/wiki/The_Twilight_Saga_(film_series).

70. Marilyn Ferguson, *The Aquarian Conspiracy*, op. cit., p. 280.

71. "Come Out From Them and Be Separate" at: www.crossroad.to/HisWord/verses/topics/separate.htm.

Chapter 16: How to Guard Against Immorality & the Occult

1. A Pro-Family Forum—no longer online.

2. Jay McInerney, *Bright Lights, Big City* (New York, NY: Vintage Contemporaries, 1984), pp. 6-7.

3. Neil Postman, *Amusing Ourselves to Death* (New York, NY: Viking Penguin, Inc., 1985), vii-viii.

4. Aldous Huxley, *Brave New World and Brave New World Revisited* (HarperCollins Edition, 2004), p. 267.

5. Jim Trelease, *The Read-Aloud Handbook* (New York, NY: Penguin, 1987 edition), p. 40.

Chapter 17: When Popular Music Becomes Obscene & Immoral

1. Larry DeBruyn, "The Music and the Mystical" (Guarding His Flock Ministries, http://guardinghisflock.com/2010/06/29/the-music-and-the-mystical).

2. Nevill Drury, *Music for Inner Space* (Dorset, CA: Prism Press, 1985), p. 21.

3. Ibid., 28.

4. Ibid., p. 54.

5. Chief Shoefoot, *I'll Never Go Back (Don Shire Ministries, can be purchased at: http://www.lighthousetrails.com).*

6. Kathleen Donnely, "Giving Voice to the Magic of Africa's Talking Drums" (*San Jose Mercury News*, 7 April 1989).

7. Nevill Drury, *Music for Inner Space*, op. cit., p. 18, citing A. J. Langguth, *Macumba*, 1975, p. 70.

8. Nanci des Gerlaise, *Muddy Waters*, op. cit., p. 94.

9. Manfred Clynes (ed.), *Music, Mind and Brain* (New York, NY: Plenum Publishing Corporation, 1982), p. 174.

10. Nevill Drury, *Music for Inner Space*, op. cit., p. 18.

11. Jeff Lilley, "Dabbling in Danger" (*Moody Monthly*, March 1989), p. 17.

12. *Wikepedia*: http://en.wikipedia.org/wiki/Heavy_metal_music.

13. Ozzy Osbourne, "No Bone Movies" (Blizzard of Ozz, Jet Music Ltd., CBS, 1981).

14. Joe Schimmel, "Ozzy Osbourne" (Good Fight Ministries: http://www.goodfight.org/a_m_osbourne_ozzy.html). You can also watch a film presentation of Schimmel's talk at his website.

15. Joe Schimmel, "Backstreet Boys" (Good Fight Ministries, http://www.goodfight.org/a_m_back_street_boys.html).

16. Ibid.

17. Ibid.

18. Ibid.

19. Ibid.

20. *Webster's New World Dictionary of the American Language* (New York, NY: The World Publishing Company, College Edition, 1964), p. 968.

21. "Rock 'n' Roll's Leading Lady" (*Time* magazine, December 16, 1974), p. 63. Note: Although it was many years ago that Joni Mitchell disclosed "Art," this information sits on her website today, where she calls Art her "shrine of creativity." (http://jonimitchell.com/library/view.cfm?id=757&from=search).

22. *Rock and Roll: A Search for God* video cassette with Eric Holmberg (Reel to Real Ministries, P.O. Box 44290, Pittsburgh, PA 15205), quoting Angus Young (Hit Parade, July 1985), p. 60.

23. The DVD *They Sold Their Souls for Rock n' Roll* can be obtained at: http://www.goodfight.org. Good Fight Ministries has a rating on the film of 14 years or older.

24. Paul Proctor, "A New Song" (October 22, 2003, http://www.

crossroad.to/articles2/2002/proctor/new-song.htm).

25. "Daily Media Use Among Children and Teens Up Dramatically From Five Years Ago" (http://www.kff.org/entmedia/entmedia012010nr.cfm).

26. Peggy Mann, "How Shock Rock Harms Our Kids" (*Reader's Digest*, July 1988), p. 102, citing Dr. Joseph Stuessy.

27. "MacPhisto, Who the Devil?" (http://www.canadanne.co.uk/macphisto/who.html).

28. "Bono Bites Back" (*Mother Jones* magazine, May 1989, http://www.motherjones.com/media/1989/05/bono-bites-back), p. 35.

29. Elliott Nesch, "U2 Frontman Bono: Christian or Antichrist?" (August 12, 2012, http://www.holybibleprophecy.org).

30. Ibid.

31. Ibid.

32. Cited from *The Submerging Church*: DVD 2 by Joe Schimmel. A trailer of this can be seen at: http://www.youtube.com/watch?v=0PQOMb5T76A&feature=channel&list=UL. The DVD set can be obtained at www.goodfight.org or at www.lighthousetrails.com.

33. David Dombrowski, "In View of the Recent Tragedy, a Timely Message"(Lighthouse Trails blog: http://www.lighthousetrailsresearch.com/blog/?p=10511).

34. Marc Gunther, "Power Pastor: Will Success Spoil Rick Warren?" (*Fortune Magazine*, October 2005, http://money.cnn.com/magazines/fortune/fortune_archive/2005/10/31/8359189/index.htm).

35. Michelle A. Vu, "Evangelical Movement at 'Head-Snapping' Moment, Says Scholar" (*Christian Post*, http://www.christianpost.com/news/evangelical-mov-t-at-head-snapping-moment-says-scholar-41337).

36. Roger Oakland, *Faith Undone* (Eureka, MT: Lighthouse Trails Publishing, 2007), p. 65.

37. Yaconelli, Mark (2011-03-22). *Contemplative Youth Ministry: Practicing the Presence of Jesus* (Youth Specialties) (Kindle Locations 2592-2596). Zondervan/Youth Specialties. Kindle Edition.

38. Douglas LaBlanc, "A Troubadour and His Guitar" (*Christianity Today*, October 22, 2001, http://www.christianitytoday.com/ct/2001/octoberweb-only/25.103.html), interviewing John Michael Talbot

39. John Michael Talbot, *Come to the Quiet: The Principles of Christian Meditation* (New York, NY: Tarcher/Putnam, 2002), p. 8.

40. http://www.contemplative-life.org/audio-for-teaching-children-to-meditate/open-our-hearts-christian-meditation-for-children-9-10.html

Chapter 19: Mystical New Age Thrills Enticing Children

1. Glenn Alexander Magee, *Hegel, and the Hermetic Tradition* (Ithaca and London: Cornell University Press, 2001), pp. 1-3. This Hermetic Tradition originated in Egypt. According to the Gnostic Society, "The Hermetic tradition is usually understood as a form of 'pagan Gnosticism,' developing in Egypt during the same historical period that saw the flowering of the Christian Gnostic tradition." (From: http://www.faculty.umb.edu/gary_zabel/Courses/Phil%20 281b/Philosophy%20of%20Magic/Arcana/Gnostic%20Texts/ lectures.html).

2. Mark Blanchard, "Family Yoga Practice" (November 4, 2006, http://web.archive.org/web/20090620224738/http://www.pro-gressivepoweryoga.com/blog/2006/11/family-yoga-practice.html).

3. http://www.markblanchardsyoga.com/about-mark-blanchard. html

4. Mark Blanchard, "Family Yoga Practice," op. cit.

5. Mini Yogis: Yoga for Kids: http://www.miniyogis.com/clients. htm.

6. Yoga Ed. in Action: http://www.yogaed.com/action.html.

7. "Yoga Causes Controversy in Public Schools" (Associated Press, January 28, 2007, http://www.msnbc.msn.com/id/16859368/ns/ health-childrens_health/t/yoga-causes-controversy-public-schools/).

8. Alessandra Stanley, "Same Street, Different World: 'Sesame' Turns 40" (*New York Times,* November 3, 2009, http://www.nytimes. com/2009/11/08/arts/television/08stan.html?pagewanted=all&_ r=0).

9. Starhawk, *The Spiral Dance*, op. cit., pp. 193-196.

10. *Encyclopedia Britannica*, Volume 11 (Chicago, IL: William Benton, 1968), p. 15. Based on A. Machain, *Celtic Mythology and Religion* (1917); E. Hull, *Folklore in the British Isles* (1928).

11. "Halloween" (*Encyclopedia Britannica*, http://www.britannica. com/EBchecked/topic/252875/Halloween).

12. *Ancient Wisdom and Secret Sects* (Alexandria, VA: Time-Life Books), pp. 17-19.

13. Ibid.

14. Ibid., p. 10.

15. Merle Severy, "The Celts" (*National Geographic*, May 1977), pp. 625-626.

16. Ibid.

17. "Who We Are" (Girl Scouts History: http://www.girlscouts.org/who_we_are/history).

18. On a twelve-page brochure for their 2010 National Council Session.

19. "Music, Turning Harmonies Into Memories" (http://www.girlscouts.org/for_adults/volunteering/music.asp).

20. "Girls Walk Their Talk" (*Leader Magazine*, Spring Summer 2007, http://web.archive.org/web/20101222200014/http://girlscouts.org/for_adults/leader_magazine/2007%20spring-summer/SP07_Leader-web.pdf), p. 22.

21. Girl Scouts, http://www.girlscouts.org/fitsinn—quote is on home page.

22. "Weighing In" (Girl Scouts of the United States of America, 2004, http://www.girlscouts.org/research/pdf/weighing_in.pdf).

23. Ursula Castrillon, "Volunteering—From Yoga to PR" (Girl Scouts of the United States of America, April 16, 2003, http://www.girlscouts.org/news/stories/2003/natl_volunteers_day.asp).

24. Emily G. Kelting, "Become the Best You Can Be" (Girl Scouts of the United States of America, Winter 2003, http://www.girlscouts.org/for_adults/leader_magazine/2003_winter/become_the_best.asp).

25. "GSUSA Partners with The Ashland Institute" (http://web.archive.org/web/20110604033539/http://www.girlscouts.org/strategy/leadership_from_the_inside_out.asp).

26. "Introduction To: Attunement—Creative Energy Practice" (The Ashland Institute, http://id.mind.net/~tai/pdf/Attunement.pdf).

27. "Retreats & Programs: Coming Into Your Own" (http://id.mind.net/~tai/retreats.html).

28. "Coming into Your Own: A Program for Women" (http://

id.mind.net/~tai/pdf/CIYO2008inviteUS.pdf).

29. "Mentorship Circles" (http://id.mind.net/~tai/pdf/circles.pdf).

30. The Fetzer Institute: http://www.fetzer.org.

31. "Publications and Other Resources" (http://web.archive.org/web/20090224221303/http://www.fetzer.org/Resources.aspx?PageID=Resources&NavID=1).

32. The Ashland Institute: http://id.mind.net/~tai/resources.html.

33. "Kid Contemplatives: UW Neuroscientist's Project Aims to Give Middle-Schoolers Tools of 'Mindfulness' and Meditation" (*Capital Times*, November 9, 2007, http://psyphz.psych.wisc.edu/web/News/captimes_11-8-07.html).

34. Ibid.

35. Ibid.

36. Ibid.

37. Ibid.

38. Ray Yungen, *For Many Shall Come in My Name*, op. cit., p. 66.

Chapter 20: How to Guard Against Mystical New Age Thrills

1. "Yoga Causes Controversy in Public Schools" (*Associated Press*, http://www.msnbc.msn.com/id/16859368/ns/health-kids_and_parenting).

2. Gail Williams, "Christian Parents Group to Sue School Over Yoga Classes" (*Examiner*, December 19, 2012, http://www.examiner.com/article/christian-parents-group-to-sue-school-over-yoga-classes).

Chapter 21: Becoming Aware of Spiritual Deception in the Church

1. Leonard Sweet, *Soul Tsunami*," pp. 74-75. www.crossroad.to/Quotes/Church/postmodern/leonard-sweet.htm.

2. Philosophy: Inspiring World Changers at http://kidmo.com.

3. Raymond Houghton, *To Nurture Humaneness: Commitment for the '70s* (The Association for Supervision and Curriculum Development of the NEA, 1970), pp. 46-47.

4. David Krathwohl, *Benjamin Bloom and Bertram Massia, Taxonomy of Educational Objectives, The Classification of Educational Goals, Handbook II: Affective Domain* (McKay Publishers, 1956), p. 55.

5. Julian Huxley, "UNESCO: Its Purpose and Its Philosophy," (Preparatory Commission of the United Nations Educational, Scientific and Cultural Organisation, 1946, http://unesdoc.unesco.org/images/0006/000681/068197eo.pdf).

6. "Inspiring World Changers" (http://www.kidmo.com/kidmo-kollege/philosophy.aspx).

7. Mike Yaconelli, "The Problem of Parents" (http://www.youth-specialties.com/articles/Yaconelli/parents.php).

8. John Goodlad, "Report of Task Force C: Strategies for Change," Schooling for the Future, a report to the President's Commission on Schools Finance, Issue #9, 1971.

9. James Becker, Editor, *Schooling for a Global Age* (New York: McGraw-Hill Book Company, 1979), xiii, xvii, citing John Goodlad.

10. The article Megan was referring to was "Piling on the Millstones," written by the late Mike Yaconelli in September 2001, which can be found on page 65 in the book *Getting Fired for the Glory of God* compiled by Karla Yaconelli (Youth Specialties, 2008). The article can be accessed at: http://faithworksministries.org/jfydec2002d.html.

11. Roger Oakland, *Faith Undone,* op. cit., p. 91.

12. Richard Kirby, *The Mission of Mysticism* (London, UK: SPCK, 1979), p. 7.

13. Michael Anthony, *Perspectives on Children's Spiritual Formation* (Nashville, TN: Broadman & Holman Publishers, 2006), p. 82, quoting Carlson and Crupper.

14. Ibid., p. 83.

15. Ibid., p. 85.

16. David Steindl-Rast, "Recollection of Thomas Merton's Last Days in the West" (*Monastic Studies,* 7:10, 1969).

17. Rob Baker and Gray Henry, Editors, *Merton and Sufism* (Louisville, KY: Fons Vitae, 1999), p. 69.

18. "Contemplative Prayer" (*PrayKids*, NavPress, issue #25).

19. Marcus Borg, *The God We Never Knew* (New York, NY: HarperCollins, First HarperCollins Paperback Edition, 1998), p. 25.

20. "An Epidemic of Apostasy—Christian Seminaries Must Incorporate 'Spiritual Formation' to Become Accredited" (Lighthouse Trails Special Report, November 2011, http://www.lighthousetrailsresearch.com/blog/?p=7733).

21. The State of the World according to Gorbachev at www.crossroad.to/text/articles/tstotw1196.html.

22. Richard and Linda Nathan, "Children of the Inklings—Emergent 'Christian' Fiction" (Kjos Ministries website, 2007, http://www.crossroad.to/articles2/007/nathan-fiction.htm).

23. Dan Wooding, "I'm Not Coming Back to America in Case I Get Shot" (*Assist News*, March 10, 2005, http://web.archive.org/web/20051026235707/http://www.assistnews.net/Stories/s05030046.htm).

24. Review on: http://web.archive.org/web/20060826033722/http://www.christianmusicplanet.com/magazine/viewarticle.asp?id=184.

25. *Shadowmancer* on Amazon: www.amazon.com/exec/obidos/ASIN/0399242562/102-7411094-3751360. Actually the setting might be in the 18th century.

26. *Shadowmancer*, "Description" at http://cbw.strang.com/c.cgi?ProdID=6132&Source=INTNET.

27. Mike Oppenheimer, "Making Way for the New and Improved Church" (2002, at www.letusreason.org/Current58.htm).

28. 2006 interview between Brian McLaren and Leif Hansen, http://www.lighthousetrailsresearch.com/brianmclarenandthecross.htm, (transcript and audio file).

29. Brian D. McLaren, *A New Kind of Christian* (San Francisco, CA: Jossey-Bass; 1st edition, 2001), pp. xx-xxi.

30. Pastors.com website: Issue #214, July 6, 2005, http://web.archive.org/web/20081227043708/http://legacy.pastors.com.RWMT/?ID=214.

31. "The 25 Most Influential Evangelicals in America" (*Time* magazine, February 7, 2005, http://www.time.com/time/specials/packages/article/0,28804,1993235_1993243_1993300,00.html).

32. Brian McLaren, *Finding Our Way Again* (Nashville, TN: Thomas Nelson, 2008), p. 133.

33. Ibid.

34. Rick Warren, "What Do You Do When Your Church Hits a Plateau?" (original Pastors.com website, June 14, 2006), no longer online.

35. Brian McLaren, *Finding Our Way Again*, op. cit., p. 139.

Afterword—The First and Final Deception

1. James Wasserman, *Art and Symbols of the Occult: Images of Power and Wisdom* (Rochester, VT: Destiny Books, 1993). p. 16. Read about the Hermetic Order of the Golden Dawn here:www.crossroad. to/Excerpts/books/lewis/inklings-williams.htm and www.crossroad. to/articles2/2003/occult-rpg.htm.

2. Ibid., p. 59. Those occult words are attributed to Hermes Trismegistus (the Egyptian version of the ancient Greek messenger god, Hermes) who has been the symbolic idol of occult orders and secret societies through the ages.

INDEX

A

abortion 28, 56, 65, 73, 127
Addy, Obo 225
Africa 77, 224, 226
"Age of Aquarius" 81, 88
AIDS education 71
Aladdin 100
aliens 137, 139, 159
altered states of consciousness 39, 146, 239, 245
America 4, 14, 17, 29, 31, 35, 65, 70, 76, 77, 78, 92, 93, 99, 108, 135, 145, 211, 217, 224, 236, 243, 246, 254, 285
American Academy of Pediatrics Subcommittee on Children and Television 133, 148
American Girl Doll Company 160
American Girl Yoga doll 161
American Humanist Association 27
American Indian religion 28
American Library Association 219
America's public schools 17
ancestral spirits 100
ancestral worship 101, 185
ancient
    Canaan 119
    Israel 190

occultism 24
    rituals 187
Ancient Wisdom 255
A New World Order 77
Angel Wars 106
Ankerberg, John 140
Antichrist 25, 88, 139
anti-Christian policies 94
Aquarian energy 14
Aquino, Michael 150
Archbishop of Canterbury 82
armor
    see God's armor
"as above, so below" 172, 195, 200
ascended masters 103, 105, 140, 142
Ashland Initiative 252, 253
Ashland Institute 253
astrological signs 243
astrology 110, 185, 187
Atlantis 102, 103, 104, 105, 106, 298
atonement 25, 213, 214, 270
August Burns Red 227
auras 15
Aurora Borealis (Northern Lights) 192
Avatar 110, 111, 112, 113
avatars 84
Awana Clubs 268, 269, 270

B

baby-boomers 243
Backstreet Boys 228, 229

Note: Because of their frequency in the book, certain terms such as Bible, New Age, occult, television, media, etc. are not in this Index.

59, 60, 64, 86, 201
values education 59, 70
values transformation 54
vampires 210
"vintage" Christianity 234
violence 107, 109, 131, 148,
149, 150, 153, 154, 155, 163,
164, 166, 170, 178, 184, 223,
226, 231, 236, 283, 286
visualization 37, 50, 84, 94,
110, 171, 190

W

Walsch, Neale Donald 13, 14,
15, 16, 212
Warren, Rick 206, 209, 233,
264, 278, 279
Warrior Cats 187
Washington, George 76
Weldon, John 140, 301
Western civilization 35
Western democracy 79
White, James Emery 206, 209
Williamson, Marianne 14,
212
white magic 209
Winfrey, Oprah 150
Wood, Audrey and Don 218
Willow Creek 278
witchcraft 36, 113, 114, 173,
189, 190, 201, 202, 203, 204,
205, 207, 208, 218, 238, 242
witches 109, 115, 156, 191,
192, 193, 203, 208, 248
world consciousness 81
world cultures 39, 85
World Magazine 306

world peace 16, 18, 94
world's population 87

Y

Yaconelli, Mike 265, 266
Yanamamo
    see Chief Shoefoot
yin-yang symbol 172
Yoga 23, 24, 39, 45, 50, 104,
160, 161, 172, 235, 242, 244,
245, 246, 252, 254, 255, 257,
258
YogaEd 244
youthful lusts 237
Youth Specialties 265, 266
Yungen, Ray 97, 161

Z

Zen 222

RECOMMENDED RESOURCES

BOOKS

Twist of Faith by Berit Kjos—on the New Age

The Invisible War by Berit Kjos

Persecution Stories for Children by Berit Kjos

For Many Shall Come in My Name by Ray Yungen—on the New Age

Yoga and the Body of Christ by Dave Hunt—on Yoga

Faith Undone by Roger Oakland—on the emerging church

A Time of Departing by Ray Yungen—on contemplative spirituality and mystical meditaion

False Christ Coming: Does Anybody Care? by Warren B. Smith—on the New Age/New Spirituality

Strength for Tough Times by Maria Kneas—for comfort, encouragement, and exhortation in the faith

Muddy Waters: an insider's view of North American Native Spirituality by Nanci des Gerlaise—on Native Spirituality and the new missiology

Seducers Among Our Children by Patrick Crough—on protecting our children from sexual predators

DVDS

Searching for the Truth on Origins by Roger Oakland (on creation)

The Emerging Church lecture series by Roger Oakland

The New Face of Mystical Spirituality with Ray Yungen

WEBSITES

Kjos Ministries: www.crossroad.to.

Good Fight Ministries: www.goodfight.org.

Let Us Reason Ministries: www.letusreason.org.

Deception in the Church: www.deceptioninthechurch.org.
Herescope Blog (Discernment Group): http://herescope.blogspot.com/
Lighthouse Trails Research Project: www.lighthousetrailsresearch.com.
Spiritual Research Network: http://www.spiritual-research-network.com
Understand the Times, International: www.understandthetimes.org.

Forcing Change Ministries: www.forcingchange.org

ONLINE ARTICLES

"When is Yoga, Yoga – And How is it Affecting Children in Public Schools?" By Roger Oakland: http://www.understandthetimes.org/commentary/c119yoga.shtml.

"Indigo Children—And Conversations With God" by Berit Kjos: http://www.crossroad.to/articles2/05/indigo.htm.

"Christian Leaders Giving Mysticism to Our Youth" by Ray Yungen: http://www.lighthousetrailsresearch.com/blog/?p=1043.

"Karate, Kids, and the Culture: Your Child and the Martial Arts" by Richard and Linda Nathan: http://www.crossroad.to/articles2/05/karate.htm.

"5 Things You Can Do to Protect Your Kids From Sexual Predators" by Patrick Crough: http://www.lighthousetrailsresearch.com/blog/?p=11392.

continued on next page

RESOURCES ESPECIALLY FOR CHILDREN

BOOKS

The Invisible War by Berit Kjos

Treasures of the Snow and *The Tanglewood's Secret* by Patricia St. John

In My Father's House by Corrie ten Boom and *Trapped in Hitler's Hell* by Anita Dittman can be read by 13 years and up as well as by adults.

DVDS

The Adventures of Jakes Farm—Broyden Bros. Pictures

Appalachian Trial—Unusual Films

Sheffey—Unusual Films

Nikolai (a young boy in Communist Russia learns to stand for his faith)

Treasures of the Snow (DVD)

Pilgrim's Progress by John Bunyan

God of Wonders by Eternal Productions (on creation—wonderful for the family)

Learn the Truth About the Spiritual Formation Movement!

Spiritual Formation and the Mystical Revolution
by Ray Yungen
author of
A Time of Departing

RELEASE DATE: WINTER 2013

Spiritual Formation: A movement that has provided a platform and a channel through which contemplative mystical prayer is entering the church. Find spiritual formation being used, and in nearly every case you will find contemplative spirituality. In fact, contemplative spirituality is the heartbeat of the spiritual formation movement.

Spiritual Formation and the Mysical Revolution will unveil the underlying roots of the Spiritual Formation movement, which has now been introduced into the majority of Christian colleges, seminaries, and universities, as well as many churches and organizations.

TITLES BY
LIGHTHOUSE TRAILS PUBLISHING

BOOKS

Another Jesus (2nd ed.)
by Roger Oakland, $12.95

A Time of Departing
by Ray Yungen, $12.95

Castles in the Sand (a novel)
by Carolyn A. Greene, $12.95

Faith Undone
by Roger Oakland, $12.95

For Many Shall Come in My Name by Ray Yungen, $12.95

Foxe's Book of Martyrs
by John Foxe, $14.95, illustrated

How to Protect Your Child From the New Age & Spiritual Deception
Berit Kjos, $14.95

In My Father's House
by Corrie ten Boom, $13.95

Let There Be Light
by Roger Oakland, $13.95

Muddy Waters
by Nanci des Gerlaise, $13.95

Seducers Among Our Children
by Patrick Crough, $14.95

Stolen from My Arms
by Katherine Sapienza, $14.95

Stories from Indian Wigwams and Northern Campfires
Egerton Ryerson Young, $15.95

Strength for Tough Times
by Maria Kneas, $7.75

The Color of Pain
by Gregory Reid, $10.95

Things We Couldn't Say
1st Lighthouse Trails Edition
by Diet Eman, $14.95, photos

The Other Side of the River
by Kevin Reeves, $12.95

Trapped in Hitler's Hell
by Anita Dittman with Jan Markell, $12.95, illustrated, photos

DVDs

The Story of Anita Dittman
with Anita Dittman
$15.95, 60 minutes

The New Face of Mystical Spirituality lecture series with Ray Yungen—3 DVDs, $36.95 set

Quantum Lie
with Warren B. Smith and Bob DeWaay, 4 lectures, $29.95

For a complete listing of all our books, DVDs, and CDs, go to www.lighthousetrails.com, or request a copy of our catalog.

To order additional copies of:
*How to Protect Your Child
from the New Age & Spiritual Deception*
send $14.95 per book
plus shipping ($3.95 for 1 book, $5.25 for 2-3 books,
$10.95 for 4-16 books) to:

Lighthouse Trails Publishing
P.O. Box 908
Eureka, MT 59917

Call or go online for information about quantity discounts.
You may order online at
www.lighthousetrails.com
or
Call our toll-free order number:
866/876-3910 (USA & Canada order line)

For all other calls, including all international calls:
406/889-3610
Fax: 406/889-3633

How to Protect Your Child from the New Age & Spiritual Deception, as
well as other books by Lighthouse Trails Publishing, can be ordered
directly from Lighthouse Trails or through all major outlet stores,
bookstores, online bookstores, and Christian bookstores. Bookstores
may order through Ingram, SpringArbor, Anchor Distribution, or
directly through Lighthouse Trails.
Libraries may order through Baker & Taylor.

Quantity discounts available for most of our books.
International orders may be placed either online, by phone, through
e-mail, or by faxing or mailing order form.

Please visit the author's websites for extensive research:
www.crossroad.to and www.howtoprotectyourchild.com.

Lighthouse Trails Publishing and Research Project
www.lighthousetrails.com
www.lighthousetrailsresearch.com